# Public Management in an Information Age

# THE PUBLIC MANAGEMENT AND LEADERSHIP SERIES

Series Editor

**Zeger van der Wal, Leiden University**

The Public Management and Leadership series aims to provide a set of key texts to meet the changing needs of the growing range of graduate and executive courses at Public Policy Schools, Civil Service Colleges, and professional Training Institutions, as well as concise and accessible readings for busy practitioners. Books in the series will address the essential topics of leadership and management, collaboration, innovation and modernization, as well as specific and timely areas of interest, such as information technology and data, networks and partnerships, political-administrative relations, diversity, and ethics management.

International in scope and conception; accessible in style and presentation; and drawing on case examples and insights into best practices from a wide variety of jurisdictions and policy sectors, each title offers an authoritative review of the state of theory and practice, identifies key challenges and the most promising strategies, and practices to tackle them.

Other Titles in the Series:

# Public Management in an Information Age

*Towards Strategic Public Information Management*

### Albert Meijer, Alex Ingrams and Stavros Zouridis

BLOOMSBURY ACADEMIC
LONDON • NEW YORK • OXFORD • NEW DELHI • SYDNEY

BLOOMSBURY ACADEMIC
Bloomsbury Publishing Plc
50 Bedford Square, London, WC1B 3DP, UK
1385 Broadway, New York, NY 10018, USA
29 Earlsfort Terrace, Dublin 2, Ireland

BLOOMSBURY, BLOOMSBURY ACADEMIC and the Diana logo
are trademarks of Bloomsbury Publishing Plc

First published in Great Britain 2023

Cover design by Eleanor Rose
Cover image © Getty Images

A catalogue record for this book is available from the British Library.

A catalog record for this book is available from the Library of Congress.

ISBN:     HB:      978-1-3503-4388-7
          PB:      978-1-3503-4387-0
          ePDF:    978-1-3503-4390-0
          eBook:   978-1-3503-4389-4

The Public Management and Leadership Series

Typeset by Integra Software Services Pvt. Ltd.

To find out more about our authors and books visit www.bloomsbury.com
and sign up for our newsletters.

# Contents

# List of Figures, Tables and Boxes

## Figures

## Tables

# Boxes

# Notes on the Authors

**Albert Meijer** is a professor of public management at Utrecht University. He is also co-editor-in-chief of the journal *Information Polity*.

**Alex Ingrams** is an assistant professor at Leiden University. His research concentrates on technology, governance reforms and comparative public administration.

**Stavros Zouridis** is a professor of public administration and law at Tilburg University and a member of the Dutch Safety Board.

# Preface

The original spark for *Public Management in an Information Age* came appropriately enough from a fortuitous moment of information exchange. Even though we know each other really well, only by chance in 2019 the authors connected the – hitherto rather hidden – dots and discovered that we already had initial sketches underway for two very similar books. The two projects both had the same core idea: the pressing importance of moving questions of technology to the front stage of public management. Technology cannot be ignored nor reduced to a technological issue. We all wanted to find a way to bring technology to the core activities and attention of public managers. Needless to say, it did not take long to realize that the best approach was to combine our efforts into one book.

We are all scholars with a mixed background who have become interested in technology because of its implications for government and society. We are intrigued by these relations and feel that these are of great importance for the future of government. In governments all around the world we observe a historically unprecedented technology push. Technology nowadays shapes government and governance but it does not by itself reveal the politics and values embedded in the information systems and communication networks. The technology push needs to be countered by a real public management approach guided by values such as democracy, legitimacy and accountability instead of the IT specialists. These core convictions create the want to write a book about technology that does not have a technological angle. We feel that those working in and around public administration need a 'language' to talk about technology that emphasizes social processes and human beings rather than artefacts and gadgets.

Given our wish for a book that is firmly focused on the daily practical challenges of public managers, it made sense for us to try to meld our vast array of case knowledge from around the world into chapters based on the main domains of public management work from policymaking and politics to risk management and human resources. In so doing, the book is an ideal introduction to the main themes of public information management for public managers in master's- and executive-level training as well as students in public administration and public policy master's degrees.

We aim to address what we see as a gap in the market for textbooks on digital technology challenges and public administration. Our experience as teachers and academics is that there are already many good books on technology in government or policy, but these are generally not well connected to the literature on public management. Rather, the technological perspective dominates. We want to approach questions of technology in government from a public management perspective where the relevance of those challenges could be carefully explained and applied. These matters are far too critical to the future of government to be left to drawing of insights from different texts that do not take advantage of the rich stream of public sector knowledge and expertise. Moreover, we want to make our message clear: public managers cannot effectively achieve their goals while ignoring the impact of technology on their organizations.

We owe many individuals and organizations a debt of thanks for their help in producing this book. Marcel Thaens was an early collaborator on the book but needed to step out due to pressing duties in his work as Chief Information Officer for the province of North Brabant. While Marcel was not able to work with us as a co-author, the book was initially developed with his help and would not have been the same without him. We would like to thank two of Albert's student assistants, Roos Hofstra and Friso Selten, in particular for their editorial support for the manuscript. Roos and Friso's influence was very timely coming as it did when new sets of eyes could offer new critiques and perspectives and editorial improvements. Zeger van der Wal provided an excellent and thorough review of the manuscript, which resulted in a broad range of improvements to the organization of chapters and new content. Finally, the support of members of the Bloomsbury team and editorial team, in particular, Milly Weaver, Almudena Gutiérrez and Becky Mutton, Liz Holmes, Joanne Rippin, and Sarah Norman was invaluable to improving the quality of the book and keeping us on track with deadlines.

*Utrecht/The Hague/Tilburg*
*March 2022*

# List of Abbreviations

| | |
|---|---|
| ACA | Affordable Care Act |
| AFST | Allegheny Family Screening Tool |
| AI | artificial intelligence |
| BPM | business process management |
| BYOD | bring your own device |
| CAS | Crime Anticipation System |
| CCTV | closed-circuit television |
| CEO | Chief Executive Officer |
| CIO | Chief Innovation Officer |
| CISO | Chief Information Security Officer |
| COMPAS | Correctional Offender Management Profiling for Alternative Sanctions |
| CoP | communities of practice |
| CRM | customer relationship management |
| CYF | County Office of Children, Youth and Families |
| DEG | Digital Era Governance |
| DLT | distributed ledger technology |
| DSB | Dutch Safety Board |
| ENISA | European Union Agency for Network and Information Security |
| ERP | enterprise resource planning |
| FEMA | Federal Emergency Management Agency |
| GCP | Google Cloud Platform |
| GPS | Global Positioning System |
| HCI | human computer interactions |
| HDB | Housing and Development Board |
| HRM | human resource management |
| I-labs | Innovation labs |
| ICT | information and communications technologies |
| IT | information technology |
| KNOMAD | Knowledge Partnership on Migration and Development |
| KPIs | key performance indicators |

| | |
|---|---|
| LSI-R | Level of Service Inventory Revised |
| ML | machine learning |
| NBER | National Bureau of Economic Research |
| NGOs | nongovernmental organization |
| NPM | New Public Management |
| OECD | Organization for Economic Co-operation and Development |
| OMB | Organization Management and Budget |
| PbD | Privacy by Design |
| PET | privacy enhancing technology |
| PICMD | Policy and Institutional Coherence for Migration and Development |
| POI | points of interest |
| PRC | People's Republic of China |
| reps | representatives |
| RFID | radio-frequency identification |
| ROUTETOPA | Raising Open and User-friendly Transparency-Enabling Technologies for Public Administrations |
| SDGs | Sustainable Development Goals |
| SIS | Schengen Information System |
| SPIM | strategic public information management |
| SWOT | strengths, weaknesses, opportunities, threats |
| TfL | Transport for London |
| UK | United Kingdom |
| US | United States |
| WHO | World Health Organization |
| WMD | Weapons of Math Destruction |
| WPRDC | Western Pennsylvania Regional Data Center |

# 1

# Public management in an information age: a daunting task

*This chapter introduces strategic public information management (SPIM) as a key challenge for public managers. With the increased use of information and communications technologies (ICT), information has become fundamental to managerial work. We argue that the challenge of managing information does not concern merely operational processes but, mostly, the strategic role of information in the public sector. SPIM is introduced by discussing its four defining elements: strategy, publicness, information and management. This chapter then identifies seven key questions for SPIM and links them to the core domains of managerial work: organizational performance, public policy, public services, regulation, risks, politics and innovation. Together, these questions indicate how the work of managers needs to be updated to meet the demands of the information age. These seven questions will be answered across the subsequent chapters.*

## Neglected domain of public management

The nature of the public sector is rapidly changing with the introduction of robotics, predictive algorithms and big data analytics (Kuziemski and Misuraca 2020). What do these continual waves of technological change mean for the work of public managers? Many textbooks on public management stress that the agenda of public managers is filled with structuring organizations, allocating financial and human resources, enhancing the quality of public services, performance management and social interactions. In this book, we argue that these aspects of public management are increasingly conditioned, mediated and structured by ICT.

Public organizations are digitized organizations: old paper-based offices have been complemented and, in some cases, entirely replaced by computerized habitats (Plesner, Justesen and Glerup 2018). Most public servants spend a great portion of their time interacting with a computer: they communicate, enter activity reports, write policy documents, search for information, plan and coordinate activities and process requests from colleagues and citizens via their computers. Many traditional activities remain but have taken on new shapes and forms, while simultaneously, entirely *new* activities are increasingly shaping the daily routines of public managers. The computer has drastically changed the interaction between people to the extent that many – maybe even most – of these interactions take place through computerized interfaces. According to the Netherlands Scientific Council for Government Policy, government should be reconceptualized as an ensemble of information architectures and processes of information exchange (WRR 2011) and digital and algorithmic systems need to be seen as infrastructures that influence and condition all social, political and organizational processes (WRR 2021).

Even if public organizations are not supplanted by such information architectures, they have become highly dependent on ICT (Nograšek and Vintar 2014). The management of information is a major challenge for managers on all levels, and in all policy realms. It is crucial for the organizational routines and processes, management control and accountability, as well as policy development and co-creation in governance networks. Organizations stumble in the dark when their information supplies do not work adequately: they risk inefficiencies, policy errors, loss of control and lack of accountability. As a result, their legitimacy may be at risk. In short, a public organization without sound information management is effectively a blind and deaf organization.

Yet, in reality, many public managers have only a rudimentary understanding of the core technologies of information management: ICT (Hu 2018). Although the use of iPads and social media is omnipresent in our professional as well as private lives, the inner workings of these technologies are still by and large seen as an issue for engineers and other 'techies' (Roman et al. 2019). Public managers prefer to be 'people managers', financial managers or performance managers rather than the managers of new technological information and communication systems. ICT are regarded as tools that should simply work, much like the buildings around us should not collapse and the electricity supplied by power companies should be reliable. Just like with cars, public managers assume that they are not required to fully understand how ICT technologies work. If necessary, public managers can always turn to support staff; they do not need to know the details of technological issues. 'Why should I have knowledge about these technologies if I have skilled specialists working for me?' is a sentiment often expressed by public managers.

Interestingly, the argument that public managers do not require specialist knowledge is seldom used when it comes to financial matters or human resources. These domains of public management also require specialist knowledge of accounting, psychology and workplace safety. Public managers do rely on their support staff for detailed knowledge, but it is common sense that they should have a basic understanding of financial issues to be in control of the organization. The realization that information resources and communication infrastructures are just as important to the very survival of their organization has only slowly begun to sink in.

## Box 1.1: Importance of implementation: Healthcare.gov

Healthcare.gov was a crucial system for the implementation of US president Barack Obama's Affordable Care Act (ACA). The system was designed to facilitate the sale of health insurance plans and offer subsidies to citizens with a low income. However, the system was marred with problems and it was difficult for citizens to sign up for healthcare insurance. The Obama Administration took a long time to fix these technological problems, which resulted in serious political problems for the presidency. The president himself addressed these issues in a press conference on 20 October 2013. His opponents used these problems as an argument against the ACA; and, thus, making the system work became key to Obama's political survival. Although the system still faces safety and performance issues, most problems seem to have been solved (for the time being).

*Source:* http://en.wikipedia.org/wiki/HealthCare.gov

The example of Healthcare.gov (see Box 1.1) highlights the importance of information management: if the system had functioned smoothly from the beginning, it would have been much easier to obtain support for the implementation of the ACA. Box 1.1 clearly illustrates that the success and failure of public management increasingly depends on both high-quality information as well as the technologies that produce and process information. The success of a policy programme depends on the capacity to craft sound information and communication structures. The ACA in the US can only be successful if the information system works. The public managers in the Obama Administration did not need to be data scientists or 'techies' but they did need to be in control of the technology and had to be able to 'translate' issues of public management into information and communication issues and vice versa. Public management in an era of information government requires managers to be able to connect their familiar worlds of human and financial resources with the world of information and communication management.

No public organization can function without ICT. The integration of ICT into every aspect of the public sector over the past three decades is striking and has radically altered interactions both within government organizations as well as with stakeholders (Plesner, Justesen and Glerup 2018; see Box 1.2 for an overview of how information and communication technologies touch upon every aspect of public organizations). Every organizational and policy decision is preconditioned and influenced by the availability of information and communication, and ICT infrastructures are crucial to the success of public organizations and government policies. Whereas the ICT context of public managers has changed dramatically, public management education and theory seems to largely ignore the transformation of government (Hu 2018; Liou and Hu 2019).

This first chapter of the book begins by sketching the enormous technological and accompanying social turbulence that public managers are facing in the twenty-first century. We continue by arguing that this means that information management is therefore no longer only a support function but key to the organizational strategy and therefore the responsibility of each public manager. We present SPIM as a key domain for public managers: managers do not need to know all the technological aspects but do need to be able to strategically position information management in their organization.

## Box 1.2: Omni-presence of information in organizations

Information has become a strategic resource in the public sector. Public organizations depend on the management of this resource for tasks as diverse as ensuring organizational performance, developing and implementing policies, providing services and organizing regulation. The omni-presence of information means that managing risks related to information and information technologies become important tasks for managers and ongoing technological turbulence means that public organizations need to continuously innovate their processes. Finally, the unmediated link between sensitive information and political debates means that information is directly related to the interface between public organizations and politics. For example:

- *Information for organizational performance.* Police officers have integrated the use of information systems in their daily work when they report crimes and observations and retrieve information to guide their work. The police force cannot perform adequately without these information systems.
- *Information for effective policies.* In their development of policies for domains as diverse as safety, social security and infrastructure, government organizations rely on information about current and future situations and developments to make information-based policy decisions.
- *Information for public services.* Most services to citizens and companies are not offered primarily in government offices but through government websites such as portals for filling in income tax forms and even specialized apps, such as those that are used to identify citizens.
- *Information for regulation.* Government regulation of processes such as food safety and traffic flow are based on extensive forms of data collection through sensors and automated inspections and this data forms the basis for regulators who make their inspection choices based on big data analysis.
- *Threat of information risks.* The continuous threat of security risks and malfunctioning systems are ongoing concerns for

public managers. Recent hackings of public organizations highlight that these risks are very real and can paralyse an organization.

- *Political implications.* The leaking of sensitive information poses a risk, as does the level of quality of information in sensitive political developments. For example, when a minister does not have insightful information about developments in their department, they risk misinforming parliament which could result in serious political damage.
- *Managing innovation.* Technological development never ceases, it is continually changing. Current waves of algorithms and datafication demand public organizations to revise and innovate their organizational processes in order to embrace these new technologies.

These various processes illustrate how information management is directly related to the core tasks of public managers. They form the basis for the chapters in this book which will analyze the implications of the omni-presence of information for the work of public managers.

# Technological and social turbulence

Technological change is a matter of existential survival for both public and private organizations. Examples of private organizations that missed crucial trends – think of Kodak which produced films for photo cameras (Ho and Chen 2018) – are well known. While public organizations may not go bankrupt, their effectiveness and legitimacy are constantly and increasingly challenged by assertive stakeholders (Van der Wal 2017). Indeed, some government organizations have become obsolete or simply replaced by computers; many public organizations used to have a library but those librarians who did not become data experts have disappeared from these organizations; huge numbers of administrators have been replaced by computers. Information is a strategic resource for all public organizations and appropriate management of this resource is crucial to the realization of organizational objectives (Chan et al. 1997). This is nothing new. What is new is that novel technologies have radically changed the management of this resource. Complex information systems have been changing the management of information for the past few decades but, more recently, network technologies and social media have added a new dimension to public information management: open data, big data and social media have become the new game, creating great opportunities but also posing risks and challenges. Public organizations will need to reposition the management of their information resources in an open and networked society to retain their effectiveness and legitimacy.

Throughout history, public administration co-evolved with technological developments, which enabled governments to, for example, win wars and better administer taxes. The complexity of systems such as collecting taxes, registering land ownership, managing infrastructural systems and providing public services are directly connected to the use of new technologies. In his historical overview *The Control Revolution*, Beniger (2009) links the expansion of imperia such as the Roman and Inca empires to the use of information systems for communication and registration such as scripture and archives. Modern information technologies such as computerized systems have played an important role in the expansion of government bureaucracies in the second half of the twentieth century and this trend is only set to continue. However, this ongoing information revolution can result in technological turbulence (see Box 1.3).

## Box 1.3: Technological turbulence: distributed ledger technology[1]

In the 2020s, one of the most promising technologies that managers should be cognizant of is 'distributed ledger technology'. This technology may have a huge impact on the way information is managed within government organizations and within networks in which government organizations participate.

A distributed ledger is essentially an asset database that can be shared across a network of multiple sites, geographies or institutions. All participants within a network can have their own identical copy of the ledger. Any changes to the ledger are reflected in all copies within minutes, or in some cases, seconds. The assets can be financial, legal, physical or electronic. The security and accuracy of the assets stored in the ledger are maintained cryptographically through the use of 'keys'

---

[1] First reported by the *Guardian* newspaper in December 2015. See https://www.theguardian.com/us-news/2015/dec/11/senator-ted-cruz-president-campaign-facebook-user-data.

and signatures to control who can do what within the shared ledger. Entries can also be updated by one, some or all of the participants, according to rules agreed by the network. Underlying this technology is the 'blockchain'; a distributed ledger technology that creates encrypted records of digital transactions. Distributed ledger technologies have the potential to help governments collect taxes, deliver benefits, issue passports, record land registries, assure the supply chain of goods and generally ensure the integrity of government records and services.

In a report by the UK Government Chief Scientific Adviser on this technology, it was stated that algorithms that enable the creation of distributed ledgers are powerful, disruptive innovations that could transform the delivery of public and private services and enhance productivity through a wide range of applications. Furthermore, it was suggested that

> we may be witnessing one of those potential explosions of creative potential that catalyse exceptional levels of innovation. The technology could prove to have the capacity to deliver a new kind of trust to a wide range of services. As we have seen open data revolutionize the citizen's relationship with the state, so may the visibility in these technologies reform our financial markets, supply chains, consumer and business-to-business services, and publicly-held registers.

*Source:* UK Government Office for Science (2016)

It is not so much the technologies themselves that matter, but the fundamental transformation caused by digitalization that contemporary societies are witnessing. Taken together, these technological trends point to a fundamental process of digitalization of our societies, economies and our governments. Digitalization encompasses three interconnected phenomena:

- *Algorithmization.* Decisions on policy development, policy implementation and enforcement, and even policy evaluation, are increasingly made by computers. Ever since the 1970s computers have taken over decision-making processes in the public sector (e.g. Bovens and Zouridis 2002). Initially, only simple administrative decisions were made by computers such as the calculation of a welfare benefit or a traffic fine. During the 1980s and 1990s, more sophisticated algorithms have been developed for policy implementation in many realms. Today, implementing public policies is unimaginable without computers also making decisions. While the initial algorithms were fairly basic and static, these algorithms now include machine learning and other forms of artificial intelligence (AI). Algorithms are already widespread in industries such as chemical plants and aviation but the reach of digitization has broadened and now covers almost all production optimization and distribution of goods and services. Operational and managerial decisions in public organizations increasingly rely on algorithms (Schuilenburg and Peeters 2020; see Box 1.4).

- *Datafication.* Digitization has triggered an explosion of data. Algorithms are fed with massive collections of digitally recorded data. In the digital era, collecting and processing data has been compared with mining and refining fossil fuels during the industrial era (Mayer-Schönberger and Cukier 2013). Many interfaces and new sensing techniques translate the images, sounds, smells and any other signals of the state of humans, animals, nature or machines into data in order to record them, exchange them and process them digitally. This can be both structured data, which has a machine-ready form for being read and handled, and unstructured data, which has no pre-set form and tends to be more complex. The larger the amount of data, the more aggregate patterns can be derived from the data. Big data analysis techniques also enable managers to produce personalized information (e.g. Doppelganger research; see Stephens-Davitowitz 2017). Commercial data brokers have expanded and become players in a global economic data market. Our personal data are continuously gathered, traded and processed for commercial reasons (Goodman 2015; Zuboff 2019). The Cambridge Analytica scandal shows that even political parties buy the information on individual voters from commercial data brokers (see Chapter 6, Box 6.4).

- *Networking.* In a digital era, computer-made decisions and data collection and processing are not isolated processes but are intensely connected by networks via the internet. This connection adds a particular dynamic to computer-made decisions and big data because both humans and computers respond to each other which in turn generates new data (e.g. Kelly 1998). Networks and interconnectedness thus add reflexivity to both data and decisions on a historically unprecedented scale and with historically unprecedented speed. Financial markets and in particular high frequency trading may provide a glimpse into a future reality. Within nanoseconds, computer-supported algorithms decide to buy and sell large amounts of stocks in order to benefit from even the smallest price fluctuations. Some even regard networking as the essence of government: government is perceived as a platform for facilitating network interactions (Styrin, Mossberger and Zhulin 2021).

This rapid and ongoing digitization confronts public organizations with a range of new opportunities but also risks that require new knowledge, skills and competencies. These challenges are highly intertwined with social and organizational developments since technologies facilitate and enable new forms of interaction within and between organizations. The introduction of a variety of social media in organizations is one example (see Box 1.5).

The use of social media communications by the police highlights how technological developments and organizational issues are directly related. Sound decision-making on, and productive use of, these new technologies requires an understanding of both the technological dynamic and the organizational implications. The availability of these technologies puts the

---

## Box 1.4: Algorithms in the public sector in Korea

One of the countries at the forefront of the use of algorithms is South Korea. The use of algorithms in the private sector is stimulated and algorithms are also being introduced in government. The development and use of algorithms is diverse, as the following two examples illustrate:

- The Ministry of Justice has launched an online chatbot service called Bubby. This chatbot service provides legal information on real estate, leases, layoffs and inheritances
- The Korean government is working on the development of so-called 'killer robots' in cooperation with the Korea Institute of Science and Technology and an industrial partner

The use of algorithms has triggered debates on fairness, ethics and accountability, suggesting that their use requires open deliberation and not just instrumental application.

*Source:* Shin (2019)

## Box 1.5: Social media in policing

Police organizations in Europe and North America have started to use social media such as Facebook and Twitter to obtain information from citizens for their investigations, to improve their public image and to engage citizens in neighbourhood safety. The introduction of social media raises technological questions related to security, effectiveness, integration and privacy but also organizational questions concerning the right tone of communications, control over external communications and the need for a code of conduct for social media communications to avoid damage to either the image of the police or to their investigations. A critical issue is whether community police officers should be allowed to use social media for external communications: the Toronto Police Service feel this is important to establish a direct link between police and citizens while the Boston Police Department highlights the loss of control over external communications.

*Source:* Meijer and Torenvlied (2016)

organization of external police communications in a new perspective. Is a centralized model preferable or should the police rely on the professional competencies of individual officers to communicate responsibly through social media? What mode of organization offers the best fit with the changing nature of our (information) society? Consideration of issues requires the capacity to analyze new developments which we conceptualize as *socio-technological challenges*.

Socio-technological challenges concern issues – both problems and opportunities – that have a simultaneously technological and social dimension (Meijer and Lofgren 2015). Well-known socio-technological challenges at society level are energy production and food safety. Various technologies offer opportunities to generate energy but they all come at a price and all need to be embedded within a society. The technological manipulation of genes may guarantee food safety, but the risks need to be weighed up, and contingency plans need to be developed. In a similar vein, organizations face socio-technological challenges when they consider using new technologies to make their organizations more effective, efficient and legitimate; however, these technologies also need to be organized and embedded in organizational strategies and operational activities. Moreover, technology often provides a solution to a specific problem, while at the same time generates new problems and challenges or 'unintended consequences' of the technology (Cheeseman, Lynch and Willis 2018). This is what Edward Tenner (1997) calls 'the revenge of technology'. Forging a productive connection between the technological and the social system is thus an important challenge for public managers.

Many discussions around information and communication technologies in the public sector focus on the implications of technological developments in the form of technological challenges. What should public managers do with social media? Can they design an open data strategy? How should public organizations use big data? What can be done to ensure that a web-based system will be reliable? These approaches foreground the technology and analyze organizational responses within the context of these technologies. While this type of analysis may be powerful in promoting a sense of urgency, one disadvantage is that the issues are not framed as socio-technological ones: the organizational side of these developments receives only secondary attention. Managers need to identify the relations between the technological and social issues to successfully integrate technologies in their organizational strategies (Meijer and Lofgren 2015).

With full acknowledgement of the importance of technological developments, we position socio-technological challenges at the heart of information management. The debate about social media in the police (Box 1.5) highlights how police managers should not only be concerned about the technological system, they should also rethink the way they have organized their communication with citizens. These challenges have profound effects on the effectiveness and efficiency of organizations and governance arrangements, on the checks and balances within government, on power relations and on legitimacy. Public information management may be seen as the domain of 'geeks' and 'techies' but it demands in-depth knowledge about administrative, political and organizational processes to make deliberate and effective choices about the core technology of governance.

# Information management as organizational strategy

*Public Management in an Information Age* stresses that it is increasingly important for every public manager – and not just those responsible for ICT – to engage with information management since this has become crucial strategically. The role and use of information within organizations have changed and are changing rapidly due to expeditious technological changes such as algorithmization, datafication and networking. This also means that the focus of information management has changed. Twenty years ago, managing information was still mostly concerned with providing support for internal processes, but since then it has broadened its scope and has now become essential to the efficiency of the organization, and to realizing its strategic goals. This makes information management more complex than previously and, simultaneously, touches upon strategic issues and leads to new questions for the organization and to new management challenges. Public managers need to understand the strategic aspects of information management to connect it to the strategic vision and priorities of the organization (see Box 1.6). For that reason, this book consistently conceptualizes information management as an activity that connects the support of operational processes to broader issues of organizational strategy.

## Box 1.6: Smart street lighting: strategic choices about data and collaboration

The City of Amersfoort in the Netherlands is one of the many cities in the world exploring the possibilities of smart street lighting. The fundamental idea of smart street lighting is that the costs of street lighting can be reduced drastically if street lights are only turned on when necessary. Thus, street lights are connected to sensors that measure different movement and traffic flow. Sensors and data analysis mean the lights provide only what is needed for pedestrian and road safety, making it a sustainable and cost-effective solution. At the same time, this also means that enormous amounts of data about movement and traffic flow in cities need to be collected. The City of Amersfoort is struggling with the issue of how best to organize their collaboration with a high-tech company so that these new technologies are used adequately without compromising privacy or the data becoming openly available. Who will own and control the data? What are the rules for access? It also needs to develop ways of using the data for traffic and safety policies and integrating this type of 'knowledge' with the expert knowledge.

*Source:* Authors' own research

In the 1950s, computers in both the private and public sectors were used mainly for supporting operational and administrative processes within the organization (Van den Bogaard et al. 2008), but since the development of technology, the application range of this technology has increased. Increasingly, ICT are being used to support a variety of related processes such as logistics, payroll processing and HRM. From the 1990s onwards, however, the use of ICT has come to have a broader meaning than just supporting and controlling business processes. Information that is collected and stored in the organization is no longer used only within the limited context of payroll management but also for supporting other processes such as public services, accountability, decision-making, policymaking and implementation. The use of ICT is not only about keeping a grip on processes but also raising the effectiveness and the efficiency of the entire organization.

Today there is almost no single activity taking place within an organization that is not supported by ICT in one way or another (Rooks, Matzat and Sadowski 2017). Information management aims to explore new possibilities of the use of modern ICT for supporting all kinds of processes in the organization. The goal is to develop an infrastructure to support and control the breadth of processes in the organization, and the crux of information management is how to craft new connections between organizational activities to enhance the efficiency of the organization. Efficiency is often defined at the level of the network of organizations since information infrastructures increasingly occur in collaborations between various organizations.

Today, our use of information has taken on altogether new shapes and forms. Due to technological advancements such as social media and the decreasing costs of data storage, organizations often try to collect as much information as possible, including 'unstructured data' like tweets, pictures, movies, soundbites and Facebook messages. Within the context of our networked information society, organizations use all of these different data to achieve their own goals. For public organizations, the background is that of 'governance' instead of 'government'. The government-to-governance shift implies that new processes of policymaking and policy implementation emerge, alongside new ways of organizing governance processes and new accountability structures. The idea is that intensive collaboration between different public (and often also private) organizations is necessary. This is because nowadays no public organization alone can solve societal problems independently – collaboration is always needed. And the use of information has also changed because of those new opportunities to collect, store, share and analyze information.

At the same time, with this increasing amount of data, the analytical power of the tools used in editing and analyzing data has also expanded enormously (Mayer-Schönberger and Cukier 2013). This means that organizations can now leverage massive amounts of data – data they already have stored in their own databases or in the cloud, and also from external resources. This opens up possibilities for new technologies like big data and blockchain. However, the use of information is not limited to the internal context of the organization. It is no longer just about making the organization more efficient; new options are available for making the organization more effective in relation to its environment (citizens, private companies and other organizations). This means a more strategic use of information in which it is no longer used primarily for solving organizational issues, but has become an instrument to find solutions for policy and societal issues. For public organizations this often also means raising their own legitimacy.

In just a few decades, digitization has created a twofold shift with regards to information and information management. Information and information management shifted from a technical matter dealt with by support staff to the core activity of public organizations; what was once a technical and administrative issue for which support staff could even be hired now encompasses all processes in any public organization. It has also shifted from the operational level of the organization to the tactical level (enhancing organizational efficiency) and more recently even to the strategic level (strengthening legitimacy), rendering other orientations obsolete. For their business processes, organizations still rely on information, and information management may still contribute to the efficiency of the organization.

In sum, the context in which information management takes place has changed from supporting internal organizational processes to networks in which organizations closely work together to realize their common goals but also their own individual goals. ICT moved from the realm of support staff to the core processes of public organizations and simultaneously expanded from the operational level to the tactical and strategic levels of the organization. These changes lead to new questions and challenges, some examples of which are presented in Box 1.7.

## Box 1.7: Six challenges for information management

Rapid technological and social changes and the shift from government to governance have resulted in a repositioning of information management in public organizations. These changes have also resulted in a shift in roles and responsibilities and generated new challenges for public managers.

*Building an information infrastructure for networked collaboration.* For a long period of time, information managers were mainly responsible for connecting the business side of the organization (demand) with the ICT side (supply). In view of the additional strategic function of information management they now also have to play another role: on a strategic level they now bring together different actors and organizations who can play a joint role in solving societal problems by using information. Public managers have to be able to establish information infrastructures that contribute to the development of strategic collaborations between networks of organizations.

*Weighing different values in the use of ICT.* With their enhanced strategic focus, ICT have to contribute to balancing, realizing and securing public values like equality in law, legal certainty, legality, effectiveness, efficiency and goal-orientation. With a more intense exchange of information between many stakeholders, it often becomes more difficult, while at the same time more necessary, to weigh these – often conflicting – different values. Think, for instance, of the common discussion about privacy and security around using cameras in the public domain. Information management should focus on the difficult question of how fairness can be established with respect to both equally important values.

*Balancing process control and innovation.* Even from the early days of ICT within organizations, process control has been the main starting point for information management. With other dimensions of information management coming forward, renewal and delivering public value are added to process control. Sometimes it looks as if renewal is more important or more valued than maintaining adequate control of business processes while in fact both are equally important for organizational survival. For this reason, it is important that information management ensures that process control as well as renewal takes place within an organization. It means that in practice public managers have to change processes while they are being carried out, organize time for reflection and ensure this is used directly in the change process. In this way improvement and renewal occur simultaneously, which differs from the current starting point of process control. Working within so-called 'living labs' or 'pilots' supports this perspective on renewal.

*Connecting data to professional knowledge.* Data are but one source of knowledge in organizations and are valuable when they are connected to other forms of knowledge. More than ever, information management should address the question of how data can lead to knowledge. With the availability of large volumes of unstructured data (in addition to structured data), the options are almost without constraint. But how do we turn this enormous sea of information into valuable knowledge? What does this require from the organization and its employees? And what kind of employees does the organization need? Think, for example, of data scientists. Turning data into knowledge means that the data needs to be interpreted by experts and connected to their knowledge. Interesting new developments here are organizing data sessions where hard data are interpreted on the basis of the knowledge and experience of different people, and capturing soft data in data systems by collecting stories and providing more room to add interpretations and experiences to hard data in systems.

*Explosion of information challenge.* Managers have to find a way to deal with the enormous amount of information. The number of email and social media communications is huge but these communication streams can provide vital information for managers. Interesting approaches to this challenge are both of a social and a technical nature: social approaches entail training managers to scan these streams on the basis of certain indicators – risky processes, risky persons, crucial events – to quickly capture important information; while technical approaches include analysis of social media communication on the basis of preferences of managers or even learning algorithms.

*Reality challenge: what is real?* Probably the biggest issue in information management is to establish what is real. Big data analysis can lead to the illusion that every problem can be handled by using big data. At the same time, the notion that only in-depth stories with qualitative insights provide the 'real story' should also be treated with care. The philosophical debate about the truth has kept great thinkers occupied for centuries but managers have to determine on what information they will rely. Triangulation approaches that consist of checking information by relating it to information from a different source appears to be the most promising way of dealing with this challenge.

# Strategic public information management

Strategic public information management (SPIM) is a key domain for public managers, and the previous section connected this to a series of challenges for managers. SPIM means managing human interactions in order to connect the potential of information resources to the strategic priorities of the public organization. Throughout this book, the implications of SPIM for ensuring organizational performance, developing and implementing policies, providing services, organizing regulation, mitigating risks, managing politics and ongoing innovation will be discussed. We will introduce the building blocks of SPIM as a basis for the following chapters. To clarify SPIM, we will define the four letters – S, P, I and M – by answering the following questions:

- How can we understand information management as a *strategic* rather than an operational activity?
- How is *public* information management different from information management in the private sector?
- How is *information* an element of social activities rather than technical processes?
- How can *management* be understood as a process that takes different aspects of human interaction into account?

This section will briefly delve into some big, often philosophical, discussions. We will present various overviews to underline our message that SPIM requires a rich understanding of complex social processes. We need a multi-perspective understanding of SPIM that acknowledges the many sides of human interactions, rather than a narrow, technological view, to link information management to public management.

The first building block of SPIM is 'strategy': how can we understand information management as a strategic rather than an operational activity? While many people have debated what a strategy is, Mintzberg (1987, 11) suggests that we should not try to come up with one definition of strategy: 'Explicit recognition of multiple definitions can help practitioners and researchers alike to maneuver through this difficult field.' Mintzberg (1987) distinguishes the five Ps of strategy: a rational analysis of the options available to the organization and their match with the organization's aspirations (plan); an organizational-political analysis of influencing developments and actors (ploy); an environmental analysis of realizing a fit between itself and the environment (position); a practice that emerges from these implicit choices and actions (pattern); and a way of thinking that influences organizational actions and responses (perspective). Mintzberg's (1987) 5P model shows that SPIM is not only about developing and executing rational plans but also about being smart in organizational politics, determining how the organization wants to position itself in the environment, managing implicit choices that emerge from organizational actions and influencing the organizational culture. A key aspect of this perspective is that it emphasizes both rational as well as social elements such as political action ('ploy'), building relationships ('position') and making sense of patterns ('pattern' and 'perspective'). Box 1.8 provides an illustration of these approaches to strategy.

## Box 1.8: Applying Mintzberg's (1987) 5P model to strategies for leveraging big data

The possibilities of using big data for organizational strategies raises the question of how public managers can develop a big data strategy. The following example illustrates how Mintzberg's (1987) 5P model can help us to understand what the S in SPIM means.

- The *plan* perspective highlights that investments are needed to ensure that the organization will have the information systems it needs for obtaining value from big data. These investments should be based on an analysis of needs and developments and indicate which technological systems will be maintained, developed or acquired and how big data resources will be managed. The relation between big data analysis and long-term organizational objectives is the key focus.
- The *ploy* perspective stresses that the big data strategy should be based on an analysis of the willingness of organizational departments to share their data to contribute to organizational objectives. This perspective also emphasizes the need to ensure political and public support for big data practices. An issue such as privacy demands extra focus in order to maintain political and public support.

- The *position* perspective suggests that government organizations should consider their relations with the environment in view of the opportunities of big data. Big data collaborations could result in a restructuring of the public organization's network or the collaborative chain. In addition, the organization needs to reconsider the public value proposition of the organization.
- The *pattern* perspective turns the focus of strategy from a top-down managerial view to a view on big data practices that are being set up on the organization's shop floor. The role of management is not to set out new lines but to support, enhance and facilitate successful big data practices in the organization. By stimulating these to grow, a big data strategy emerges in the organization.
- The *perspective* perspective emphasizes that big data means that the organization needs to reconsider its identity. The Vehicle Tax Agency, for example, could start seeing itself not as an organization for tax collection but rather a centre for data about mobility. It could also view all its transactions with citizens and stakeholders as opportunities to collect data relevant to mobility.

The second building block is 'public': how is public information management different from information management in the private sector? To answer this question, we need to understand how public is connected to information – public information – and how it is connected to management – public management.

- *Public information* means that, in contrast with the private sector, the information system does not only serve the organization but also parliamentarians, journalists, interest groups and citizens outside the organization in the public sphere. Contemporary societies assume that since the information was collected with public money it should be publicly available (Henninger 2013). This means that the information can be requested on the basis of Freedom of Information Acts or Open Government initiatives and that organizations should make an effort to make the data 'open' to the public. See Box 1.9 for an example.
- *Public organizations* are different from private organizations with respect to four organizational dimensions: its environment, its goals,

its structures and its staff (Dorsman et al. 2015). The environment of public organizations is more political and thus political pressure is a continuous force on it. Due to the lack of market incentives, conflicting demands and policy complexity, public organizations have more ambiguous goals than private organizations (Pandey and Wright 2006). The structure of public organizations is more bureaucratic in terms of hierarchy, formal rules, differentiation and control than private organizations. Finally, there is a motivational difference between the staff of public and private organizations (Perry 1997; Christensen and Wright 2011; Wright, Moynihan and Pandey 2012). Staff in public organizations have a greater motivation to specifically serve the public interest whereas private sector staff focus on the demands of the individual customers (Boyne 2002, 102).

The third building block is 'information'. This term is much used by engineers and IT specialists in a technical sense; however, here we need to understand the social nature of information. How is information an element of social activity rather than technical process? Information is one of the words that

## Box 1.9: Open data in Pittsburgh

After he assumed office in early 2014, Pittsburgh mayor William Peduto's administration began an effort to make the city's data open and accessible by joining the existing vanguard of cities with open data programmes. Spurred on by the traditional adage that a good government is an open one and a desire to move towards transparency after the controversially opaque administration of his predecessor, Peduto's mandate was to ensure a more responsive city government. In order to do so, his administration has sought to equip residents and neighbourhood organizations with the tools and information they need to work toward stronger, more equitable communities. In joining forces with the surrounding Allegheny County and the University of Pittsburgh, the City of Pittsburgh launched the Western Pennsylvania Regional Data Center (WPRDC), the country's first truly regional open data platform, which has emerged as a national model for open data collaboration among municipalities, public authorities, nonprofits and community groups.

*Source:* Dayanada and Burack (2017)

we talk about all the time that has many different meanings (see Floridi 2010 for an overview). To understand the social nature of information, we build upon different disciplines:

- *Economists* highlight that information is directly related to the reduction of uncertainty in decision-making processes (Simon 1947). Decisions risk being suboptimal if they are not based on perfect information and therefore organizations need to develop business information systems (Laudon and Laudon 2000).
- The field of *cognitive psychology*, and more specifically, human computer interactions (HCI) – highlights that information is provided by machines but processed by humans (Winograd and Flores 1986). This means that we need to understand how people process information on the basis of their knowledge, attitudes and practices.
- *Political scientists* highlight that information is a source of power. Information is a scarce resource like money, buildings and personnel, and this resource is to be used to strengthen an organizational actor's position vis-à-vis other actors (Homburg 1999).
- For *anthropologists*, information is needed to position ourselves in the world and to explore who we are. Feldman and March (1981) stress that information is not only a signal to be used in (rational) decision-making processes but also a symbol to show that our actions are rational and thus deserve to be supported.

The key message from all these disciplines is that we need to understand how human beings work with information, rather than focusing only on the technology, to understand information management. Box 1.10 provides an illustration.

The fourth and final building block is 'management'. This often-debated term generally refers to organizing collaboration to achieve certain goals, though many authors have suggested that this definition risks overemphasizing the rational aspects of management. How can management be understood as a process that takes different aspects of human interaction into account? Building on Bolman and Deal (2017), management is not only about rational analysis of the organization and structuring the design of new systems (structural frame); it is also about motivating personnel (human resource frame), managing conflict (political frame) and providing meaning to people (symbolic frame). Bolman and Deal (2017) stress that managers should be able to switch between these different frames to generate information systems that actually 'work' for the organization. Their warning

# Box 1.10: Understanding information about school performance as a human process

All over the world, schools are required to publish information about their performance. But how should we understand this information?

- *Information for decision-making.* Information about school performance can help school managers make better decisions about the methods used in the curriculum and the use of educational resources. This information is also seen as crucial to the decisions of parents and students. The dominant argument for publishing information about school performance is that it will result in better decision-making for school choice.
- *Human processing of information.* The School Inspection Service in the Netherlands has studied the use of information about school performance to develop visualizations that support how people make decisions about schools. In addition, the inspection service has studied how directors and teachers perceive the information to understand the impact on schools.
- *Strategic action through information.* Publishing the information about school performance is a means for the School Inspection Service to stimulate compliance of schools to their standards. Schools tend to resist the transparency of school performance since they see it as an infringement on their autonomy in communicating about the school with stakeholders.
- *Making sense of performance information.* The symbolic meaning of publishing information about school performance is that it stresses that schools are concerned with striving for high performance. The idea that education can have many different meanings disappears from view when the functioning of a school is reduced to a set of (seemingly objective) performance indicators.

*Source:* Meijer (2007)

is that a technocratic perspective on organizations may seem rational but it is bound to produce a variety of problems that cannot be solved from a structural perspective.

A common thread in our discussion of strategy, information and management is that focus on the human side of information management is essential. As per Bolman and Deal (2017), four frames – four roles – of SPIM can be summarized: the engineer, the coach, the mediator and the reverend. These roles provide a basis for thinking about SPIM as much more than rational analysis and action (see Box 1.11).

## Box 1.11: Four roles of SPIM

### Skill set 1: Engineer

The engineer aims to build effective information systems on the basis of a rational analysis. The following assumptions constitute the core of this frame:

- Information is a commodity that needs to be managed effectively to realize effective and legally compliant government.
- Managing information means to ensure the fit between organizational processes and information systems.
- Strategic planning entails exploring future requirements and making plans to cater for these requirements.
- The central criterion for measuring the success of SPIM is its contribution to the cost-effective and rational implementation of public tasks.

### Skill set 2: Coach

The coach emphasizes that information and digitalization should match the needs of employees and stimulate their engagement and commitment to the organization. The following assumptions summarize the key idea of this frame:

- Data exists in systems but information is what people – in our case, public servants – make of it.
- Managers need to understand how people process information to develop information strategies that fit their needs.
- Information systems can strengthen the engagement of people to the organization's objectives, but can also disconnect them.

- Strategic planning is a combination of analyzing future requirements (top down) and facilitating and stimulating developments on the work floor (bottom up).
- Successful SPIM results in motivated personnel and a high-performing organization.

### Skill set 3: Mediator

The mediator accepts that information is seen as a scarce resource and that the development of information systems will usually result in conflict. The following assumptions indicate what this frame is about.

- In and between organizations, information is a scarce resource that provides power to the ones that control it.
- Managing information in organizations means finding a way to mediate conflicts and stimulate fair practices.
- Developing an information strategy means ensuring legitimacy for it in and outside the organization and finding ways to deal with resistance.
- SPIM can be regarded as successful if it contributes to public support – legitimacy and collaboration – of the organization.

### Skill set 4: Reverend

The reverend acknowledges that information systems need to provide meaningful information to actors in and outside their organizations. The suppositions below provide an overview of the line of thinking in this frame:

- Information is not only a signal to be processed but also a symbol of who we are and what the organization is.
- Managers have a leading role in providing sense to what people do with information and how they give meaning to the information.
- The process of developing an information strategy is not only about instrumental issues but also about the broader question: what is the position of this organization in society?
- The criterion for measuring the success of SPIM is whether it helps the organization to produce public value.

A public management professional is simultaneously an engineer, a coach, a mediator and a reverend.

# Outline of this book

As argued, public information management has become a crucial aspect of the work of public managers on all levels in any organization. The idea that information management can be delegated to support staff specialists is outdated. The digitization of government certainly includes technology but in the organizational context it also deals with socio-technological challenges. In an era when digitalized information systems are fundamental to the performance, effectiveness, efficiency and legitimacy of public organizations, these systems should be the key focus of public managers. This book enables public managers to address the new challenges caused by digitization. It provides insights that are needed to deal with the strategic issues that arise from the social and technological shifts ICT encountered in public organizations. As we show, public management can no longer be understood without addressing digitization and information management. The key lessons from each chapter are summarized at the end of it.

The rapid introduction of new technologies, their connection with social and organizational processes, the strategic character of decisions and the unpredictable patterns of usage make SPIM a highly complex task. Our key objective is to provide the insights that will assist the reader to shape SPIM in the context of the public organization they lead. We will discuss a wide variety of technological developments within the context of organizational issues, such as innovation, control, collaboration, policy and self-governance, as well as technological developments such as big data, open data and social media.

The use of these theories here is pragmatic: they are not explained for their own sake but to help public managers understand the challenges of the information age. The key function of these theories is that they help public managers to 'reframe' issues (Bolman and Deal 2017), to prevent becoming caught up in a one-dimensional instrumental logic and to provide action repertoires. For this reason, each chapter introduces different frames that help public managers to analyze issues of SPIM from different angles and to avoid being caught in a singular logic. Table 1.1 presents an overview of these frames. Our objective is not to provide an overview of all academic knowledge but to highlight key lessons for public organizations and to illustrate these on the basis of examples and cases from all around the world. The cases serve as illustrations of arguments about the various aspects

**Table 1.1** Overview of the frames presented in the various chapters.

| Chapter | Frames |
| --- | --- |
| Chapter 2: Managing information for organizational performance | Digital bureaucracy<br>Organizational community |
| Chapter 3: Managing information for public policy | Policy production<br>Policy network |
| Chapter 4: Managing information for public services | Proactive services<br>Co-production of services |
| Chapter 5: Managing information for regulation | Algorithmic regulation<br>Politics of regulation |
| Chapter 6: Managing the risks of information and technology | Rational analysis of risks<br>Human perspective on risks<br>Politics of risk management<br>Risks and organizational culture |
| Chapter 7: Managing information in a political environment | Instrumental opportunities<br>Normative challenges |
| Chapter 8: Strategic public information management as innovation challenge | Bright and dark sides of innovation<br>Phases of innovation process<br>Capacities and attitudes of managers |

of SPIM, and how they are connected to several different tasks in public organizations:

- *Managing information for organizational performance (Chapter 2).* A key objective of information management is to strengthen management control by providing full and accessible information about the inputs, throughputs and outputs of work processes. This requires that organizations establish a balance between 'hard' and 'soft' information. Information management not only provides managers with information, it also facilitates collaboration between employees within the public organization. The challenge here is to cater to the needs of employees while, at the same time, ensure that they work towards organizational objectives.
- *Managing information for public policy (Chapter 3).* Information is needed to develop, implement and evaluate government policies. Public organizations are pressured to enhance the evidence base of policies and strengthen the real-time monitoring of implementation. This challenge discusses the power but also limitations of policy informatics to provide information for policymaking. This challenge discusses the need to use both comprehensive policy information and common sense.

- *Managing information for public services (Chapter 4).* A cornerstone for public organization performance is the quality of services to citizens. The demands, routines and preferences of citizens are changing rapidly and confront public service providers with the need to continuously adapt their services. The challenge is how to use new technologies such as websites, social media and apps in contacts with citizens to enhance the quality of service but also strengthen the efficiency of the organization.
- *Managing information for regulation (Chapter 5).* The information resources of government organizations are public resources and access can be demanded by external users on the basis of freedom of information legislation. The challenge here is to use the variety of information sources in an effective and legitimate manner to strengthen the various forms of government regulation.
- *Managing risks (Chapter 6).* The enhanced storage of information about citizens and companies confronts public organizations with new responsibilities. The challenge is to protect data against international hackers and fulfil privacy requirements without creating bureaucratic barriers for flexible performance.
- *Managing politics (Chapter 7).* Since public managers always operate in a political context, digitization affects and reshuffles this. Information is not a neutral resource but often has great political value (and thus presents political risk). The challenge is to manage political sensitivities in such a way that democratic legitimacy is guaranteed in a complex and dynamic political environment.
- *Managing innovation (Chapter 8).* The introduction of new technologies and new ways of working in public organizations requires managers to manage these processes of innovation. New procedures and services are created but these often demand new capabilities and expertise. The challenge is to create opportunities for change and renewal while at the same time warranting the quality and legitimacy of work.

# KEY LESSONS FROM CHAPTER 1

- The integration of ICT in every aspect of the public sector has radically altered interactions both within government organizations as well as in all interactions with stakeholders.

- Current developments – algorithmization, datafication and networking – compound this trend of ICT integration and generate a whole new set of opportunities and challenges.
- For this reason, managing information technologies and information resources is just as important to the survival of public organizations as managing finances or human resources.
- In view of the strategic importance of information resources, it is increasingly important for every public manager – and not just the CIO – to engage with information management.
- SPIM means managing human interactions in and around public organizations in order to connect the potential of information resources to the strategic priorities of the public organization.
- Crucial to understanding SPIM is that it acknowledges the many aspects of human interactions – such as human cognitions, power struggles and processes of meaning-making – rather than a narrow, technological view on information management.
- This perspective on SPIM can be used to present new tasks for public managers in domains as diverse as organizational performance, public policy, public services, regulation, risks, politics and innovation.

# 2

# Managing information for organizational performance

*How can information be managed to realize successful organizational performance? In line with our approach to strategic public information management (SPIM), we argue that successful organizational performance requires different perspectives. This chapter stresses that information management needs to be aligned with a manager's perspective on their organization. When a public organization is managed as a* **monocentric organization**, *performance is about the quality of organizational processes and the digital bureaucracy presents a model for information management. When the manager directs the public organization as a* **polycentric organization**, *the quality of relations is at the heart of performance and the organizational community forms the basis for information management. We highlight the instrumental and also ethical implications of these models in the work of public managers.*

## Introduction

Public managers share the common concern of improving the quality and performance of their organization. Information and communication technologies have become crucial to maintaining and improving organization performance in various dimensions. A relatively recent example is the executive dashboard (see Box 2.1). This dashboard is highly attractive since it implies that managers have direct access to all the real-time information they need to be in full control of the organization. Should, then, all public managers immediately implement this type of dashboard in their organizations?

Various new technologies are presented to public managers as effective tools in performance management. While their value is undisputed, they do confront managers with questions such as:

- How can I benefit from new techniques for big data analysis and how can I implement these in my organization?
- Will my organization benefit from groupware and how does this affect the performance of teams?
- Is an enterprise resource planning (ERP) system valuable to my organization and how do I make this work?
- How can I use social media to support exchanges of information between employees and how will this contribute to organizational performance?

Obviously, performance management is concerned with information and data, and IT specialists in and around public organizations have eagerly come to dominate this domain with their expertise. As the previous chapter shows, performance management should not be left to IT specialists who are not trained to understand the publicness of the organization, its strategy or management. As with any field of public management, giving too much power to 'techies' or relying too heavily on data specialists is definitely a recipe for failure; although, on the other hand, ignoring their expertise can mean that opportunities for improving organizational performance are missed. How technologies can help to improve organizational performance is a question that requires input from both IT specialists and people with knowledge about organizational processes, and an understanding of the strategic importance of public sector performance and political and organizational dynamics. As argued in Chapter 1, the notion of performance requires specific attention in the public sector since it is often ambiguous and contentious. Organizational performance also depends on the stakeholder perspective on the role and the mission of the organization.

In this chapter, we argue that the technologies used to improve organizational processes should be aligned with the organization and its performance management approach. While the development of technological tools for performance management is an IT matter, the alignment of these tools with the organizational model and the approach to performance management is pre-eminently a matter for public managers. For an example of a link between an IT tool and a perspective on measuring organizational performance, see Box 2.1. Since this is not a book on organizational science or performance management, we will provide a rudimentary overview of what organizational performance in public organizations entails.

Building on the literature on performance management, we start by distinguishing two approaches of performance management. Each approach connects with a particular type of public organization. We introduce the monocentric organizational model (digital bureaucracy) and polycentric organizational model (organizational community) and show their links to performance models. We elaborate on digital bureaucracies and organizational communities to enable the reader to grasp the richness of these perspectives. The models, however, do not have only instrumental consequences; we also highlight the ethical issues that arise from the use of technological systems for strengthening organizational performance. We will finish with a summary of the main argument and key lessons.

## Box 2.1: Executive dashboards: does every public organization need one?

An executive dashboard is a visual representation in graphs and tables that gives executives a quick and easy way to view their organization's performance in real time. In *Forbes* magazine, Dave Lavinsky (2013) argues that every business needs an executive dashboard, and highlights the following five key benefits:

1. *Visibility.* An executive dashboard gives you great visibility and insight. You know exactly what's going on in all aspects of your business. This allows you to better manage it.
2. *Ongoing improvements.* One of Peter Drucker's most famous quotes is 'if you can't measure it, you can't improve it' – executive dashboards allow you to measure your performance throughout your organization and thus improve it.
3. *Time saving.* Many executives spend countless hours logging into business systems and running reports. Conversely, the right executive dashboard shows you the latest results from each report you need, saving precious hours each month.
4. *Judge performance against your plan.* Many executives spend time creating a business plan for their organization to follow. However, that's just the first step to success; the second is making sure your company is performing to your

plan's expectations. Your executive dashboard could do just that – that is, you can automatically show your goals from your business plan versus your actual, real-time results.

5. *Employee performance improvements.* When employees know their performance is being judged in a dashboard, and can see their own results, they innately start to improve their work.

Does this mean that every public organization needs a dashboard? This chapter argues that a dashboard fits well within the monocentric perspective on organizations since it is built upon the idea that central management should have direct access to the information it needs to direct the organization. However, although the dashboard can be valuable, it certainly won't automatically turn an organization into a high-performing one. This requires much more focus on supporting (teams of) professionals.

# Digital bureaucracy and organizational community

To understand the different approaches to organizational performance, we need to introduce two models: the monocentric and the polycentric organization. The monocentric model builds upon the idea that management entails the coordination of an organization's activities in order to achieve defined objectives. The managerial process starts with defining objectives for the organization and developing a strategy to realize these objectives. Managers should then organize, plan and control the organization to ensure the policies are implemented as intended. These classic key functions are especially important in what Mintzberg (1992) has called 'machine bureaucracies'. The organizational model associated with this concept is the organization as a *machine* with inputs, processes and outputs. The manager is the person who controls this machine and performance management entails, raising the ratio of outputs vis-à-vis the inputs (Morgan 1986).

Key features of this organizational model are hierarchy, a focus on the organization's tasks, formalized communication that enables the organization to account for its decisions and actions and a reliance on rules, routines and procedures. In this model, workflow systems enable public managers to optimize the production process, customer relation systems enable them to meet the demands of citizens and ERP systems facilitate public managers to improve the allocation of resources. In this perspective – which builds on a *monocentric organizational model* – ICT add a layer of instant information on organizational processes that feed managerial decision-making. The division and coordination of tasks within the organization takes place from a central – management – position. Within this context, information systems are designed to support individual tasks that contribute to the goals of the organization. The systems structure and steer the work of individuals.

Critics of the monocentric model argue that public organizations do not operate as mechanical machines as it ignores both the benefits of human creativity and entrepreneurial behaviour. The fragmented, dynamic and organic nature of public organizations requires a different organizational model and a different approach to performance management. The organization is not a machine but a *community*; it is about people being willing and able to collaborate. The division and coordination of tasks occurs in a dynamic fashion throughout the whole organization. For this reason, some public organizations have replaced or complemented performance information with a performance dialogue that connects the performance information with human intelligence and team interaction.

The metaphor of the community – the *polycentric perspective* – is a good match with recent technological developments such as community software and social networks. The fundamental idea is that an information infrastructure facilitates the real-life interactions of members of an organization. A WhatsApp group is a key example of this: it facilitates the exchange of information and collaboration in a group of people by providing a generic infrastructure that can be catered to specific requirements. While previous forms of information management fitted neatly within bureaucratic modes of organizing based on formal roles and hierarchical structures, new information technologies challenge this structure. An in-depth study of the use of email in government highlights that this medium is primarily used for personalized and horizontal communication and thus polycentric interactions; a notion also highlighted in recent studies of social media (Meijer and Thaens 2013).

Monocentric and polycentric models are fundamentally different ways to organize relations between people (see Figure 2.1), and both

*Monocentric organization*                    *polycentric organization*

**Figure 2.1** Monocentric and polycentric organization models.

present different perspectives on organizing information, and incorporate different technological tools. We want to emphasize that public managers should strive for alignment of their organizational model, their approach to performance management and the technological tools they use for performance management. To help achieve this alignment, we will now outline the different types of technologies connected with the different organizational models and approaches to performance management.

# Information management for the digital bureaucracy

The digital bureaucracy was first given serious attention in the 1990s, when computers were introduced rapidly into government organizations. Zuurmond (1994) referred to these expeditious changes as the rise of 'infocracy'. Infocracy entails the bureaucracy implementing policy decisions while supplementing – or even replacing – the hierarchical and centralized structures with an information structure. Workflows and requirements in systems dictate the work of civil servants rather than procedures and orders. Zuurmond describes how social welfare workers are steered by digital forms to take certain decisions about benefit applications. Deviating from the system is no longer possible – or at least highly complicated – since the system dictates administrative behaviour: 'Computer says no.'

Digital bureaucracy was still in its infancy when Zuurmond (1994) studied it, but became a reality in the early twenty-first century. Increasingly,

## Box 2.2: Digital bureaucracy and the response to the Covid-19 pandemic in Singapore

As countries around the world struggled with their responses to the Covid-19 pandemic, the digital bureaucracy in Singapore was widely regarded as good practice. It consisted of a variety of measures implemented by Singapore's digital bureaucratic organization, including:

- Turning many medical examinations into online counselling sessions
- Using advanced technology to follow up and diagnose cases of Covid-19 infections
- Sending the robot dog 'Spot' to public spaces to inform people about virus risks to help reduce cases of infection
- Requiring travellers arriving from abroad to wear an electronic monitor in order to avoid having to isolate at a government-designated facility
- Using sensors and cameras to monitor a variety of things from the cleanliness of public spaces to crowd density and the precise movement of each locally registered vehicle
- Developing a national digital check-in system that allows workplaces, shopping centres, restaurants and supermarkets to keep track of the individuals who enter their premises

Abdou (2021, 7) comments that 'digital machinism helps public administration to enhance transparency and accountability, while bureaucracy machinism helps government to operate with efficiency and effectiveness', clearly highlighting how a digital bureaucracy can provide a direct, stable and effective response to a crisis situation.

*Source:* Abdou (2021)

fewer employees work with guidebooks, procedures or receive training in the working procedures of the organization. Instead, employees learn to work with the ICT system and rely on the rules implemented in this system. This means that managers rely on these systems for their control over organizational processes. Dashboards with information about key domains in the organization are the basis for managerial control. For management control, the use of hard information such as management reports and key performance indicators (KPIs) on the basis of integrated information systems are of great importance. Managers need structured information about budget, personnel and performance for decision-making and control. The popularity of business process management (BPM) systems such as SAP in the public sector can be explained by their capacity to support business processes and present useful information to managers (Gulledge and Sommer 2002).

The development of smart systems for managerial control continues unabated (see Box 2.2). It remains to be seen whether managers are still physically needed in the digital bureaucracy since control of the organization can be embedded within an algorithm (see Box 2.3).

In the monocentric model of organizations, public managers select, develop and implement the information systems that support the successful outcome of their organizing, planning and control functions. The selection and implementation of an ERP system (see Box 2.5) is a key task for managers, which requires a comprehensive analysis consisting of six phases (Laudon and Laudon 2000, 346–53):

## Box 2.3: Meet your new boss: an algorithm

We have become used to developments in automation such as software programmes telling us what information we need to enter when completing a form or going to a meeting. Recent developments suggest that this will only continue and that the future manager may be an algorithm that can prompt and organize us in more complex ways:

> Companies say the new tools make them more efficient and give employees more opportunities to do new kinds of work. But the software also is starting to take on management tasks that humans have long handled, such as scheduling and shepherding strategic projects. Researchers say the shift could lead to narrower roles for some managers and displace others.

> When Shell wanted help evaluating digital business models in the car-maintenance sector, executives plugged the project into an algorithm that scanned for available Shell staffers with the right expertise—and assigned the job with a click. Shell uses

machine-learning software designed by Boston-based Catalant Inc. to match workers and projects. The program tracks and evaluates their activity so it can refine the next round of matches.

The key managerial task of controlling the work of employees could well be taken over by a computer.

*Source:* Schechner (2017)

1 *System analysis.* 'The systems analysis is the analysis of the problem that the organization will solve with an information system' (Laudon and Laudon 2000, 347). A problem could be the scattered knowledge about citizen requests for assistance from local government. A systems analyst will then map all the different interactions between local government officials and citizens and how they record information about these interactions. Building upon this and on the available technological solutions, s/he will indicate what kind of system is needed to coordinate these requests. In sum, this phase typically entails identifying problems and opportunities, specifying a solution and establishing information requirements.

2 *Systems design.* The systems design reveals how the information system can fulfil the objectives defined following the systems analysis. Expanding on the example in the previous point, the system design will result in a plan for a system that supports the coordination of citizen requests by highlighting the processes in which it will be used and the information that will be processed. Whereas organizational analysis was the key activity in the first phase, this phase is about technological design and will result in specific design specifications – or specifications for package selection – that can be used for actually building or selecting an information system.

3 *Programming.* This phase probably requires the least involvement of the manager since it entails the translation of the system specifications into programme code. It is important in this phase to keep track of progress and prevent long delays as a result of technical difficulties – progress reports are vitally important here. More agile working methods can shorten this phase and better connect it to the next phase to ensure that programming results in value for the organization. See also Box 2.6.

4 *Testing.* Testing is concerned with establishing whether the system produces the desired results under known conditions. Laudon and Laudon (2000, 351) highlight that this phase consists of three activities: unit testing (i.e. testing each programme separately), systems testing (i.e. testing the whole system and thus also the interactions between the programmes) and acceptance testing (i.e. the evaluation by users, technical staff and managers). Specific areas of testing include file storage, handling peak loads, recovery and restart procedures and security measures.

5 *Conversion.* Conversion is a seemingly rather technical but nevertheless important activity to achieve organizational stability. Conversion refers to changing from an old to a new system. A key issue here is whether the system will work effectively under real-life conditions. A variety of strategies can be used to minimize the risks of the introduction of the new system under real conditions: the parallel strategy, direct cutover strategy, pilot study strategy and the phased approach strategy. A conversion plan is important to manage this phase and minimize organizational risks.

6 *Production and maintenance.* Although the system has been introduced, the work is not over – the system needs to be reviewed periodically to assess whether it still meets expectations or needs to be adjusted and improved. Does the system actually help to process citizen requests for assistance? Errors need to be detected and processed, system efficiency needs to be checked, etc. This phase can be especially demanding and time-consuming if there were problems at the system analysis and system design phases.

Taken together, these stages should be seen as iterations. Production and maintenance are not a final stage but, in time, result in new forms of system analysis. This is indeed a challenging aspect of managing information for organizational performance: the job is never done. Systems are continuously in a state of redevelopment and therefore public managers need to regard this cycle as an ongoing aspect of their work. Key concerns of public managers such as information security and privacy protection need to be integrated in this systematic process. The design specifications, for example, will need to contain distinct indications of security concerns such as access controls, catastrophe plans and audits trails (Laudon and Laudon 2000, 350). In addition, these designs need to be based on privacy legislation and preferably integrate state-of-the-art approaches such as *privacy by design* to ensure that privacy concerns will be properly dealt with (see Box 2.4).

The monocentric organization model provides a systematic and consistent perspective on SPIM for organizational performance but it also has some important limitations and drawbacks (e.g. Wilson 1989). One key limitation is that it is built for stability rather than dynamic changes (which is why there is a call for more agile organization: see Mergel et al. 2018 and Box 2.6). The bureaucracy provides structure, as does infocracy, but its ability to respond rapidly to changes in the environment is limited. Another

---

## Box 2.4: Privacy by design

The European Union Agency for Network and Information Security (ENISA) is a centre of network and information security expertise for the EU, its member states, the private sector and European citizens. Its aim is to offer advice and recommendations on good practice in information security; an important theme of which is privacy by design.

The term 'privacy by design', or its variation 'data protection by design', identifies a development method for privacy-friendly systems and services, thereby going beyond mere technical solutions by also addressing organizational procedures and business models. Privacy should be taken into account throughout the entire engineering process from the earliest design stages to the operation of the productive system. Privacy by design is neither a collection of general principles nor can it be reduced to the implementation of privacy enhancing technologies (PETs). In fact, it is a process involving various technological and organizational components, which implement privacy and data protection principles. These principles and requirements are often derived from law, even though they are frequently underspecified in the legal sources (ENISA 2014).

Ann Cavoukia, former Information and Privacy Commissioner of Ontario (Canada), coined the term 'Privacy by Design' (PbD) and has described its seven foundational principles:

1. *Proactive not reactive; preventative not remedial.* PbD does not wait for privacy risks to materialize, nor does it offer

remedies for resolving privacy infractions once they have occurred – it aims to prevent them from occurring.

2. *Privacy as the default*. If an individual does nothing, their privacy remains intact. No action is required on the part of the individual to protect their privacy – it is built into the system, by default.

3. *Privacy embedded into design*. PbD is embedded into the design and architecture of IT systems and business practices. It is not bolted on, like an add-on, after the fact. The result is that privacy becomes an essential component of the core functionality being delivered.

4. *Full functionality – positive-sum, not zero-sum*. PbD seeks to accommodate all legitimate interests and objectives in a positive-sum 'win-win' method, rather than through a dated, zero-sum approach, where unnecessary trade-offs are made.

5. *End-to-end security – lifecycle protection*. Having been embedded into the system prior to the first element of information being collected, PbD extends securely throughout the entire life cycle of the data involved — strong security measures are essential to privacy, from start to finish.

6. *Visibility and transparency*. PbD seeks to assure all stakeholders that whatever the business practice or technology involved, it is, in fact, operating according to the stated promises and objectives, subject to independent verification.

7. *Respect for user privacy*. Above all, PbD requires architects and operators to foreground the interests of the individual by offering such measures as strong privacy defaults, appropriate notice and empowering user-friendly options.

*Source:* Cavoukian (2009)

drawback is that its focus on processes means that people are adapted to processes and there is little or no room for creativity or unstructured input from individual workers. This may also result in forms of myopia in an organization where a single point of view dominates and is not challenged by rivalling perspectives.

## Box 2.5: Enterprise resource planning (ERP) systems in Malaysia

'ERP systems are the software tools to manage all the enterprise's data, and to provide information to those who need it when they need it. The systems help organizations deal with their supply chain: receiving, inventory management, customer order management, production planning and managing, shipping, accounting, human resource management and all the other activities that take place in modern business' (Ragowsky and Somers 2002, p. 11). The initial use of ERP was to serve the manufacturing company; however, due to the tremendous benefits gained from the utilization of ERP, the public sector has taken a big step by implementing this system in their organizations (Fernandez et al. 2017). ERP systems structure collaboration in organizations by providing a procedural backbone for the organization.

Fernandez et al. (2017) have studied the application of a modern ERP system within the context of local authorities in the Malaysian public sector. Their results show that the implementation of this system leads to a positive, financially beneficial impact on performance. Since ERP technology is expected to provide more timely and accurate enterprise-wide information for decision-making, the documentation and administrative costs of the organization have been reduced. Moreover, costs could also be reduced by streamlining processing and eliminating clerical duties that are automated. Additionally, the level of sophistication and user-friendliness of this system has been proven to reduce procurement and search costs. In terms of the customer perspective, results indicate that this system managed to provide a platform for more interactive customer service, improved service quality through customer direct feedback, augmented the responsiveness to customers and consequently reduced the number of customer complaints. This is due to the fact that the system managed to provide more accurate, relevant and timely information to staff, which eliminated delays and errors in fulfilling customers' businesses (Fernandez et al. 2017).

Overall, the research demonstrated that applying this latest system to the Malaysian public sector was an efficient strategy to enhance the effectiveness and efficiency of its performance.

# Box 2.6: Agile working (and Scrum)

Since the early 2000s, many companies have embraced the agile way of software development, which has changed developers' daily work routines. Agile software development is an iterative development approach emphasizing close customer collaboration to receive faster customer feedback (see Schmidt 2016). Agile software development projects foresee frequent deliveries of incremental software functionality to their customer. This is instead of a one-time release of the finalized software package at the end of the project. This development approach encourages developers to regularly integrate newly developed software and continuously invest time into quality assurance in order to guarantee that requirements are met at all times throughout the process (Schmidt 2016).

In 2001, a group of independent thinkers on software development wrote the Agile Manifesto, in order to uncover better ways of developing software by doing it themselves and by also helping others to do it (see http://agilemanifesto.org/). The Manifesto identifies four values, constituting the essence of agile software development:

- Individuals and interactions over processes and tools
- Working software over comprehensive documentation
- Customer collaboration over contract negotiation
- Responding to change over following a plan

A number of different methods for agile working were developed based on these values. Among them, Scrum and Extreme Programming are not only the most influential but the most popular today (Schmidt 2016). Scrum is a methodology for addressing complex adaptive problems by continuously delivering (intermediary) products (Schmidt 2016, 16). Scrum is often referred to as a software development method, but strictly speaking it is a project management methodology. Scrum specifies certain roles in the development team, establishes an iterative work mode which centres around development sprints and defines different artefacts that the developers use to coordinate their work (Schmidt 2016).

# Information management for the organizational community

In organizational communities, the starting point for stimulating organizational performance is not the analysis and support of business processes but rather supporting and incentivizing interactions between individual employees who collaborate in dynamic and fluid networks. This approach to information management has a much shorter history and is not as well established as the infocratic approach. Some recent work on digital communities of practice (Wenger et al. 2009) is helpful as well as more popular theories about self-organization (Shirky 2008). In the realm of knowledge management, communities of practice (CoP) and performance dialogues have received more attention and contact between public professionals is seen as the key to organizational performance and development (Wenger 1998).

The relevance of this approach to information management can be illustrated by the systems that support collaboration in groups: groupware. Groupware has been used for some time to facilitate collaborative work in (public) organizations since these tools offer opportunities to share documents and work on projects collectively. Our own experiences with students show us that they have no problems creating a workspace in Google to work on group projects. These tools still focus mostly on hard information for group work but, in addition, tools such as Twitter and Yammer, and also Facebook, are used for CoP and to strengthen knowledge management and organizational learning. These communities have an informal character and easily mix task-related and personal information. The availability and usage of these tools is becoming increasingly vital to the effectiveness and efficiency of organizations.[1]

Wenger et al. (2009, 19) discuss the connection between technology and communities as a 'positive intertwining': 'Technology has changed the way we think about communities and communities have changed the uses of technology.' Technologies are being developed in communities such as the Linux community and new technologies facilitate community working. In

---

[1] The fact that many of these tools function in the cloud raise important questions about data ownership. We will come back to this issue in Chapter 7.

this context, the task for a manager is not so much organizing and planning, but rather mostly facilitating the professionals so that they can do their work in the most effective way possible. In some cases, this means stimulating them and providing the necessary resources and focal points for attention. It may also entail removing the barriers that hinder them in their work and making sure professionals collaborate effectively and engage with each other's perspectives. Collaboration is conceptualized as a network activity that emerges out of contact between public professionals in – or even outside – an organization. Virtual communities at different levels are crucial to facilitating this type of organization (see Box 2.7).

The community perspective on organizational collaboration results in a different approach to performance management. The focus on hard information in organizational performance is replaced by a focus on enabling teams, intra-organizational and even inter-organizational groups to discuss organizational performance and collaborating in order to improving it. The manager dashboard is replaced with software that allows or provokes new ideas on improving performance and dialogue in which the proposals are discussed and implemented. These communities in turn affect human processing of information since processing is a social process. The communities can also be regarded as an approach to dealing with an overload of information by focusing only on the information that is highlighted by others in their networks. In addition, these communities of individuals both reproduce and challenge power structures by sharing information in traditional yet innovative ways. Finally, communities of individuals change the identity of organizations and result in new (sub)cultures. Managing these (virtual) communities and providing sense demands new skills from public managers (see Box 2.8).

The perspective of the polycentric organization means that managing information for organizational performance is about enabling public professionals to collaborate in communities. The polycentric model of organizations highlights that the key task of managers is to select, develop and implement information systems that contribute to smart and high-performing teams. Wenger et al. (2009) emphasize that the management of information in this model should be understood as technology stewardship. In contrast to the systematic analysis in the monocentric model, managers need to stimulate forms of technology stewardship in their organization to encourage interactions

## Box 2.7: Examples of virtual communities at different levels

Virtual communities can play a role at different levels of organization: in one public organization, in the public sector of a whole country or internationally connecting civil servants in different countries.

- *Virtual community in a public organization: Yammer.* VicRoads, an Australian state government authority in Victoria, uses Yammer to stimulate the exchange of information between employees. Yammer is a social network for organizations and helps employees to share information with their colleagues, to point out relevant resources, to collaborate around issues and to engage in debate (Fabre 2015).
- *Virtual community in a whole country: Pleio.* The Pleio system has been developed to facilitate collaboration between civil servants in different public organizations in the Netherlands. Pleio offers building blocks for teamwork and knowledge sharing and can be adapted to specific preferences. This platform facilitates teamwork between civil servants who work in different organizations and even at different levels of government. For more information, see www.pleio.nl.
- *Virtual community in all Spanish-speaking countries: Novagob.* Novagob is an international platform for collaboration between Spanish-speaking public professionals. It offers opportunities for publishing blogs, forming groups, to advertise events and for organizing debates. In addition, it offers a Wiki page with relevant information. Novagob is quite unique in its ability to facilitate international collaboration at an individual level. For more information, see novagob.org.

These examples highlight that the logic of organizational community does not always correspond to the boundaries of formal organizations: collaborations often cross the boundaries and platforms facilitate new networks.

in the networked organization. Wenger et al. (2009, 26–7) highlight that technology stewardship consists of five interconnected streams of activity:

1 *Community understanding.* The first stream of activity is about understanding the needs of the community and responding to

# Box 2.8: Email and the networked bureaucracy

Email communication (still) poses a challenge for bureaucratic procedures: personal and organizational communication are mixed, context-information is lacking, lines of communication are not respected, etc. At the same time, email has become an indispensable tool of communication in bureaucratic organization and civil servants spend a large deal of their time communicating with others in and outside the organization this way. How can we understand this paradoxical relation between email and bureaucracy?

An empirical study in the Netherlands analyzed the interaction between email use, communication patterns of civil servants and two bureaucratic characteristics – formalization and hierarchy. Previous research suggested that the use of email leads to less formalization and hierarchy, but empirical research in three bureaucratic organizations in the Netherlands led to different conclusions. First, the use of email leads to informal formalization: the style of communication is more informal but the content focuses less on personal issues and emphasizes efficient recordings of agreements. Second, the use of email leads to hierarchical horizontalization: horizontal contacts take a more central position in bureaucratic organizations but these are tightly linked to vertical structures. The result of the interaction between email and government bureaucracy is horizontal communication directly linked to vertical structures. Thus, electronic communication turns government agencies into late-bureaucratic organizations.

What do these changes in organizational communication mean for the role of public managers? A key finding is that public organizations need this type of electronic communication to provide links between systems of vertical and horizontal communication and enable bureaucratic organizations to be both flexible and accountable. In practice, this means that managers need to assume a more monitorial role in the organization rather than discussing all the action in advance; they can follow streams of communication and intervene when needed.

*Source:* Meijer (2008)

expressed and unexpressed needs with respect to technology. Who needs to participate? What are the key activities in the group? A community with a focus on exchanging knowledge will need another type of support than a network that organizes the development of a new service.

2 *Technology awareness.* The second is about knowing technological opportunities. Wenger et al. (2009, 26) describe this stream of activities: 'Technology awareness requires an informal but ongoing scanning of the technological landscape – through personal experience, playfulness, conversations, reading, or participation in technology-oriented communities.'

3 *Selection and installation.* The third is concerned with making informed choices about the use of technology for supporting community interactions. These decisions can be small – testing out a new tool – and big – using a new platform for interaction. This stream of activities may require substantial technological expertise to install the technology in a specific organizational environment.

4 *Adoption and transition.* The fourth is about actually implementing the technology and using it in the community interactions. This consists of activities such as training the members, providing manuals, stimulating the use of the technology, adapting the technology to specific user requirement, etc. This is a critical set of activities since community members may be likely to reject the technology rapidly if it is not convenient to their activities.

5 *Everyday use.* The fifth and final stream focuses on all kinds of (often less-visible) activities that are needed to support the everyday use of the technology: technological aspects, such as tool management, upgrades, access and security, and back-ups, and also social aspects, such as onboarding newcomers, craft agreements about technology use and building capacity for stewarding in others.

These activities take place within an organizational setting that provides both resources and restraints for technology stewardship. Resources such as the technological infrastructure and access to databases, standards for the use of technology or even for community interactions and the interplay between organization and the community condition the opportunities for technology stewardship. The key task for managers can thus be summarized as providing stimulating conditions for technology stewardship in organizations (see Box 2.9 for an example).

# Box 2.9: Bring your own device

Bring your own device (BYOD) is a trend that fits perfectly within the polycentric model. BYOD basically means that professionals in public organizations have the freedom to assume the responsibility for selecting and implementing the tools they need for their work. In a traditional bureaucratic organization, the organization provides the employees with everything they need to do their work (office space, desk, pencils, computer, software, etc.). The idea of BYOD is that individual employees have specific preferences and therefore it is preferable for them to select their own computer, software, apps, etc. to support their work. The organization does not provide them with the facilities but instead with a budget that they can use to purchase what they need.

Several technological trends have been drivers behind BYOD:

- *Superior consumer products.* New technologies such as mobile devices are developed first for the consumer market. While previously technologies at work were superior to technologies at home, the opposite is now often the case.
- *Apps for every task.* Generic software – apps – are now available for all kinds of processes such as planning meetings, managing projects, etc. Previously, dedicated software needed to be developed but now many programmes are (mostly) freely available.
- *Data in the cloud.* Data storage was a key facility in organizations but now storage is easily available in the cloud, often at no or limited cost. Employees can use these facilities and easily share access with others inside and outside the organization.
- *Ubiquitous internet access.* Employees now have access to the internet wherever they are and whenever they need it. They no longer depend on computers that are connected to an organizational network through cables.

Organizations will need to develop a clear policy for BYOD since it also raises some financial, technical, legal and organizational questions. Key issues are data security, organizational control over data and responsibility for data. BYOD can result in data breaches, no access to data when employees leave the organization and damage to external stakeholders when data are not adequately protected and stored.

> BYOD fits well within the paradigm of the organizational community but undermines forms of bureaucratic control. Public managers need to assess to what extent this is desirable and acceptable and how it contributes to organizational performance. The answers to these questions depend on issues such as the nature of the work and the data, the organizational culture and the (political) environment.
>
> *Source:* Meijer and Van Berlo (2014)

At the same time, public managers are also participants in these communities; and these communities provide crucial management information. The new information systems also facilitate access to 'soft' information for management control, since they have direct access to conversations that would otherwise be largely inaccessible to them. One could even talk of virtual management by virtually or electronically 'walking around'. Managers can set an example in some of these interactions by expressing the type of behaviour or input they see as desirable. One could even speak of 'e-leadership' when managers use the online environment to guide their staff (Roman et al. 2019). Managers can follow the open social media communication of their employees – Twitter, Yammer – to pick up signals and to show that the manager is present in these communications.

This section has provided a brief overview of a quite different perspective on information management in public organizations, the polycentric model. The literature on this is not as extensive as that on monocentric organizations, so we refer the interested reader to Wenger et al. (2009) for a concise overview. The basic idea of this approach is that facilitating interactions between members of an organization will result in enhanced organizational performance. The focus is on the human side of organizing and the contribution of human resources to organizational performance. Our key message is not that public managers should choose between one of the two perspectives but rather that they should find a way to provide infrastructures for both monocentric and polycentric organizations.

# Ethical issues

Managing information for organizational performance is not only about finding instrumental solutions. We stress that managing information for organizational performance raises important ethical issues that need to be acknowledged and addressed. Ethical questions have been raised in the classical work by Rob Kling (1996), who highlights that introducing new technologies always results in controversy and is about value conflicts and social choice. Managers need to choose between values such as privacy and efficiency or participation and effectiveness and avoid privacy breaches and bias (see Box 2.10). There is no simple answer to the question of how organizations should deal with these questions but the literature on responsible research and innovation provides some principles that may be helpful (Von Schomberg 2013):

1 *Apply technology assessment.* Do not let the effects of new technological systems surprise you by investigating beforehand what undesirable outcomes could arise.

2 *Apply the precautionary principle.* Assume social responsibility to protect employees and stakeholders from exposure to harm when there is a plausible risk.

3 *Engage employees at an early stage.* Let employees explore risks and trade-offs at an early stage to develop shared assessments of risks and benefits.

4 *Regard ethics as a design factor.* Do not see ethics only as a limitation but rather as a challenge to develop better technological systems.

5 *Create platforms for deliberation.* Decisions about new technologies should not only be taken in closed boardrooms; there should be ample room for deliberation.

These principles can guide public managers in making the right decision about the use of technologies in their organization. Public managers are confronted with some challenging issues when they engage with SPIM in order to improve organizational performance.

- *How much monitoring of individual activities is allowed?* Fusi and Feeney (2017) conducted research on electronic monitoring in US local governments. They point out that with the increased use of information and telecommunication technologies (ICT) in the workplace, employers can more effectively track and record employee actions through having access to all employee email, scanning employee emails, listening in on phone calls, recording phone calls, monitoring in the workplace by video camera, tracking websites visited by employees, blocking internet websites and using firewalls, monitoring data transmissions and monitoring personal social media sites (e.g. Facebook). They found that electronic monitoring is more

## Box 2.10: Bias in the COMPAS-algorithm

An algorithm that triggered much discussion is the system COMPAS that is used for decisions about parole in the US by predicting the probability of recidivism. COMPAS stands for Correctional Offender Management Profiling for Alternative Sanctions and can be used in American courts in parole decisions. This means that the probability of recidivism that results from the algorithm can have a direct impact on judicial decisions.

Journalists from ProPublica analyzed the algorithm and came to the conclusion that the algorithm has a bias towards black defendants. Their analysis indicated that black defendants are twice as likely as white defendants to be misclassified as a higher risk of violent recidivism. Although these conclusions were criticized by others, the discussion highlights the sensitivity of the use of these algorithms that sometimes contain a hidden racial bias.

*Source:* Larson et al. (2016)

intense in highly centralized or politicized organizational contexts, where it can be perceived as invasive or reinforcing top-down control, with potentially negative impacts on employee commitment and motivation. Similarly, electronic monitoring is higher when public organizations utilize external technologies, such as social media. More so, they point out that electronic monitoring can undermine individual privacy and freedom and increase stress among public employees.

- *To what extent do we let systems penetrate the life world of people?* The extensive use of technology in organizations raises the risk that these organizations also view reality mainly from a systems perspective or, in the terms of Habermas (1984), the system world. They often neglect to pay attention to the life world, the sphere within which we lead much of our social and personal life (Habermas 1984). Reasoning within the organization then takes place on the basis of the logic of the system rather than on the individual and the specific conditions of citizens. This could lead to a Kafkaesque situation in practice in which citizens get completely tangled in rules, regulations and procedures.

- *Do we accept the fragmentation of responsibility?* With the increase of the use and exchange of information within and between organizations, the risk of decontextualization occurs. This means that information gathered in a particular context and for a particular goal is now being used in a totally different context and for a totally different goal. Think for example of information that is collected for service delivery that later is being used for control and enforcement. The original context in which this information was collected is then discarded and the information is recontextualized in a different setting. But the responsibility for the quality and the reliability has not evolved in the same way. Often this responsibility is not clearly assigned to a specific organizational actor. The WRR (the Netherlands Scientific Council for Government Policy) pointed out these kinds of risks in relation to what they call 'iGovernment' (WRR, 2011).

- *How much dependency on technology is acceptable?* Technology has become so pervasive in organizations that one could ask the question whether it is possible for an organization to function if the ICT are (temporarily) unavailable. Nowadays almost every organizational activity involves the use of ICT in one way or another. That leads to a vulnerability for organizations. Organizations need to ask the question about how much vulnerability is acceptable.

An interesting overarching question here is to what extent organizational communities are seen as empowering individuals or controlling them. Wilson (1995) argued that the use of combined computer-based systems and quality management applications can result in 'insidious forms of control'. Dystopian novels such as *Nineteen Eighty-Four* and, more recently, *The Circle* and *The Every*, give us a clear idea of what type of organization we do not want. The onus is on managers to develop organizations that we do want and that are broadly supported.

# Conclusions

This chapter has argued that SPIM for organizational performance needs to be aligned with the model of the organization. A monocentric organization requires a different approach to a polycentric organization. Concrete guidelines for public managers have been provided for both models. On the basis of this discussion, we can now present some answers to the questions that managers may be struggling with.

- *How can I benefit from new techniques for big data analysis and how can I implement these in my organization?* The dominant response to this answer will be to integrate big data analysis in the bureaucratic structure of the organization and to use the data for strengthening management control over organizational processes. Our model, however, stresses that big data analysis can also support team interactions on platforms to stimulate processes of learning and professional work in the organizational community. Managers should be aware of the reflex of bureaucratic control and also consider the options that emphasize networked collaboration. In addition, our model emphasizes that implementing big data analysis in the organization requires focus on patterns of usage by both specialists and other workers. Managing the introduction as a process of change with stakeholder inclusion is crucial for connecting the technological possibilities to organizational performance.

- *Will our organization benefit from groupware and how does this affect the performance of teams?* Groupware is widely seen as crucial to supporting the performance of teams. Selecting and implementing groupware requires a systematic analysis of team interactions and the opportunities to support these. Smart teams need systems that are flexible but can operate in a stable context provided by organizational infrastructures. In addition, user participation in the selection and implementation of these packages is crucial to ensure that the software actually works for them.

- *Is an ERP system valuable for our organization and how do we make this work?* An ERP system can strengthen the support of business processes and therefore requires a systematic analysis of business processes to adapt the generic system to the specific organization. Managers will also need to ensure that the system does not drive out opportunities for team interaction and be able to adapt it to patterns of usage to ensure user satisfaction.

- *How can we use social media to support exchange of information between employees and will this contribute to organizational performance?* Social media plays a key role in facilitating network interactions in the polycentric organization. These interactions can contribute to organizational performance if employees are connected to the vision of the organization. At the same time, the public manager will need to engage in and monitor these interactions – virtual management by walking around – to check whether these interactions actually contribute to organizational performance.

Finally, we highlighted that managing information for organizational performance is not only about instrumental choices but, ultimately, about value conflicts and social choice. The key issue for public managers is to create organizations that we would all want to work in: human organizations. In that sense, a new look at McGregor's (1960) classical work about the human side of enterprise is certainly needed in this information age.

# KEY LESSONS FROM CHAPTER 2

- A broad variety of new technologies can contribute to organizational processes and hence can improve organizational performance.
- To improve organizational processes, SPIM should be aligned with the organization and its performance management approach.
- We distinguish two basic models for organizational performance – the digital bureaucracy and the organizational community – as starting points for SPIM.
- The digital bureaucracy – the monocentric organization – focuses on the realization of organizational objectives through a reliance on rules, routines and procedures.
- To achieve successful organizational performance in this model, public managers select, develop and implement the information systems that support the realization of the organizing, planning and control functions.
- The organizational community – the polycentric organization – emphasizes the need to support and stimulate collaboration between organizational professionals.
- The polycentric model of organizations requires that managers select, develop and implement information systems that contribute to smart and high-performing teams and communities.
- SPIM for organizational performance results in a set of ethical issues, and to handle these principles from responsible research and innovation may be helpful.

# 3

# Managing information for public policy

*This chapter shows that public policy is directly connected to and dependent on strategic public information management (SPIM). In line with the argument in this book, we will show that how SPIM is deployed depends on the model of policymaking. In this chapter, we distinguish between two models: policy production and policy networks. In the* **policy production model***, based on a rational analysis of problems and solutions, SPIM can be geared to improving the evidence base of public policy. The* **policy network model** *conceives of policymaking as a process of mutual adaptation of actors in a policy network. SPIM for this model guides us towards communication infrastructures to support networked interactions.*

## Introduction

Public policymaking is a key task for many public organizations. These organizations prepare policies that aim to tackle a wide range of issues such as poverty, cybercrime, environmental pollution, climate change, medicine shortages and so on. Information is one of the main resources of any policy programme. Since policy programmes aim to tackle social and political problems, defining the problem and plotting a course of action rests on the available information. If a government wants to combat crime, information is needed on the prevalence of crime, the hot spots where crime occurs and the causes of crime.

Effective policies increasingly rely on information. During its entire life cycle, a policy programme is continuously fed by information which is increasingly produced by technologies. The 'techies' and data scientists have thus entered the policy process. Since many traditional policy specialists do not understand the technologies, and the 'techies' who advocate these technologies are not familiar with the context and art of public policymaking, good alignment between both spaces is paramount.

The availability of huge amounts of information on policy interventions, target groups and changes in the behaviour of individuals and societies has dramatically affected the policy process and the content of public policies. Continuous monitoring and software that enables modelling of complex systems has provided an impetus for evidence-based policies (see Box 3.2). Evidence-based policymaking suggests that policies should be based on facts rather than ideological ideas. In addition, policy implementation can be monitored in real time through elaborate information systems. Box 3.1 highlights some of the key issues.

## Box 3.1: Big data in US educational policies

Educational policies in the US are a good example of innovation in policymaking through new forms of information processing. Even though the local community's control over primary and secondary education is an American political tradition, state and federal policymakers have strengthened their roles and centralized school district governance significantly over the past century. Metrics on student performance, parent satisfaction, quality control, etc. are now reported to national and state departments of education. This information is used to monitor the performance of schools and intervene in case of underperformance. The information is also used to analyze various specific issues, such as differences between schools in upper- and working-class neighbourhoods and between racial groups. The information from this analysis plays a crucial role in educational policymaking, since they claim to be developed on the basis of 'evidence' on the effects of school governance.

*Source:* Lavertu (2016)

Information processing has always played a key role in policy processes, and new technological developments such as big data and smart algorithms seem to generate a host of opportunities for optimizing policy processes. Public managers run the risk of being overwhelmed by the technologies and the marketing strategies of IT specialists. If the policy process and public policymaking are not aligned with the design and use of the right technologies, a public organization runs the risks of both policy and IT fiascos. This means that SPIM is important for effective policies. The following are some of the issues with which public managers currently struggle:

- How can I use big data analysis for designing better policies?
- How can I use information systems to evaluate the effectiveness of my agency's policies?
- Can social media analysis contribute to policy monitoring?
- Do smart algorithms contribute to better policy designs?
- How can I use diverse information sources for policy evaluation?
- Can network technologies improve the communication in policy processes?

The domain of policy informatics focuses on the relation between information management and the policy process (see Box 3.2). Dawes and Janssen (2013, 251) present the following definition: 'Policy informatics is an analytical approach that comprises concepts, methods, and processes for understanding complex public policy and management problems. Policy informatics uses modern computational methods to process vast quantities of data, mine data from single and multiple sources, seek patterns in multidimensional data, and develop models of various phenomena.' Johnston (2015, 6) stresses that policy informatics is built upon the fundamental premise that information can be efficiently and effectively mobilized to enable evidence-driven policy design, implementation and analysis in a legitimate government environment. This means that the focus of SPIM switches to the domain of policymaking. Johnston (2015) stresses that policy informatics is not only about traditional policymaking by single organizations but also about building governance infrastructures for the next generation of public organizations (see Box 3.2).

The dominant mode of thinking about policy processes is the policy production model (Stone 1997): information about the policy problem and policy solutions is used to design the best possible policies. This model is closely connected to the rational approaches to organizing discussed in Chapter 2, and the monocentric model of organization presented in Chapter 3. Policy analysts develop plans, organizations need to implement them and policy evaluators need to asses them to check whether they have

## Box 3.2: Center for Policy Informatics at Arizona State University

The relation between new technologies and public services has been well explored in e-government studies, and the relation with organizational performance has been studied in information systems research. The value of information systems for policy processes has received much less attention, though this appears to be changing. *Policy informatics* is a promising new field of research. Erik Johnston, one of the pioneers in this field, has set up a Center for Policy Informatics at Arizona State University, which focuses on the following questions:

- How can models and simulations aid individuals and groups when developing new policy plans and making policy choices?
- What are the dynamics of policy decisions for building and sustaining collaborations in civic, business and academic contexts?
- Can we use complex systems methodology and theory using agent-based modelling as a complement to traditional quantitative and qualitative research methods for policy analysis?

The work at this centre highlights that complex approaches to modelling policy systems are becoming more accessible for policy analysis because of the availability of data and rapid developments in these systems. The link between policy analysis and complex systems will become increasingly important in the near future which means that public managers will need to develop a basic understanding of system models in order to assess their value for policy design. This research points us to a big challenge: public managers need to change their mental models of policy systems from relatively simple cause and effect relations to complex feedback loops and interactions.

For more information, see https://sustainability-innovation.asu.edu/research/project/center-for-policy-informatics/.

generated the desired results. The production paradigm of policymaking has traditionally focused on policymaking as a design process. It builds on a succession of policy design, policy implementation and policy evaluation. Information plays a key role in all these phases. A strong analysis of the nature of the problem and possible solutions is at the heart of policy design; information is needed to steer and monitor the policy implementation and information is needed to evaluate the outcomes of the policies. The opportunities for new technologies seem clear: better information results in more effective policies.

At the same time, this perspective on the policy process has been criticized for emphasizing too heavily the linear and single actor nature of the policy processes. Organic approaches to policy processes foreground policy processes as more iterative and more interactive. This model for understanding public policy is connected to the symbolic and political perspectives in Chapter 2 and the polycentric model of organization in Chapter 3. All these approaches highlight the political, sociological and psychological dimensions that shape social, organizational and policy processes. In these network models, policymaking is not separated by implementation and evaluation. Instead of a linear process, these approaches emphasize a continuous and iterative flow of social activities to develop, implement and evaluate public policies. Network management has been presented as an alternative to the traditional model of government. In these policy network models, information also plays a key role but in quite a different manner owing to the fact that the information does not come from one actor; rather, it flows in different ways through the network. This necessitates that communication technologies and other means of combining and exchanging information from different sources are crucial to the policy process.

These two approaches to policymaking highlight that managing information for effective policies requires a rich understanding of policy processes. This chapter begins by introducing the key characteristics of these approaches, which will be referred to as the policy production and the policy network models. We will further elaborate on these models framed as the policy machine and the policy network. The two perspectives are related to the frames of the engineer and the mediator that we developed in Chapter 1. We will end this chapter with a summary of the main argument and key lessons.

# Policy production and policy interactions

Mechanical approaches to policymaking consider it to be a design process that follows an assembly line logic. Policy plans are drafted on the basis of an expert analysis, the plans are approved by decision-makers, implemented and then finally evaluated. This assembly line metaphor highlights that policies pass successive stages on their way to producing the desired outcomes. Effective policies result from solid designs grounded in evidence as well as adequate implementation. The key responsibilities for public managers is to hire the experts, provide them with an infrastructure, control the policy process and ensure that the successive stages are well coordinated.

The conceptualization of the policy process as a design process has been highly influential both in academia and in practice since the post-Second World War era. In the 1960s and 1970s, the effectiveness of public policies was enhanced by developing approaches for policy design, policy implementation and policy evaluation on the basis of academic work. Policy analysts are trained in rational design and evaluation, according to academically tested methods. The rationalization during these decades resulted in a professionalization of both policy analysis and policy analysts. At the same time, the assembly line metaphor of the design process has helped to strengthen the legitimacy of policy processes by drawing a clear distinction between political choices and administrative work. The political choices for policies are made by elected or mandated politicians whereas the development and implementation of specific plans occur on the basis of professional expertise. In the end, expertise plays a role in evaluating the impacts of policies and these evaluation studies play a key role in the process of political accountability.

In the policy production model, policies ideally result from a number of successive stages and processes (Hoogerwerf 1998, see Figure 3.1):

1 *Agenda-setting.* Processes inside the organization, political dynamics and processes in society determine whether policy issues reach the agenda. Many issues never reach the policy agenda and, for this reason, are not tackled through policies.
2 *Policy design.* The quality of the policy design is crucial to its success which means that it needs to be based on information and expertise, and a strong and comprehensive analysis of policy problems and solutions by policy experts with extensive knowledge on the policy field.

3  *Policy decision.* A decision is made on the basis of the policy design. The decision specifies the objectives and means of the policy. It also provides indications about the timing of interventions. The policy decision is made by those responsible for the specific issues on the basis of information from different sources.

4  *Policy implementation.* Policy implementation needs to be carried out in line with the policy plan. This means that control over the implementation of policy plans is of great importance. Are the interventions carried out according to plan and to the timeline?

5  *Policy evaluation.* The policy evaluation is crucial for accountability and learning as it forms the input for new or adjusted policy plans. Information for the policy evaluation has to be collected continuously and made available to independent evaluators.

In each stage, information is crucial because more and better information supports the experts to make a finer analysis of the policy problem and possible interventions, to maintain control over policy implementation and to evaluate the outcomes of policies. A variety of information systems have been developed to strengthen the policy process, such as Geographical Information Systems for spatial planning, Intervention Monitoring Systems for policy control and Data Warehousing to support policy evaluation. These systems help experts and strengthen the policymaking capacity of public organizations.

The value of this approach to policymaking is widely acknowledged, but mechanical approaches to policymaking have also been criticized. A

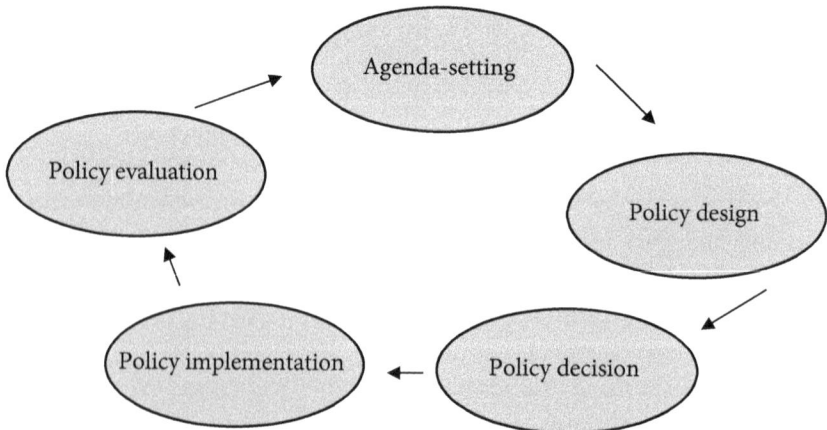

**Figure 3.1** Policy production model: stages of the policy.

first point of criticism is that this approach presents a false image of how policymaking actually takes place in practice (John 1998). A well-known example is Kingdon's (1984) idea of a 'policy window' which highlights how policy entrepreneurs connect streams of problems with streams of policies to obtain support for new policies. This perspective is quite different from the idea of the design process since it does not acknowledge the consecutive stages of problem analysis and design of solutions. Kingdon acknowledges that this approach may be a valuable normative ideal but it does not adequately describe practices of policymaking. A second point of criticism is that the design metaphor focuses on the central role of government – and more specifically, policy experts – and does not acknowledge the active role of other stakeholders in the policy process. Critics and empirical research on governance networks show that policies are often developed in collaborative settings where government officials negotiate and deliberate on the nature of the problem and possible interventions.

Critics have suggested many alternative approaches to policymaking, describing them with terms such as interactive governance (Torfing et al. 2012), process management (De Bruijn, Ten Heuvelhof and In 't Veld 2010) or network management (Kickert, Klijn and Koppenjan 1997). The key idea of these policy network models is that the quality of policies lies in coordinating engagement and the expertise of various stakeholders in a collaborative process. De Bruijn, Ten Heuvelhof and In 't Veld (2010) highlight the following core dimensions of this interactive approach to the policy process (see Figure 3.2 for a graphic overview):

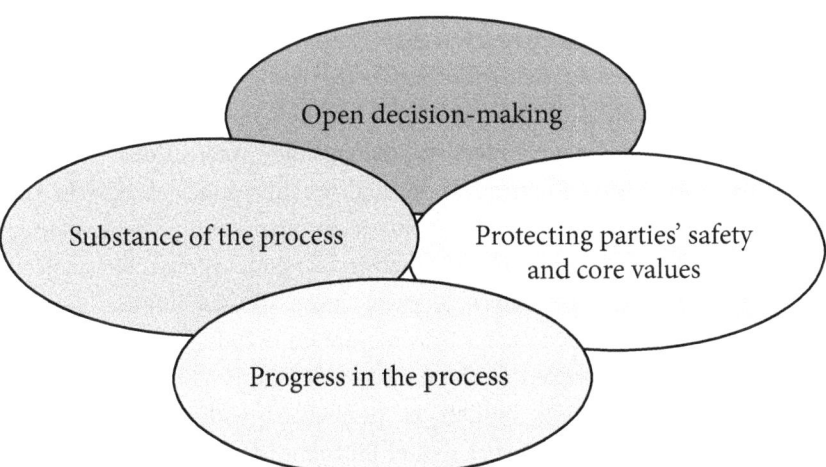

**Figure 3.2** Policy network model: dimensions of the collaborative process.

1  *Open decision-making.* The process needs to be designed and implemented in such a way that it offers the correct openness at the right moment in the process. It is imperative that all relevant actors are involved, that there are process agreements as a means to make substantive choices and there is transparency of the process to all stakeholders.

2  *Protecting parties' safety and core values.* When stakeholders are prepared to engage in an interactive policy process, there need to be guarantees that their safety and core values are protected. Crucial here is to achieve commitment to the process rather than to the result, the possibility to postpone commitment to sub-decisions and the establishment of exit rules.

3  *Progress in the process.* A major risk of interactive policy processes is that insufficient progress is realized and processes may stall. Several elements can help to realize progress: early participation, prospect of gain as an incentive for collaboration, creating quick wins, transferring conflicts to the periphery of the process and ensuring tolerance towards ambiguity.

4  *Substance of the process.* Policies are developed through interactions between stakeholders but, at the same time, the outcome of these interactions should be a policy that is not only supported but also effective. Expertise is still important but in a different sense. Key issues here are how to bundle and unbundle experts and stakeholders and how to use variation and selection mechanisms to choose effective policy options.

A key implication of this approach is that the role of public servants changes radically from a focus on their substantive expertise – their ability to design, manage and evaluate policies – to a focus on their managerial expertise – their ability to engage stakeholders and manage their interactions.

Information is a vital resource for high-quality policy design in the production models of policymaking, hence technologies should be developed to enhance the quality of the information. Organic approaches instead emphasize the social production of policy programmes: implementation and evaluation. These approaches thus require quite different technologies. In general, one could argue that the monopoly of information technologies in the policy production models is supplanted with communication technologies in the policy network model. Since the latter focus on managing interactions between stakeholders, this means that there is another need for information than that in the policy design metaphor. For one thing, relevant information is not only produced by government organizations but also by other participants in the interactive process. This means that information sharing becomes a key focus in supporting the policy process. In addition, communication between stakeholders is crucial in the various stages of the process and information and communication systems can play an important role in facilitating communication.

# Information management for policy production

The promise of SPIM is that it can improve the information basis of policymaking. The use of more and better information can help to design policies that are more likely to realize their goals. The *information machine* is to be designed in such a way that it provides optimal support for policy design during the whole policy process (see Box 3.3 for an in-depth discussion of this metaphor). This means that the information collection, processing and visualization need to be well attuned to the policy process (see Box 3.4). We will discuss the successive stages of policy design and demonstrate how the policy machine contributes to more effective policies.

## Box 3.3: Three meanings of the metaphor 'machine'

The metaphor of the machine has been used by Dijstelbloem, Meijer and Besters (2011) to describe the use of information and communication technologies in migration policies in the Netherlands and Europe. They analyze how the implementation of these policies is directly connected to all kinds of information processing and exchange. Complex inter-organizational and international information systems such as the Schengen Information System (SIS) have been developed to support the work of immigration officers.

The term 'machine' is used in three different ways. The first emphasizes that the technologies are used to strengthen the performance of government bureaucracies. Dijstelbloem, Meijer and Besters (2011, 5–6) state: 'Applying technological and computerized methods can help to ensure that borders are better monitored, that applications are dealt with more quickly and that procedures are used more efficiently.' The ideal of an impartial, rational implementation of government policy is here expressed through the metaphor of the machine.

The second, however, emphasizes that the machine may not function as well as planned: it is a malfunctioning device that undermines the quality of policy implementation. Dijstelbloem, Meijer and Besters (2011, 6) comment that 'technology is sometimes an unreliable ally, leading to undesirable side effects. If information files are unreliable, impossible to adequately check or correct, migrants may unjustly be refused entry.' The risk of a non-transparent and malfunctioning machine is expressed through the metaphor of the machine.

The third stresses that technology has a mechanizing effect on the implementation of migration policies. Substantive considerations fade into the background and instrumental considerations related to exposing whether a migrant is telling the truth become central to the work of migration officers. The migration machine becomes a 'lie detector' which enables officers to see through the fictional stories of migrants. The risk of a technology that dominates our thinking rather than support our work is presented through the metaphor of the machine.

The advice for public managers is that they should consider the various elements of the machine and not focus solely on the idea that the use of technology strengthens policy implementation. Public managers need to reflect on the instrumental risks of reliance on technological systems and on the substantive risk that mechanistic thinking may come to dominate policy processes.

The first issue that the information machine can tackle is **agenda-setting**. Agenda-setting is the process through which issues are identified as problems that need to be tackled through policies. The process of agenda-setting is highly complex and political, and information about problems plays an important role. Technologies may enhance the situational awareness of policymakers by providing information on policy problems, contributing in at least three ways to the problem definition: by providing 1) access to organizational data; 2) data about the online behaviour of people; and 3) data from various other sources and organizations.

First, organizational data such as registration data and data produced by transaction and workflow technologies offer a precise and valid account

## Box 3.4: Visualization of spatial data

Data visualization plays an increasingly important role in presenting information about a policy sector. An example of this is the data visualizations of the Netherlands Environmental Assessment Agency, which is the national institute for strategic policy analysis in the fields of the environment, nature and spatial planning. Until a few years ago, this agency would produce mainly extensive reports with comprehensive analysis of data about developments in the physical environment to provide policymakers and society with the information they need to identify policy problems. Former director Maarten Hajer, however, decided that the agency needed to put much more emphasis on visualizing situations to convey their information in a more accessible manner. The agency invested in building up the capacity they needed to visualize data and started to experiment with visualizations as a means to present complex information, such as the realization of the Sustainable Development Goals. The United Nations has formulated an agenda for 2030 and has expressed the ambition to realize seventeen Sustainable Development Goals (SDGs). Information about these goals is crucial to inspiring collaboration between a broad variety of actors and the challenge is to do justice to the abstract world of the many interdependencies between the SDGs while remaining in touch with human imagination, inspiration and collaboration. Therefore, the Netherlands Environmental Assessment Agency made a 'storyboard' that depicts scenes of human–nature interdependency and cooperation that need to be addressed in order to attain a more sustainable development. The storyboard contains brief explanations but mostly visualizations that present an overview of a problem situation.

of the problem. These types of information are the raw materials of any problem definition. How many cases of child abuse are registered, what about the number of unemployed persons, their gender and age, how much carbon dioxide is produced by what types of power plants, and so on. Since any transaction or workflow technology also registers information on cases, sophisticated data science tools allow transformation of this information into raw materials for policy programmes. It should be noted that registration and workflow of cases are highly biased by the organizational routines of the agencies involved. These biases affect the reliability and the validity of the information generated. Crime statistics provide a good example: those produced by law enforcement agencies may be claimed to represent the prevalence of crime in a city or country but these figures do not withstand real reliability tests. As Van Dijk (2007) argues, any crime statistic produced by law enforcement agencies should not be used for policy purposes even if warnings on the use of this information are included. The information derived from the registries of official agencies should thus be complemented by other types of information in order to enhance the reliability of the information.

An interesting second type of information technology for problem definition is suggested by Stephens-Davidowitz (2017). His analysis shows that reliable and relevant information for the policy can and should be derived from the behaviour of people online. In his fascinating book *Everybody Lies*, Stephens-Davidowitz argues that the truth about social realities is better disclosed by Google searches than any other source. Since people reveal their real behaviour in their Google searches, the analysis of these searches comes closer to the truth than any other source. One example is domestic violence. Experts expected that the financial and economic crisis that followed the bankruptcy of Lehman Brothers in 2007 would trigger a rise in physical abuse by parents. That the increase in unemployment following the recession would increase levels of domestic violence did sound logical, but the official statistics did not support this hypothesis. As Stephens-Davidowitz (2017, 182) argues, child protective agencies reported 'that they were getting fewer cases of abuse. Further, these drops were largest in states that were hardest hit by the recession.' But did the official statistics tell the truth about domestic violence? An analysis of Google searches (such as 'my mum beat me' or 'my dad hit me') presented 'a different – and agonizing – picture of what happened during this time. The number of searches like this shot up during the Great Recession, closely tracking the unemployment rate.' Thus, the official figures did not reflect the reality of child abuse but rather the bias of official agencies driven by their operational capacity and budget cuts. This highlights the potential value of data on online behaviour for obtaining in-depth insights about specific problem areas.

As well as the use of official information and data analysis of online sources, technologies may contribute to the problem definition phase in a third way. Data science technologies not only enable policymakers to obtain a clear picture of the situation but also to identify the predictive factors that have led to the situation. If unemployment truly correlates with domestic violence then policies may benefit from information on unemployment to predict or even prevent domestic violence. If the number of new migrants in a neighbourhood really predicts the prevalence of crime, policies can be developed to prevent rising crime figures. And so on. Modelling based on real data enables policymakers to use sophisticated forecasting techniques.

Traditionally, the collection of information about problems was a largely centralized endeavour by expert organizations. Several dedicated government agencies had the task of collecting information about social, economic, spatial and environmental developments to identify relevant trends and problems. In the 1960s and 1970s, many of these agencies were created in several countries to rationalize government intervention and to generate information for policymakers. The Social and Cultural Planning Agency in the Netherlands, for example, continuously collects information through surveys about perceptions of citizens of their work, their life, their environment, etc. In parallel, dedicated research institutes generate information about problematic situations in order to put them on the policy agenda. These efforts fitted with the idea that the allocation of scarce government resources needed to be based on a rational analysis of the urgency of problems in society.

More recently, the collection of data on policy problems has become much more fragmented. The costs for the collection and analysis of data have dropped dramatically and so there are many more actors providing this information. Civil society organizations, research institutes, media platforms and many others have set up information systems to provide information about issues as diverse as environmental pollution, school quality, traffic safety and sexual harassment. The fact that government organizations have been opening up their datasets to the public facilitates the processes of collecting information about policy problems. An interesting development in this respect is the generation of information by individual citizens collaborating in loose networks. Citizen-generated data about issues such as noise from airports or traffic pollution can help to put these issues on a policy agenda (Meijer and Potjer 2018).

This means that public managers need to include and assess a variety of information from numerous sources to determine which problems are most urgent. Information management is not only about collecting and analyzing the organization's information but also the information from various other sources. Techniques of big data analysis may help to analyze this variety of data and identify relevant problems. As indicated above, these approaches also have significant drawbacks related to the limitations of data and the fact that the nature of the analysis may not be transparent.

Information and communication technologies not only feed the problem definition phase of the policy process but also **policy design**. In countries all around the world, there is much emphasis on evidence-based policies and the idea is that better information can help to develop policies that are based on evidence for interventions (Pawson 2006). Ideas on evidence-based policy are based on parallels with evidence-based medicine and the argument is that all available information has to be collected and analyzed in a systematic review to assess what evidence is available for the effectiveness of policy interventions (Young et al. 2002). Policy design has always been based on information but traditionally the information was collected and analyzed in a less systematic way. The current emphasis on evidence highlights the need to generate strong information – preferably based on the gold standard of having a group and a control group and an ex-ante and ex-post measurement of the intended effects of the intervention – to realize the most effective policy interventions.

Policymakers should be cautious and handle evidence-based policy tools with some care. Many policies aim to realize long-term objectives and these can only be assessed after a long period of time. This means that good evidence only becomes available after several years. This reduces the timeliness of evidence-based policies, especially in a context that continuously changes because of technological and societal developments. A more fundamental criticism of evidence-based policy is highlighted by Baumgartner and Jones (2015), who argue that evidence-based approaches represent an attempt to censor information and to include only 'good' information in the debate while other, 'softer' forms of information are left out. The authors stress that rich information is needed since we need to acknowledge the complexity of policy domains and interventions. Focusing on certain lines of argument will result in tunnel vision and, in the end, failing policies. For this reason, knowledge-based policies seems a more realistic ambition. This means that different types of knowledge are admitted into the policymaking process. This knowledge can be weighed and assessed but its value does not depend on the question of whether it presents evidence but rather whether it presents valuable insights for policymaking. More specifically, this could mean that information systems could provide the following functions to policy design (Dawes and Janssen 2013, 251–2):

- Testing policies by simulation that would be impossible to test empirically
- Mining enormous databases to extract understanding

- Using 'what if' analysis to trace out over time results that would emerge from different policies and scenarios
- Supporting counterfactual analysis to explore untried policies in historical contexts
- Making complex problems and systems understandable and manageable without oversimplifying
- Conducting iterative modelling to build understanding in stages from simple beginnings to complex understandings

Public managers should focus on ensuring that the information systems in their organizations and the information they obtain from other organizations offer a strong basis for knowledge-based policies, such as information for local sustainability policies. Information systems need to provide information about current and future air pollution, traffic and industry, preferably at a fine-grained scale, and also information about the effectiveness of different types of measures. Rational policy designs are based on comprehensive information about the problem situation – environmental pollution – and the effects of measures such as traffic restrictions. The broad variety of new techniques for data management and analysis such as data warehousing and big data analysis is of great importance to generate the desired information for policy design.

Information technologies may also support **policy decision-making**. The policy decision is made by higher civil servants and politicians on the basis of information about the policy plan and its expected implications and outcomes. Policy decisions are tightly connected to policy designs but they generally involve the inclusion of other actors and therefore the requirements for information may be different. Decision-makers generally have limited time and often lack the skills to analyze complex datasets, therefore it is key that they have quick access to the information required for their decisions. New technologies offer advanced facilities to present data in different visual formats and even generate dynamic overviews. The consequences of different options for traffic flows, for example, can easily be presented through dynamic visualizations (see Box 3.5).

Data visualizations offer many opportunities but they also generate risks. Presenting data in an accessible format also means that the data are being framed. The data are biased by these frames and the design choices made with regard to the visualization. A very simple example is the presentation of a trend over time. A trend is always presented from a start date to an end date, thus the choice for the start data is an important one. The choice for the scale and the cut-off point at the y-axis is also important and can

## Box 3.5: Traffic visualizations

Traffic visualizations can form a basis for decision-making about policy plans. Various industry and research projects work on improving these traffic visualizations.

> Living Cities is basically a web project that visualizes traffic in a time-lapsed format over the course of 24 hours, in five different global cities, namely, Mumbai, London, Chicago, Rome and Helsinki. The project anonymized data from the HERE platform of Nokia and allowed CartoDB to visualize traffic movements over a period of one month. CartoDB made the visualizations a lot more happening by offering users an experience to hear the sounds of the road besides pop-up windows with stats and trivia relating to the Metro along with its Points of Interest (POI). All this besides providing insights into the traffic pattern in the city. Even the colors of the map turn bright and dark in line with the weather and time of day … Well, clearly Nokia is targeting governments and other agencies that could utilize such data – think traffic planners and logistics companies like DHL and more! They could all benefit from such data and analysis.
>
> (http://geoawesomeness.com/living-cities-project-a-beautiful-dynamic-visualization-of-traffic-from-nokias-here-and-cartodb/)

> Employees of Datatonic, a Europe-based data analytics consultancy, recently participated in a week-long hackathon ('Data in Motion Hack Week') organized by Traffic for London (TfL), the city's official transport authority. As you might expect, the goals of the hackathon included stimulating developer creativity to overcome, through innovative use of public-cloud infrastructure and open data, high-priority TfL challenges such as limited overall transport capacity, endemic road congestion and air-quality degradation … Most of the other teams chose to focus on data mashups or visualizations to give London residents information for making better route decisions during their commutes. The Datatonic hackers, in contrast, looked to machine learning (ML). By augmenting real-time data visualization with an ML model, they found they could predict areas of congestion during the morning and evening commutes, which currently stand at 30 million daily journeys, and more than 1 million net-new journeys expected by 2018. Their solution uses Google Cloud Platform (GCP) for storage and data processing and provides

insights based on 3 months of data from 14,000 traffic sensors across London, amounting to well over 100 billion rows.

(https://cloud.google.com/blog/big-data/2016/11/real-time-data-visualization-and-machine-learning-for-london-traffic-analysis)

result in very different interpretations of a trend. Stone (1997) indicates how presentations with numbers are political constructions that reflect choices concerning what is measured, what scale is used, how the numbers are presented, and so on.

The policy machine can play an important role in rationalizing policy decisions by providing decision-makers with more accessible information. We mentioned a similar point in the previous chapter in our discussion of management dashboards. A policy dashboard may support the policy process, and the OECD has developed an interesting policy dashboard for measuring policy and institutional coherence for migration and development (see Box 3.6). The policy dashboard will not remove the political element from decision-making but it does promise a more information-based debate about the pros and cons of certain policy measures.

## Box 3.6: OECD policy dashboard

The OECD has developed a dashboard of indicators for measuring policy and institutional coherence for migration and development. They see this as a **stock-taking tool for policymakers**:

The dashboard of indicators for measuring policy and institutional coherence for migration and development (PICMD) is a user-friendly tool that has been developed by the KNOMAD Thematic Working Group on Policy and Institutional Coherence. The dashboard aims to measure the extent to which public policies and institutional arrangements are coherent with international best practices to minimise the risks and maximise the development gains of migration, and can be used by domestic policymakers and other stakeholders such as researchers, civil society and international organisations. For policymakers, the dashboard should serve as a particularly useful tool during the policy formulation, evaluation and adjustment process.

With the recognition that countries face unique national contexts presenting distinct opportunities and challenges – and furthermore find themselves at different stages of policy development vis-à-vis migration and development – the purpose of the dashboard is not to label governments' policy interventions as 'right' or 'wrong'. Rather, the dashboard aims to help countries:

- take stock of their existing policies and institutional arrangements in different sectors related to migration and development;
- consider what policies and institutions may be needed to maximise the positive impact of migration on development.

*Source:* https://www.oecd.org/dev/migration-development/knomad-dashboard.htm

The information machine also supports **policy implementation**. The implementation of policies in large-scale bureaucracies was one of the first domains heavily influenced by the introduction of information systems in the public sector. Administrative policies such as tax policies and student loans have been transformed in information processes. For some decades most tax files and applications for student loans in the Netherlands have not been assessed by a human civil servant: computers manage the process and make the decisions. This does not hold for other policy domains such as policing, education, healthcare or refuse collection but these policy implementations are also increasingly driven by information systems. Intelligence-led policing, for example, is a term more frequently used to indicate that the work of individual police officers is increasingly steered by information systems (Ratcliffe 2016).

Information plays a different role in policy implementation:

1 *Information as input for policy.* Information about clients, requests, concrete problems, etc. is needed to implement the policy.
2 *Information as output of policy implementation.* The policy implementation generates all the kinds of information needed to monitor or steer the policy implementation.

Since the 1960s, government organizations have been developing information systems to assist them in collecting and processing the information they require. In the early days, information management for policy implementation emphasized the use of internal information. The tax department of the agency for student loans would collect information from their policy processes and use this to steer the processes. From the 1990s onwards, information management for policy implementation began emphasizing the collaboration between various agencies. Chain informatization became important (Grijpink 2010): standardization of information to facilitate exchange and collaboration between agencies. More recently, information management has started to foreground information from fragmented sources. Information is collected through organizational information systems, open data, social media. The domain of safety policies provides an example: data from various sources as diverse as tax compliance, school truancy and refuse collection play a role in safety policies. The Living Lab Stratumseind (see Box 3.7) and Taiwan's response to the Covid-19 pandemic (see Box 3.8) illustrate how a broad variety of information is used for safety management regarding urban and health hazards.

For the role of the policy machine in policy implementation, this means that information management for policy implementation is not only about managing the organization's own information resources, but, more importantly, obtaining access to additional information from external sources. Managing access to relevant internal and external information and,

## Box 3.7: Living Lab Stratumseind

The City of Eindhoven in the Netherlands has transformed one street in the centre of the city into a laboratory for the use of new technologies for safety management. The use of data plays a key role in this living lab. The following list provides some examples of the data that are collected and combined as well as the means by which these data are collected.

- *Cameras* have been positioned at the five entrances of Stratumseind. The video images are not preserved but are used to count numbers of people.
- *Specific software* is used to convert the video images into information about the number of visitors to the area.
- Wireless *noise detectors* have been positioned in the same five positions as the cameras. The data from these detectors can be used to generate a three-dimensional image of the noise in the area.

- *Light sensors* for measuring light intensity are planned to be positioned at two or three positions.
- When a user has chosen to access Bluetooth or Wi-Fi on their mobile phone, a *macadres reader* can read the telephone's unique code. Five readers have been positioned in the same places as the cameras and noise detectors, and since these readers work up to 150 metres, the whole area is covered.
- *Social media analysis* is also part of the living lab. In collaboration with a commercial firm, a web crawler has been developed to search for tweets and posts with search strings such as 'Stratumseind', 'Stratum' and the names of the bars. The software analyzes these tweets to generate a sentiment analysis which indicates whether the posts are generally positive, negative or neutral.
- The *perceptions of the inhabitants* of the neighbourhood will be measured on a weekly basis with a digital survey, which is designed to measure the subjective perceptions of the situation in Stratumseind.
- Data about the *location where mobile phones are purchased*. Aggregate and anonymized data about the town where people live are bought from Vodaphone. These data provide insights in the origins of the visitors to Stratumseind.
- The intelligence of the Eindhoven police department provides *police reports* about Stratumseind. Respondent 1 – the project manager – would like these to be more specific in order to pinpoint exactly where incidents took place, though he thinks this will demand too much from police reporting.
- Data from the *garages* in the area provide information about traffic flows at certain times and the number of visitors who go to Stratumseind by car.
- The Municipal Cleaning Department provides information about the *amount of waste and glass* collected at Stratumseind per day.
- The beer breweries who provide the beer to the bars provide information about *beer consumption*.
- The *public events calendar* provides insight into specific events in the city that may have an impact on the number of visitors or the timing of their visit to Stratumseind.

*Source:* Meijer and Thaens (2018)

---

## Box 3.8: How Taiwan used surveillance to fight the Covid-19 pandemic

In the early stages of the Covid-19 pandemic, the high number of travellers from mainland China to Taiwan posed a serious health risk. To manage this risk and make responsible decisions, real-time surveillance with rapid risk assessment was one of the pillars of the Taiwan Center for Disease Control's strategy. Once the Center's surveillance team had detected the outbreak by social media surveillance, it continued collecting relevant information to monitor the progress in China on a daily basis. This information ranged from outbreak news from social media to government reports and official press releases. The information was used to periodically update a rapid risk assessment tool for decision-making at the provincial level. These forms of surveillance were of great importance for Taiwan's management of the pandemic.

*Source:* Cheng, Li and Yang (2020)

---

in parallel, producing information for internal and external stakeholders is key to strong information management for policy implementation.

Another important role of the information machine is to provide the basis for **policy evaluation**, the independent evaluation of policy processes (Pawson 2006). In the pre-digital era policy evaluation was complex and expensive as large sets of data needed to be collected through targeted research. The information explosion has greatly facilitated the evaluation of policies. The evaluation may build on the information collected during the policy implementation but also on a variety of other online sources that register behaviour. The role of information in the evaluation process follows a pattern that is quite similar to that identified in the stage of problem definition.

The ideal policy machine facilitates instantaneous evaluation: all the information is collected in real time and made available to evaluators. We see this trend in the private sector with an increased emphasis on 'real-time accounting' (Rezaee, Ford and Elam 2000); accounting is not a process that happens periodically in annual cycles but rather a continuous process of control. The cycle of the policy process is increasingly condensed and the rational ideal is the continuous adaptation of policies on the basis of real-time information about its effects.

An overview of the role of information management in the production model of policymaking is presented in Table 3.1.

**Table 3.1** Role of information management in the production of policy.

| Phase in policy production | Key issue for policy process | Role of information management |
|---|---|---|
| 1. Problem definition | The key challenge is to build a precise and valid account of the policy problem | Collection and analysis of data from different sources provides the basis for the identification of the most urgent policy problems |
| 2. Policy design | Policy design needs to result in the best possible policy plan to tackle the problem situation i.e. evidence-based public policy | Systematic assessment of the evidence for different policy intervention provides the basis for policy plans |
| 3. Policy decision | Decisions about policies need to be made on the basis of rational considerations | Information management provides information about the costs and benefits of various policy options |
| 4. Policy implementation | Policy implementation needs to be carried out in line with the policy plan | Information management provides information about the implementation of policy |
| 5. Policy evaluation | Evaluation needs to provide a comprehensive assessment of the effectiveness of the policy | Information management provides information about policy progress and goal attainment |

Ideally, SPIM connects these stages in a policy cycle: the evaluation feeds back into the problem definition which then results in an adjustment of the policy (Hoogerwerf 1998). The information that is produced in the various stages can also be used in the later stages: information collected during the implementation, for example, is also used for the evaluation and possibly for the identification of problems for the agenda. The use of information systems that can generate real-time information may speed up the policy cycle since evaluation and readjustment can occur almost instantaneously. This means that public managers should manage information in such a way that these continuous processes of policy learning result in the required outcomes and new technologies offer them various facilities to strengthen this information management.

New information technologies offer good opportunities for managing information in the design of public policies but this approach also has some limitations. The emphasis on quantitative information is risky and may result in myopia. For that reason, it is important that organizations develop approaches to combine hard and soft information for policy processes (see also Chapter 1). Observations, focus groups, discussions with policymakers and citizens and many other forms of collecting more narrative information are crucial to be able to interpret the quantitative information that is produced by the policy machine.

A more fundamental criticism of the policy machine is that it ignores the fact that policymaking is to a large extent an interactive and political process. Organic approaches to the policy process thus present the policy network as an alternative perspective on policymaking. This alternative perspective results in a set of different tasks and considerations for SPIM.

# Information management for the policy network

The network model of policymaking emphasizes the political and social process that produces policy programmes, the implementation and the evaluation of these policies. In the network model policy networks interact on policies and these networks provide for implementation and evaluation as well. The policy network requires support in the form of information management to stimulate interactions between different stakeholders. Information and communication technologies may provide an infrastructure that facilitates communication, deliberation, exchange of information and interactive or even collaborative decision-making. While the production model requires technological tools for policy design this approach requires technologies that facilitate the policy process. These technologies support at least four dimensions of the policy process.

First, **open decision-making** is technologically supported. This is the idea that the structure of meeting and interactions facilitates the inclusion of a variety of stakeholders in the process so as to create the basis for an effective and legitimate process. Information and communication technologies are needed here to provide a platform for these interactions. A strong feature of these technologies is that they do indeed provide these platforms. We see that our students have become very capable in using platforms such as Facebook and WhatsApp to facilitate their collaboration and to easily connect to a broad variety of actors. Platforms such as Slack offer all kinds of opportunities for collaborative work. These types of platforms offer opportunities for both open collaboration and collaboration by invitation only and therefore are useful for managing access to decision-making arenas (see also Box 3.9). The Covid-19 crisis has triggered a boom in online collaborative work and technologically mediated communication and decision-making.

The policy network can help to generate the infrastructure for open decision-making. The rules for inclusion in the platform are important and demand attention. Choices about access to certain groups need to be clear and based on criteria of both effectiveness and legitimacy. An intermediate approach can be that the members are listed and part of the discussion is open to the public. In fact, new media offers opportunities to manage access in a much more sophisticated manner than one could achieve in real-life situations and therefore they are suitable for supporting interactions in policy networks.

## Box 3.9: Consensus-oriented decision-making in a collaborative setting

A key challenge for policy networks is making decisions in a multi-actor setting. These decisions require deliberation and mutual recognition of positions. Empathy is an important aspect of these decision-making processes since actors have to 'feel' what is important for other stakeholders. The Center for Policy Informatics (Arizona State University) is working on developing a computer-mediated synthetic environment as a deliberation space for individual participants to explore different perspectives, arrive at a consensus and make decisions for sustainable outcome under conditions of uncertainty. Stimulating mutual empathy is a key focus in this approach. The case they have used to show the value of developing interactive simulation models for consensus-oriented decision-making is the policy for water demand and supply in the Phoenix Metropolitan Area. The model that they have developed can be used for: 1) providing a virtual context to complex dynamics embedded in water management; 2) exploring the effectiveness and efficiency of different water policy decisions and their impact on future water availability; and 3) exploring various challenges and uncertainty associated with human-induced climate change, urban growth and urban developmental polices. In this way, actors can interact around this problem situation and develop a shared understanding of the problem and possible interventions.

Secondly, the policy process should protect **parties' safety and core values** and technologies can safeguard fair interactions on the platform. The emphasis is on:

- *Network rules.* The rules of network interactions are partly coded into permissions of different participants. Access to certain information may be limited to certain participants, participants may or may not have the right to add or delete information, the identity of participants may or may not be visible, etc. Network rules may also be more informal and indicate what can or cannot be expected from the different participants. Can all participants be expected to react within a day on certain questions?
- *Network moderation.* A moderator of the platform has specific tasks in managing and stimulating interactions on the platform. The moderator can ask participants for contributions, s/he can provide summaries of debates and ask new questions but the moderator can also make the rules for interaction explicit and take measures if behaviour is not in line with these rules. The moderator can also give participants rights or take these away from them.

Network rules and moderation play a key role in creating an atmosphere that is open, productive and safe. This may especially be an issue in more open forms of collaboration where different types of actors can engage in discussions and the risk of conflict is higher.

The literature on social media emphasizes the importance of moderation for the quality of interactions on digital platforms. The role is rather new for policy interactions and does not have a clear counterpart in the offline world. Distinctions can be made between pre-moderation (check posts before posting), post-moderation (check after posting), reactive moderation (checks posts when they have been flagged by the community), distributed moderation (relying on a system of community scores of posts) and automated moderation (automated check of posts on the basis of keywords or algorithms). It is crucial to have clear guidelines and a system that is effective and seen as legitimate in the network. A third dimension that needs to be safeguarded is **progress in the process**. The technological communication infrastructure can also support this dimension. The platform and the moderator should stimulate closure of perceptions and decisions on key issues in the network. Interesting approaches to collaborative decision-making have been developed on the internet. An important point here is that progress needs to be made visible so that it can be debated in the network. Visualization technologies are of great importance since they can easily show what progress is being made in the network. It is preferable that these visualizations align the progress with expectations from different actors.

Another issue is the question of what can be done to stimulate progress in the governance network – the ability to organize and summarize discussions and to highlight key issues in the governance network. This means that discussions need to be managed, which can be done through some of the different forms of moderation we presented above: concentrated process management by one or more moderators, fragmented process management by the whole community and automated process management by algorithms. The choice for a form of process management depends on the effectiveness and legitimacy of the mechanism.

The fourth and final dimension is the **substance of the process**. The policy network processes information about different problem perceptions and possible courses of action. This information can be provided by experts but also by stakeholders and is generally coloured and incomplete. Network interactions are needed to make sense of this information and to construct both shared problem definitions and shared perspectives on courses of action. An interesting point here is that substance is not the same as the evidence that we discussed for the policy machine. Young et al. (2002) highlight that the idea of providing evidence for policy fits well with a perspective on policymaking as a design process but not so well with the idea that policies emerge from interactions between different stakeholders. The interactive model stresses that perspectives on the 'world' depend on the perspectives of stakeholders and therefore objective evidence has a much more limited meaning in the process which is geared at constructing a shared image of the world rather than obtaining information about an externally existing world. Communication and sense-making are important functions, but these are often ignored when information is regarded as evidence. This also means that facilitating systems should not emphasize one perspective but present different perspectives on a situation or problem (see Box 3.10).

## Box 3.10: Governance informatics

Overall, a development that is specifically related to information management for the policy network is known as 'governance informatics'. Koliba and Zia (2015, 189) discuss how information technology can help to deepen situational awareness of 'wicked problems' and eventually help to develop new policy designs: 'Governance informatics is predicated on the assumption that by building the capacity to describe governance processes of heterogeneously interacting agents in complex inter-organizational environments, network managers will enhance their situational awareness to adaptively manage the wicked problems surrounding the accountability and performance of inter-organizational governance networks.' They suggest that governance informatics projects include the following:

1. Clarification of initial boundary conditions
2. Undertaking of participatory modelling sessions with stakeholders
3. Development of early scoping models
4. Visualization of new design considerations and scenarios
5. Construction of pattern-oriented, agent-based models
6. Continuous engagement with stakeholders

This indicates that the new technologies offer a range of functions that could support the management of interactive policy processes. Koliba and Zia (2015) show how this approach can help to strengthen projects with multi-stakeholder collaboration and they discuss a transportation planning project and a watershed management project as two examples.

The communication infrastructure needs to provide opportunities for sense-making. Sense-making can take place both in online and offline environments. It is important to have 'data sessions' in which the patterns in the data are discussed and analyzed on the basis of different kinds of expertise. Interpretation of patterns requires the input of formal expertise but also of local knowledge. The City of Utrecht in the Netherlands, for example, organizes data sessions around topics such as urban safety and health. The data analysis department presents analysis of data and input from security and healthcare experts but also area managers are used to

## Box 3.11: Social Platform for Open Data

In the context of the European Project ROUTETOPA (Raising Open and User-friendly Transparency-Enabling Technologies for Public Administrations), we have developed a Social Platform for Open Data. The basic idea of this social platform is that the meaning of patterns in open data needs to be discussed to develop a shared understanding. Discussions in this platform also focus on questions such as how the data can best be visualized and what additional data is needed to develop a shared understanding.

To facilitate the interactions on this platform, we created a 'cocreation room' and an 'agora'. The 'co-creation room' has restricted access and enables stakeholders in a team to discuss the data and to collectively develop an understanding of the subject matter at hand. The 'agora' is a public room where external stakeholders can react on the data visualization that are produced by the stakeholders.

The Social Platform for Open Data is an example of a platform that focuses not only on the computational aspect of data – how can the data be analyzed? – but also on the construction of shared meanings on the basis of open data – what do the data tell us?

*Source:* Working group, 'Route to PA', http://routetopa.eu/

attribute meaning to the patterns in the data. In networked governance, it is crucial to have a 'digital room' that enables participants to discuss the data (see Box 3.11) and to organize offline sessions. The objective of these sessions is to develop a shared understanding that can form the basis for network collaboration.

An overview of the role of information management for the policy network is presented in Table 3.2.

This table highlights the two key components of the tasks of public managers: selecting (or constructing) an adequate platform for interactions between participants and facilitating (and moderating or steering) safe interactions on this platform, so that they result in adequate progress and that there is enough room for sense-making (or discussing the veracity of information). These activities are quite different from those in the policy production in that they focus on creating a digital environment that contributes to the quality of the policy network.

**Table 3.2** Role of information management in the policy network.

| Dimension of the policy network | Key issue | Role of communication infrastructure |
|---|---|---|
| 1. Open decision-making | Designing and implementing the process in such a way that it contains the correct openness at the right moment in the process | Communication infrastructure should offer opportunities for open and closed collaboration |
| 2. Protecting parties' safety and core values | Creating guarantees in the process for protecting the safety and core values of stakeholders | Communication infrastructure needs to contain rules and moderators that generate a safe environment for interactions |
| 3. Progress in the process | Preventing collaborative processes from stalling | Communication infrastructure needs to provide functions for visualizing the performance of the network as a basis for managing progress |
| 4. Substance of the process | Ensuring that the process generates a broad knowledge base for the selected policy option | Communication infrastructure needs to provide elaborate function for collective sense-making of data |

# Ethical issues

The general perspective on ethical issues in SPIM for policy processes is similar to the approach we developed in the previous chapter for information management in organizations. The principles of responsible research and innovation form a starting point for tackling these issues (Von Schomberg 2013): apply technology assessment, apply the precautionary principle, engage stakeholders at an early stage, regard ethics as a design factor and create platforms for deliberation. At the same time, key issues can be identified for the policy process:

- *To what extent can access to collaborative platforms be limited?* Open access to governance networks seems attractive from a democratic perspective but it may undermine the quality of interactions in the governance network. Limiting access to a digital platform may be necessary to realize closure and to help advance the process of collaboration. This opens up the possibility, however, of opportunistic policy development based on close relations with friendly stakeholders.

- *How much value should be attributed to advanced scenarios and modelling?* Information and communication technologies have already generated a host of new opportunities for computing and visualizing scenarios and models. These may be helpful for developing policies but their advanced character may also undermine the possibility of democratic debate since these models become the 'truth'. One could even argue that these models should be rather 'raw' to highlight their fictional character.

- *Can social media be monitored to mine information for policy design?* Monitoring the social media communication of citizens and stakeholders is an attractive way to obtain relevant information for the policy process. At the same time, this could be seen as a form of 'eavesdropping' on communication that was not meant for government officials. The issue here is how governments can deal with the dividing line between public and private information in an information age.

- *How can big data be used in the policy process?* The use of big data for obtaining information about a policy domain requires reflection since the data may contain a number of biases. O'Neill (2016) highlights that big data may in fact only strengthen the current status quo since the data show how people have behaved in the past. At the same time, big data may also present an opportunity to challenge some current biases in policies. The key issue here is that big data should not be regarded as 'the truth' and the biases and limitations of the data need to be considered explicitly.

- *To what extent can moderators influence interactions on policy platforms?* Moderators manage communication in policy networks and therefore have the opportunity to influence the interactions. To some extent, this is desirable in view of the need to make progress in the process. At the same time, moderators may invisibly steer these interactions in the direction of certain outcomes. For that reason, the role of the moderator needs to be discussed not only in an instrumental sense but also in an ethical sense: what kind of moderation do we see as desirable?

The overarching issue here is to what extent governments should make policies *for citizens* based on expertise and knowledge or engage them in the policy process to develop policies *with citizens*. The participatory approach seems to be based on democratic traditions but one could also argue that this results in practice in strong influence on policies by a small group of higher educated people (Bovens and Wille 2017). A more paternalistic approach based on a mandate from representative democracy and neutral expertise could be seen as a way to guarantee that the interests of all citizens are considered. Should information systems support policies for the people or with the people?

# Conclusions

This chapter has shown how SPIM can be used to support policy processes. We underlined that this support can be understood in the sense of providing a 'policy machine' to support the policy design process (problem definition, preparation of policy, decision-making, policy implementation and evaluation). In addition, this support can be understood in terms of providing information and communication opportunities to support the interactions in policy networks (open decision-making, protecting parties' safety and core values, progress in the process and substance of the process). We highlighted that both sets of activities can be understood from the perspective of the engineer and the mediator and identified key rational and political tasks for the SPIM that supports policy processes.

On the basis of this discussion of SPIM for policy processes, we can now also provide some answers to the questions presented in the introduction to this chapter:

- *How can I use big data analysis for designing better policies?* A collection of data from different sources can indeed help to develop information-based policies but an exclusive reliance on big data should be avoided. Policymaking should rely on knowledge-based methods building upon a variety of types of knowledge rather than pursuing the illusion of evidence-based policies.
- *How can I use information systems to evaluate the effectiveness of my agency's policies?* Information systems play a key role in supporting the evaluation of policies and the possibility of real-time evaluation actually comes near. At the same time, the limited nature and biases of information systems need to be acknowledged.

- *Can social media analysis contribute to policy monitoring?* Social media analysis presents an important contribution to the collection of information about a policy domain. This combination can be paired with data from other sources to develop a comprehensive understanding. Organizations also need to discuss to what extent social media monitoring is ethically acceptable.
- *Do smart algorithms contribute to better policy designs?* Algorithms can certainly help in the phase of the policy design to conduct iterative modelling to build understandings in stages from simple beginnings to complex understandings. A key requirement for these algorithms is that they are transparent so that the choices in the modelling of the policy process can be discussed.
- *How can I use diverse information sources for policy evaluation?* We emphasized the combination of quantitative and qualitative data to identify patterns but also attribute meanings to these patterns. The perspective of the moderator highlighted that combining information and drawing conclusions is not only a rational process but also a political one: a focus on the legitimacy of choices for information usage is needed in policy evaluation.
- *Can network technologies improve the communication in policy processes?* Many approaches to SPIM for policy processes emphasize the use of information and modelling techniques. Our discussion of governance networks highlights the value of these platforms but also indicates that this value most often relies on a combination of online and offline interactions.

The key issue is whether SPIM supports policies for the people or with the people. A proper balance between the two seems to be an adequate response but that means that this balance needs to be discussed explicitly to prevent high-tech policy systems that drive out citizen engagement or, vice versa, volatile systems that respond only to citizens with the loudest voice. The real challenge is supporting systems for effective and democratic policies.

# KEY LESSONS FROM CHAPTER 3

- Increasingly, new advanced technologies such as virtual networks, algorithms and data analytics provide the basis for policy development and implementation.

- To ensure the value of SPIM for public policy, it needs to be aligned with the model for policy development and implementation.
- Two key models are presented in this chapter as the basis for SPIM for public policy: the policy production model and the policy network model.
- The policy production model stresses that policies are produced in different stages – agenda-setting, policy design, policy decision, policy implementation and policy evaluation – and that each stage needs to be supported by SPIM.
- For each of these stages, internal and external information resources can help to rationalize the policy processes by providing a better evidence basis.
- The policy network model emphasizes that policies are developed and implemented in collaborative networks of stakeholders and SPIM needs to support and facilitate these multi-actor collaborative processes.
- SPIM can support the policy network by providing a communication infrastructure for open decision-making which takes into account the requirements for effective network interactions.
- Ethical issues for SPIM in policy processes are identified and the principles of responsible research and innovation – apply technology assessment, apply the precautionary principle, engage stakeholders at an early stage, regard ethics as a design factor and create platforms for deliberation – can form a basis for tackling these issues.

# 4

# Managing information
# for public services

*In their everyday lives, citizens all around the world interact with public organizations as recipients of public services. Services may range from refuse collection to licensing building permits, producing passports and assigning welfare benefits. In this chapter, we explore how strategic public information management (SPIM) supports high-quality public service delivery. We will highlight how technological developments have enabled governments to restructure their services to make them more customer-friendly and efficient. More specifically, we introduce two new trends –* **proactive service delivery** *and* **co-provision of public services** *– as models for thinking about managing information for public services in an information age.*

## Introduction

Most citizens encounter public agencies if they appeal to public services. Services provide goods in domains such as education, public housing and healthcare. Unlike these tangible services, many public services are primarily information-driven transactions. Citizens need governments to obtain a passport, a student loan, a building permit, etc. These are specifically provided to individual citizens.[1] Because public service delivery is the predominant context in which citizens meet their public agencies, the quality of these services to a large extent shapes the public reputation of the agencies. It is also

---

[1] Individual services differ from collective services such as street cleaning, policing, park maintenance, national security and many other government activities. For collective services, there is no direct relation between the government agency and an individual citizen. This also means that individual services require information about individual citizens and collective services do not. As a result, the information management dynamics of these collective services are quite different and thus these services should be seen as organizational implementation (see Chapter 3).

an encounter that can have a great impact on their life and therefore public services can have a great impact on how citizens think about government.

Public services have been a key focus in the practice of e-government – public services provided over the internet – since the early 1990s. One of the main promises of the use of ICT in the public sector was that this would result in more accessible services for citizens in that they would be able to reach government 24/7 and from any location. Before the introduction of e-services, citizens needed to physically visit the agencies in their offices or through written communications. The introduction of the internet and e-government meant the introduction of a new channel of communication– the government website – and it also meant that interactions between citizens and government could proceed much more efficiently. The objectives of the digital services policy of the Western Australian Government provides an example of the promise of digital services (see Box 4.1).

## Box 4.1: E-services by the Western Australian Government

The Western Australian Government aims to provide services to citizens in a seamless and accessible manner. The idea of 'whole of government' guides this ambition: the government wants to prevent citizens from having to shop at different departments: one single point of access helps them to obtain the service they need. The following goals have been formulated for their digital services to citizens:

- Supporting the transformation of government processes and delivery of services through the appropriate digital channels
- Delivering digital services that are based on community needs and life events
- Delivering a unified consistent presence across channels to enable a better user experience for Western Australian citizens
- Delivering secure digital services that are current, reliable and accessible anytime, anywhere, using any device

These goals highlight the change of focus from government processes as a starting point for digital services to citizens' needs, life events and user experiences as the basis for e-services.

*Source:* Government of Western Australia Digital Services
Policy, https://www.wa.gov.au/government/publications/
digital-services-policy

The ambitions of the Western Australian Government illustrate that quality of service has become a key aspect of government performance. In the 1980s, the promise of new technologies merged with a wave of reforms in public sectors all around the world. New Public Management (NPM) replaced the old Public Administration. The traditional perspective on public services – now referred to as Old Public Administration – highlights the procedural correctness of government processes. Working according to regulations and procedures was regarded as good government practice since it prevented corruption and arbitrary decision-making. At the same time, the procedures resulted in government organizations that were slow and inflexible. Government services had a very bad reputation with the common notion of being sent from one office to another. This model of organizing service processes was challenged in the 1980s by NPM. NPM focuses on citizens as the customer – the client of public services – and the need to achieve better customer satisfaction to maintain the legitimacy of government (Fountain 2001).

The current debate on public services can only be understood from the perspective of NPM which promised a better, friendlier, more accessible and faster government service (for an in-depth analysis, see Bekkers and Homburg 2007). Government agencies work for citizens, hence they have an obligation to make these services customer-oriented (see Box 4.2). The key argument here is that the legitimacy of government not only depends on a fair electoral process and adherence to legal frameworks but also on the quality of government work in general and of government services specifically. This has resulted in large government programmes to strengthen public services all around the world. Benchmarking government services has become an important point of orientation for many governments (see, for example, KPMG's benchmark of city services: https://home.kpmg/xx/en/home/insights/2017/09/finding-the-courage-to-improve-benchmarking-city-services.html).

The introduction of NPM triggered a wave of reforms that aimed to supplant the traditional focus on supply with a focus on citizens' demand (Hoogwout 2010). Many public agencies aimed to replace the logic of their organizational routines with the logic of clients' situations. The key objective is the one-stop shop: citizens should not be sent from one official to the next but should receive all the services they need at the first point of contact. This change means that the organization is 'tilted' to organize itself around customer demands rather than government processes (Hoogwout 2010). This transition has had important implications for information management since it means that all the information should be available at the one-stop shop: governments needed a so-called 'de-siloization' of government

## Box 4.2: United Nations E-Government Development Index (EGDI)

The United Nations foregrounds the quality of digital services to citizens, and have developed an index consisting of three indices to measure national e-government capacities:

- *Online service index.* This focuses on the provision of service and measures a government's capability and willingness to provide services and communicate with its citizens electronically.
- *Telecommunication infrastructure index.* This emphasizes the underlying infrastructure and measures the existing infrastructure required for citizens to participate in e-government.
- *Human capital index.* This measures the ability of citizens to use e-services and calculates literacy rates and enrolment in education as proxies for citizens' abilities to use e-government services.

These measures are used to assess where governments are in their stage of e-government development and what next steps can be taken to strengthen these services. Key to the line of argument of the UN is that government services are not only about provision but also about use of the services by citizens.

*Source:* Leibniz Institute for Economic Research at the University of Munich, 'E-Government Development Index', https://www.ifo.de/DocDL/dicereport412-db2.pdf

information – removing barriers between organizational departments – to facilitate focus on clients in public services. The variety of information processes should be connected with the variety of customer demands. This is challenging for the information provision and, in response to this trend, numerous organizational transformations have occurred which enhance the customer focus of organizations and the building of new front offices, mid-offices and back offices that support the diverse connections between the various processes and customer needs.

Currently, many of the technological trends that we have introduced in the previous chapters such as big data, sensor networking, learning algorithms, social media, etc. result in new challenges for SPIM for public services. These new technologies create all kinds of opportunities but they need to be integrated into the processes of the organizations. Thus, the domain of public services results in the following set of questions for managers:

- What options does new technology provide for improving public service delivery?
- How can I use new media for contacts with citizens?
- How can organizations adapt their processes to the needs of citizens?
- How can ICT strengthen the engagement of clients in service production?

To answer these questions, this chapter will delve into the question of what public services are and how they can be strengthened. We introduce two dominant trends in public services – proactive service provision and the coproduction of services – and will then explore the key issues of SPIM for these two models, which also raises ethical implications. The chapter ends with conclusions and the answers to the questions for public managers presented earlier.

# Proactive and coproductive services

The focus on improving the quality of public services and, more specifically, customer satisfaction, forms a part of NPM that advocates the use of knowledge, methods and approaches from the private sector in the public sector. One of the key premises of NPM is that customer satisfaction is a vital element in government legitimacy: government needs to work for the people and deliver high-quality services. The reframing of citizens as clients of public organizations resulted in significant attention on focus groups to identify the needs of clients, measure customer satisfaction, etc. It also means that the front office – an e-services portal – has become a key element of e-government and one of the factors being assessed in e-government benchmarks. A flashy web portal rather than a new building has become the hallmark of a modern government agency.

The emphasis on citizens as customers has resulted in the large-scale implementation of systems for methodically managing customer relations, and a big push for using private sector technologies for public service delivery (see Boxes 4.3 and 4.4). However, this push may overlook some of the reasons public services are quite different from private services. Hoogwout (2010, 34–6) identifies some key dilemmas for public service provision, which highlight their specific nature:

- *Individual versus collective interests.* Public services are generally concerned with the redistribution of public money such as social benefits or weighing of public values such as building permits. Services that satisfy customers may conflict with collective interests since easy access to benefits or a permit to build a warehouse may not be regarded as desirable by the collective that requires strict enforcement of regulations.
- *Enforcement versus service provision.* Government organizations need to enforce regulation, for example related to safety, but also provide services to citizens and entrepreneurs. There may be conflict when an entrepreneur needs a permit as soon as possible to run his/her business while the government organization requires time to carefully check the safety criteria.
- *Education versus providing support.* In public services such as refuse collection, local governments not only want to provide easy services to citizens but also have an interest in educating these citizens to reduce and separate rubbish in a proper manner. Such educational efforts may not always be appreciated, but they are an important pillar in certain policies and long-term strategies of the government organization.

These dilemmas highlight that public services may build on the logic of private sector service processes, but they also need to take a whole host of legal and policy considerations into account (see the discussion of 'publicness' in Chapter 1). As argued in the introduction, publicness is a foundation of any public organization. The double focus on services to individuals is one of the key challenges for public service provision. The demands and circumstance of individual citizens need to be reconciled with the demands and requirements of generic regulations and organizational routines. The administrative processes need to be firmly rooted in relevant legislation and policy rules but applied in specific situations.

The proactive provision of services is a key element in digital era governance (Dunleavy et al. 2006). The perspective developed by Dunleavy and his colleagues stresses that NPM, due to its emphasis on

## Box 4.3: Customer relationship management

Information systems in the public sector generally support specific business processes and follow from an analysis of the informational needs in these processes. This type of informational support works for the process but fails to integrate the various sources of information and interaction with citizens. Information about the same citizen is often managed within many different information systems. A system for customer relationship management (CRM) centralizes all information about customers and in that sense connects the different customer processes in the organization. The key objective of CRM is to learn more about customers and to improve relationships by catering better to their needs.

CRM consists of three elements: collaborative (offering a consistent customer experience across channels); operative (streamlining processes in the back and front offices); and analytical (the organization and interpretation of customer data through data mining). The basic principles of CRM – personalization (products, information, services), integration (planning processes, business process re-engineering, service development), interaction (channels, long-term communication, surveys) and selection (identify different user groups) – completes a holistic focus on clients. CRM fits the focus of organizations on citizens as customers rather than on organizational processes.

The Housing and Development Board (HDB) in Singapore provides an interesting example of how CRM can be used in the public sector. The main task of this board is to provide affordable housing for the public. It uses CRM to: 1) ensure that both customers and HDB have a single view of each other; 2) keep consistent records of customers and be proactive in serving customers; 3) facilitate personalized interactions with customers; 4) provide customers with a selection of channels appropriate to their needs; and 5) provide database management facilities to support HDB's business analysts with business intelligence.

*Sources:* Schellong (2005); Teo, Devadoss and Pan (2006)

disaggregation, competition and performance-based incentivization, created some important limitations on the production of services. They argue a new approach has emerged to deal with these limitations which is strongly based on new technologies and focuses on integration

## Box 4.4: Blockchain

The blockchain – the basis for crypto currencies such as Bitcoin – is a technology that may have a revolutionary impact on public services. This technology promises cost and safety advantages over traditional currency and exchange systems through its distributed ledger technology (DLT). This technology can be used for identity management but also for safeguarding the reliability of documents which has increasingly become a topic of concern in the public sector. For this reason, countries around the world are experimenting with the value of this technology for improving public services.

An interesting example of the value of the blockchain for the public sector comes from Brazil. Here, forged degree certificates are a big problem. To tackle this problem, an innovative approach has been developed. The certificates get a fingerprint which is then stored in the blockchain with a signature and also possibly the courses that the student has passed. A regulatory agency in Brazil automates a smart contract in the blockchain that allows accredited universities to automatically record a certificate after completion of the right courses. It is also possible to revoke certificates if erroneous transactions are discovered. This innovation promises to reduce the number of forged certificates.

*Sources:* Scholl and Bolivar (2019); Palma et al. (2019)

and collaboration rather than fragmentation and competition. The key elements of digital era governance are:

- *Reintegration.* Digital Era Governance (DEG) is based on the fundamental reintegration of the various functions and agencies in government. The idea of the 'whole-of-government' (Christensen and Lægreid 2007) underlies efforts to ensure that government activity is not organized in silos but rather presented in a seamless way to facilitate integrated services.
- *Needs-based holism.* DEG is based on the idea that distinct client groups and their needs lead the organization of government rather than the distinctive tasks. This would mean, for example, that all welfare services for are provided in an integrated manner rather than providing access to benefits, housing, training, etc. through separate channels.

- *Digitization.* This element of DEG seems almost trivial now: all government agencies have become digital organizations. Dunleavy et al. (2006), however, stress that digitization means fully exploiting the potential of digital storage and internet communications to transform governance. The modern service organization is not a traditional organization that uses new technologies but a radically transformed organization. Processes are optimized around technological capabilities.

These elements of DEG highlight the features of modern organizations that differ radically from traditional, bureaucratic, task-focused organizations. Modern service organizations focus on their customers and use technologies to organize functions in an integrated manner around the customers. Organizationally, these demands are generally translated into the construction of a front office for customer contacts and a back office for administrative processes. Many organizations have replaced the traditional task-focused organizational structure with one that separates the front office – with customer contact – from the back office – with administrative processes – and sometimes a mid-office to bridge them (Schuppan 2009). Information management in the front office follows the logic of the individual citizens while information in the back office still follows the organizational routines.

The front office is the point of contact between government organization and client, which may be a virtual location such as a website or a social media platform. At the front office, customers receive information about the services in general and also their specific situation. Most local governments in Europe and North America have websites that enable citizens to interact with their governments and obtain the services they need. This means that the front office needs to be structured in an accessible manner for a diverse group of citizens and provide an easily structured menu. It also means that it needs to be able to present relevant information to customers and process information that is entered by citizens. The front office is connected to the back office where information is maintained and processed.

The back office consists of databases with information about citizens and software for processing the data. Overall, the back office is about applying general rules to specific situations. When a citizen, for example, applies for a building permit, the information that is collected at the front office is processed to check whether the permit is in line with legislation and existing building zones. And when a citizen applies for a social benefit, eligibility is checked in the back office. Back offices are a highly technological environment – Zouridis (2000) refers to them as 'information refineries' – in which technology plays a key role in achieving an effective and efficient process. The output from the back office is communicated to the front office where it is presented to the customer.

In the current debate, we see two seemingly contradictory trends influencing the future of public services. The first trend is *proactive service provision*: the idea that on the basis of information about citizens, services can be provided proactively by government organizations. The logic is a guiding one and can be described as providing *services for citizens*. Tax declarations in the Netherlands are an example of how technologies are used to reduce the effort that is expected from citizens. The Tax Service presents a tax form that is to a large extent already filled out with all the information that the Tax Service has about the citizens. The only thing that is expected from citizens is that they check this information and digitally sign it in order to complete their tax applications. The ideal situation for the citizen from the perspective of proactive service provision is one in which services are provided by government without even having to request them.

The second trend is the *co-provision of services*: the idea that the quality and efficiency of services can be enhanced by strengthening the engagement of citizens in their provision through the use of new technologies (Lember et al. 2019). The logic is based on collaboration and focuses on providing *services with citizens*. Notifications about problems in public spaces are examples of this trend. Local governments in the Netherlands have been developing systems that facilitate the notification of problems such as broken streetlights and holes in pavements. New apps enable them to take a picture and upload it – with GPS coordinates – directly onto the website of local government so that they know what they need to fix. An example of these types of services is FixMyStreet in the UK, a website and app that enables citizens to easily report, view or discuss local problems such as graffiti, fly-tipping, broken paving slabs or street lighting (see https://www.fixmystreet.com/; see also Box 4.8). The underlying idea is to offer a situation where citizens are able to provide their input to government whenever and wherever they are.

These trends occur simultaneously and relate to different types of services. Proactive services can be developed if government does not require input from citizens whereas co-provision of services is valuable when additional input from citizens can help to enhance the efficiency or effectiveness of services. They both represent a different underlying ideal government *for* the people or government *with* the people. The challenge for government agencies is to use new technologies in such a way that government agencies are able to provide better services for and with citizens. The opportunities and challenges for SPIM will be discussed in depth in the following two sections.

# Information management for proactive services

The first challenge that emerges in e-services is providing services for citizens by government agencies taking the lead and guiding citizens in the process. The burden of applying for services should be minimized by the use of technology to make it as easy as possible for citizens. Public services become more accessible for citizens with limited bureaucratic skills. As some pilot schemes with welfare benefits show, these proactive services are also inclusive services. The benefits can be realized by making the services 'seamless'. Seamless services means that information processing by government organizations reduces the administrative burdens for citizens. Box 4.5 highlights how seamless services have been enacted.

---

### Box 4.5: Seamless services at the Dutch Social Insurance Bank

The Social Insurance Bank in the Netherlands provides child benefits to all citizens. Citizens need to enter information into the system for their firstborn but not for their other children. The Social Insurance Bank obtains information about the birth of children from local government and automatically provides the child benefit to the parents. In this situation, the provision of the public service is fully automatic in the majority of cases and citizens do not need to apply or engage in administrative tasks.

*Source:* Van Eck (2018)

---

Proactive public service delivery implies that citizens who are entitled to certain benefits receive these benefits automatically. Proactive public services are based on new principles for information collection and processing. Information that has already been collected by the government agency does not need to be collected again. Information that does not require additional input from citizens will be processed by the agency and tentative information is presented to citizens so that they only need to validate the information rather than having to provide it all.

There are advantages and disadvantages to seamless public services. Seamless services certainly can be attractive for citizens as customers. Very few citizens voluntarily engage with administrative tasks and by automating these tasks citizens are better served. In addition, engaging in these administrative tasks requires a certain bureaucratic competence; a competence that is not exactly equally divided in society. In that sense, proactive services are specifically important and helpful for citizens with a lower level of education and/or limited digital skills. One could argue that seamless services contribute to equity in government–citizens relationships.

Proactive services, however, also pose risks and show some serious disadvantages. One significant risk is invasion of privacy: information from different sources may be collected to provide these seamless services but this can result in an invasion of the citizen's privacy. In theory, governments are able to provide the best services when they have comprehensive knowledge of their citizens. In addition, citizens seem to have more limited options to influence the services and therefore they can become more dependent on the system. Malfunctioning systems may be difficult to correct and could have a big impact on people's lives. The main challenge for government agencies is to realize the benefits in a fair and accepted manner. This requires high-quality standards for information management but also respect for legal and ethical concerns (see Box 4.6).

## Box 4.6: Social media monitoring

Social media monitoring – sometimes referred to as social media listening – is an important strategy for obtaining information about customers. This type of monitoring is frequently used in the private sector to obtain information about brand popularity and customer satisfaction with certain products. Government can monitor citizens' social media communication to gain insight on how communities feel about public services and to obtain raw and unfiltered feedback.

An example of an agency that uses social media monitoring is the Tax Department in the Netherlands. This agency uses social media monitoring to gain insight into taxpayers' sentiments about taxes and their perception of the organization and also to gain better insight into the questions and problems that clients have with their tax returns (Bekkers, Edwards and Kool 2013). The Tax Department uses keywords to scan the online environment for issues relevant to the agency and also focuses on a small set of online communities where members of important target groups communicate about tax issues. The overall aim is to collect information to improve services and the image of the Tax Department.

Social media monitoring also raises some legal and ethical issues. Bekkers, Edwards and Kool (2013, 341) highlight the following issue: 'The monitoring of networks that are perceived as private by their users, even when these forums are publicly accessible, can be seen as an intrusion into their life world.' This is the reason they emphasize that the perceived privacy, method and covert nature of monitoring need to be taken into account when organizations consider using social media monitoring.

The proactive provision of seamless services entails some important shifts in the organization of the service process.

- *From bureaucratic form to (near) natural language.* In the current situation, web forms are basically bureaucratic forms in an electronic format. The proactive provision of services aims to drastically reduce the 'bureaucratic work' of clients. New interfaces will enable clients to easily check one option or even just present their request in natural language.
- *From clients providing the information to an agency collecting the information.* Currently, clients are often required to provide extensive information about themselves whereas much of this information has already been collected. The proactive provision of services means that government agencies will collect all this information from their own or other datasets.
- *From requested services to actively provided services.* In the current situation, clients have to request services such as a parking permit or housing subsidy. Proactive services means that government agencies can identify which citizens need a parking permit or a housing subsidy and provide them automatically.

**Table 4.1** Role of information management in proactive service provision.

| Proactive service provision | Role of information management | Front or back office |
|---|---|---|
| 1. Provide opportunity for easy request of services | 1. Natural language as a basis for requesting services | Front office |
| 2. Minimize information that clients need to provide | 2. Collecting relevant information about clients from different sources | Back office |
| 3. Provide services without any client action | 3. Process information from clients and provide the service | Back office |

The implications of these shifts for the role of information management are summarized in Table 4.1.

Table 4.1 highlights that seamless service predominantly entails back office interventions. The 'invisible side' of government becomes more important than the interaction portal. One could even argue that the ideal of seamless services is an invisible government that ensures that all citizens obtain the services they need without them ever applying for these services. This type of action requires that government store and process enormous amounts of personal information from these citizens to be able to provide the right services.

# Information management for the coproduction of services

The idea of connected services is radically different from seamless services: while the role of citizens is drastically reduced in seamless services, connected services require active citizenship. The basic idea of connected services is that new technologies provide platforms for interactions between government and citizens and these platforms can be used to strengthen services. Singapore even developed an e-government strategy labelled 'Government-with-You' in order to stress that the government aims to 'facilitate a collaborative government that co-creates and connects with the people' (Linders 2012). In an extreme situation, governments can reduce themselves to the role of a platform so citizens, business and civil society organizations can then coproduce and co-consume public services on this platform (Linders 2012).

The perspective of coproduction highlights that services are not provided by government but instead result from cooperation. Citizens may play a role in the collective services such as safety – by providing information about suspects – or nature conservation – by counting birds or fish. Citizens can even help each other with advice on arranging administrative issues with the government (see Box 4.7).

---

## Box 4.7: Expatica as a community of public service support

Platforms can be used by citizens to self-organize their own forms of public service support. Expats often have difficulties finding their way in the institutional landscape of their new country. Contact with other expats may be very helpful in finding their way through the web of residential permits, schools for their children, healthcare insurance, etc. This information may also be available on government websites but may not be in their language and are often difficult to find. In many countries, expats have developed platforms to facilitate the exchange of information. These platforms can be understood as virtual communities or 'communities of public service support' which provide a basis for social learning in peer-to-peer networks. The worldwide operating Expatica (www.expatica.com) is the best-known example of such a community of public service support.

*Source:* Meijer et al. (2012)

---

Coproduction of services may also focus on individuals or groups. Bovaird (2007, 847) provides the following definition of coproduction: 'the provision of services through regular, long-term relationships between professionalized service providers (in any sector) and service users or other members of the community, where all parties make substantial resource contributions.' Coproduction of public services may take various forms. Linders (2012) distinguishes three different forms of coproduction in the age of social media with increasing citizen control: citizen sourcing (e.g. Challenge.gov, FixMyStreet, CrisisCommons), government as a platform (e.g. crime mapping, recovery.gov) and do-it-yourself government (e.g. Yelp, neighbourhood portals). See Box 4.8 for an example.

> ## Box 4.8: Apps for the maintenance of public space
>
> Local governments are responsible for the maintenance of public space. They work with maintenance plans but also on the basis of information from citizens about broken streetlights, loose paving slabs, etc. The information that citizens provide directly contributes to the quality of the maintenance. For this reason, various apps have been developed by and for local governments to collect information from citizens. Citizens can enter the information and even upload a photo with the GPS location to their local government. This information is processed and used to optimize the maintenance of public space. Examples come from various countries such as the UK (www. FixMyStreet.com), Switzerland (www.zueriwieneu.ch) and Slovakia (www.odkazprestarostu.sk).
>
> *Source:* Meijer and Potjer (2018)

The aim of government is no longer to provide individual services but rather to facilitate the coproduction of services. This means that information management provides a platform, which enables citizens to become coproduced by providing information. Information management also processes citizens' inputs and manages the interactions between various citizens.

Table 4.2 reveals that the key challenge for connected services is to provide an interface between the organization and its information resources and

**Table 4.2** Role of information management in connected services.

| Connected services | Role of information management | Front or back office |
|---|---|---|
| 1. Providing a platform for interactions between government agency and citizens | 1. Developing and maintaining a digital platform for the coproduction of services | Front office |
| 2. Informing citizens about government actions and questions | 2. Providing information to citizens about coproduction | Front and back office |
| 3. Processing coproduced inputs from citizens related to the services | 3. Processing the information from citizens | Front and back office |
| 4. Managing the community of coproducers | 4. Administrating information about the coproducers | Front and back office |

citizens and their information input. The platform for connected services needs to provide information from the government agency but also process the input, feedback, suggestions and comments from citizens and connect this to the organization's information resources.

# Ethical issues

Realizing good services for citizens is challenging and also raises a range of ethical issues for SPIM.

- *Can personal information be used to make service provision easy?* The issue here is whether a breach of privacy that works to the advantage of the client is permissible. One can think of methods to ask citizens for permission but one can also question whether this is adequate since we are so often asked for permission by websites that this hardly qualifies as informed consent.
- *Should government organization replace human interactions by robots?* Chatbots and automated decision systems are increasingly used in government organizations to replace human interaction. The issue is whether this is how we want to realize relations between government and citizens. Should there be no human contact at all? See also Box 4.9.

---

### Box 4.9: Human touch

Automated decision-making systems increasingly make decisions about student loans, housing subsidies, parking fees, child benefits, etc. without any human interference. A question of increasing concern is whether there is a right to have a human being evaluate a decision. This issue is of great importance when citizens feel that they are being treated unfairly, especially in exceptional situations when a human assessment may take into account specific considerations that a computerized system would overlook. A more fundamental issue is whether there is such a thing as a right to human contact. The Rathenau Institute emphasizes that human dignity is a key value in the contacts between government and citizens.

*Source:* Rathenau Institute (2017)

- *How transparent should the back office of government organizations be?* From a democratic point of view the back office – the operations – needs to be transparent but to realize effectiveness and efficiency government organizations may want to reduce transparency.
- *To what extent is the use of citizen profiles allowed?* Many smart approaches to proactively offering services rely on algorithms identifying profiles by analyzing similarities between users. This could mean, however, that citizens are profiled and receive different treatments by their government. The question is whether this interferes with constitutional principles such as equal treatment and universal access.
- *Is coproduction permitted even if it results in more inequality?* A key objection to coproduction is that certain groups of citizens – well-educated, vocal – will be able to improve the situation for themselves whereas less administratively competent citizens will not. An example is the app for information about public space (as discussed in Box 4.8). The risk of this app is that more maintenance will occur in neighbourhoods where it is not as necessary as it is in others.
- *Should government stimulate peer-to-peer contact between citizens?* The advantage of peer-to-peer contact – e.g. citizens giving each other information about permits and benefits – is that it reduces government expenses. At the same time, this may result in incorrect information. Is the government agency responsible for this incorrect information if it provides the platform for the interactions?

These ethical issues are complex in the sense that they require a response that relies on contextual weighing of factors and finding appropriate responses. Specific instruments for ethical decision-making such as the Data Ethical Decision Aid (https://dataschool.nl/deda/?lang=en) can help organizations to debate these issues and decide how to deal with them (Franzke, Muis and Schäfer 2021).

# Conclusions

This chapter discussed the value of SPIM for public services and highlighted trends in the provision of these services: proactive or seamless services and connected or coproduced services. Seamless services highlight the idea that information contact is cumbersome for citizens, requires specific administrative competences and that governments should aim to provide these services with limited or no effort from citizens. Connected services emphasize the collaboration between government and citizens. This approach suggests that new media could reduce transaction costs and therefore enable new forms of coproduction. Both trends occur simultaneously but generally in different domains and enable governments to work better both for and with citizens, resulting in a government that is more or less visible and also connected to citizens.

SPIM plays a key role in the transformation of services. The new media offer great potential for improving services. We can now use the discussion of the two approaches to using these new media to answer the questions posed at the beginning of this chapter:

- *What options does new technology provide for improving public service delivery?* We have shown that technology provides new opportunities for making services very easy through data warehousing and active processing of citizen data. The rapid increases in data storage and processing technologies (data warehousing, data analytics, artificial intelligence) enable service providers to develop services that require no or minimal effort from citizens. At the same time, new communication technologies such as social media platforms provide enormous opportunities for coproduction of services.
- *How can I use new media for contacts with citizens?* There are effectively two ways to use social media for public services: the first is to use social media to obtain information to enhance the quality of services. Social media monitors can be used to measure customer satisfaction and to continuously improve services. The second is to use social media as a new channel for connections between government and citizens. Social media enables new forms of coproduction of services, e.g. when citizens provide information for the police.
- *How can organizations adapt their processes to the needs of citizens?* The needs of citizens can be adapted by fully organizing all processes around the needs of citizens. The clients need to be well known, which should lead the design of government processes. The main idea is that the processes are to be structured flexibly around citizens rather than taking government tasks and responsibilities as a starting point.
- *How can ICT strengthen the engagement of clients in service production?* This chapter highlights that new technologies can be used to facilitate the engagement of large groups of citizens in the production of services. New technologies reduce transaction costs and enable organizations to interact with countless citizens.

In sum, this chapter highlights how organizing e-services is concerned with redefining the relation between government organizations and citizens. We have discussed different perspectives such as needs-based holism and citizen coproduction to provide an overview of some of the ways in which organizations can conceptualize their clients. A final observation is that government organizations can learn much from the way private sector organizations organize their service but they should always keep in mind that public services have certain features – no monopoly, equal treatment, tax money, legal implications, etc. – which make these services different. A strong perspective on citizens as clients should therefore form the basis for the organization of public services.

# KEY LESSONS FROM CHAPTER 4

- Increasingly, government services are provided online and there are various ways that SPIM can support high-quality public service delivery.
- New developments have been highlighted and two trends introduced – proactive service delivery and co-provision of services – as models for thinking about managing information for public services in an information age.
- Proactive service provision means that, on the basis of extensive information, services to citizens can be provided proactively by government organizations rather than merely reacting to specific requests.
- Three specific routes for SPIM are identified to realize proactive services: natural language as a basis for requesting services, collecting relevant information about clients from different sources and processing information from clients and providing the service.
- Co-provision of services means that the quality and efficiency of services can be enhanced by strengthening the engagement of citizens in their provision.
- To realize this co-provision of services, SPIM needs to focus on providing a platform for interactions and managing the community of coproducers.
- Ethical issues are identified and we emphasize that specific tools for assisting ethical decision-making provide value to public managers.

# 5

# Managing information for regulation

*This chapter addresses two aspects of regulation and ICT: the regulation of ICT itself and the use of ICT for regulatory practices. It highlights the diversity of challenges in both aspects for strategic public information management (SPIM). Challenges range from attempts to use ICT for shaping and nudging the behaviour of citizens and companies, to the way organizations regulate their employees with ICT, to regulating increasingly powerful technology companies. We compare rational and political perspectives as two different ways to address these challenges. The* **rational perspective** *is informed by a cybernetic concept of algorithm design in which signals are processed to steer a social system in the desired direction. The* **political perspective** *stresses that regulation is about the use of power to make other actors do what the regulator wants them to do. We discuss how the rational perspective focuses our attention on the effective use of ICT for regulation, whereas the political perspective emphasizes the legitimate usage.*

## Introduction

A key task for government organizations is regulation: ensuring citizens and companies comply with (legal) rules and taking appropriate action to keep people or organizations on track or incentivize change if needed (Jordan 2018). This traditional task of government has only become more important and complicated over the past decades as the number of rules and regulations has increased, companies increasingly work transnationally in networks and public demand for strict regulation has become stronger. Regulation has become a highly complex and politically sensitive government task in which information processing plays a key role.

Public managers have traditionally had quite a limited role in the day-to-day work of regulation, but we argue here that regulatory activity is another sphere that has gained in importance for SPIM. Information management used to be a unique organizational specialism supporting regulatory tasks on an ad hoc basis. This included tasks like defining regulatory policies, explaining them to the groups they apply to and monitoring compliance. But, today, information and the technologies used to exploit it are deeply embedded in all areas of the regulatory process. Changes in technology are shifting the responsibilities of public managers, and the range of regulatory tools available to them.

The availability of new information and communication technologies provides government organizations with powerful instruments for their regulatory tasks since the new technologies provide a broad range of opportunities for shaping the behaviour of individuals and companies and tracking and analyzing compliance. Think, for example, of the observation of non-compliant behaviour. Cameras and audio are fitted to mobile phones, which are widely used by people in professional and non-professional capacities to track, record and analyze behaviour. The ability for organizations to store, search and analyze camera and audio data is growing at a fast pace.

The new technologies provide enormous potential to improve regulatory tasks but also raise a host of ethical, legal and political questions for SPIM. There are serious concerns that ICT such as cameras, drones, sensors and wearables (see Box 5.1) will invade upon the privacy of citizens or employees and the fear of a Big Brother state is still very much a topic of discussion. Regulatory technologies may result in a bias towards certain groups in society and thus generate new levels of technology-enabled discrimination. The new technologies also result in novel regulatory tasks for government, either because previously unregulated areas of activity can be regulated or because the application of ICT itself needs to be regulated. The proper use of technology – by public agencies and companies – has become a key domain for government regulation. The regulation of privacy is a key example: governments need to observe whether companies adhere to privacy regulation in their collection and processing of data about individual persons. Another regulatory task related to technology concerns the potential abuse of the market position of tech platforms.

## Box 5.1: Regulating public health responses during Coronavirus

A recent example is the use of ICT to enforce social distance between people to reduce the spread of Covid-19. Such ICT include biometric technology to control movement, smartphone apps and wearables. In several European countries, including Italy where the pandemic struck early and in some regions particularly hard, cameras and drones were used to observe people, take temperatures and inform policing decisions. Telephone data were used to track their movements.

Such a regulatory intervention using ICT has both short-term and long-term consequences on behaviour. In the short term, surveillance drones provide information that feeds to medical and law enforcement personnel to alert them when police intervention is needed for more serious regulatory interventions. In the long term, the insights measured over time and used in combination with other statistics regarding neighbourhood or other geolocated information can give public health planners an evidence-based tool for studying whether existing regulatory practices are working. Following this, planners can implement regulatory solutions to either ease or increase public restrictions on interactions in public spaces.

*Source:* Kitchin (2020)

The potential of technology for strengthening regulation combined with the risks associated with them confronts public managers with the following questions for SPIM:

- How do ICT influence different areas of regulatory work for public managers?
- How does algorithmic regulation influence the risk of surveillance by governments and businesses?
- What politically contentious areas of ICT-driven regulation should public managers address?
- What measures should be put in place to ensure that regulatory approaches are legitimate in the eyes of citizens?
- What are the main ethical areas to address when public managers use ICT for regulation?

To answer these questions, we address how regulation and information interrelate and how SPIM can capitalize on a better understanding of this interrelation. We will consider how information technologies can create new problems and dilemmas for regulatory processes. We will compare three different trade-offs in particular: 1) centralized and diffuse regulation; 2) public and private regulation; and 3) internal and external regulation. The prospect of regulating through algorithmic decision-making tools is a growing area of interest for public managers and we will explain what this is and what its implications are for SPIM as well as how politics can negatively influence the regulatory process and what SPIM approaches public managers can take to address it. We will continue by addressing the ethical implications of the implementation of algorithms as a regulatory tool. The chapter ends with conclusions and the answers to the questions for public managers just presented.

# Types and dilemmas of ICT-informed regulation

The domain of ICT-informed regulation is highly diverse. We will map the variety of forms of regulations and show that the idea of surveillance is central to the use of information in all these forms. The strategic challenges of managing information are highlighted through three main areas of tension that characterize these dilemmas:

- Centralized and diffuse regulation
- Public and private regulation
- Internal and external regulation

*Centralized and diffuse regulation.* Regulation has traditionally been regarded from a government-centric perspective as a command-and-control system reliant on a government agency to make rules, employ an inspectorate and institute mechanisms for enforcement and punishment (Harrison 2017). An example of a centralized regulation is the requirement placed by governments on car manufacturers to only use engines that keep carbon emissions below a specific level.

However, a modern governance perspective more suitable to management of ICT and public information stresses that regulation has evolved into more nuanced and devolved forms of influence that engage public, private and nongovernment agents in processes of monitoring, reporting, persuasion and punishment (Grabosky 2013). An example of diffuse regulation is the creation of markets for cap and trade of carbon emission credits. The goal here, like engine regulations, is also to control carbon emissions, but governments provide a platform for different actors (businesses) to regulate the behaviour of the industry as a whole. The role of government in the modern situation is different: governments generally have a system responsibility rather than a responsibility for individual cases. Diffuse regulation tends to be 'softer' than centralized regulation. Rather than having hard and fast rules that come with fines and punishments, diffuse regulation may rely on reputational or social incentives that give individuals and companies space to self-regulate.

*Public and private regulation.* Private control over large parts of the internet raises the question of how the responsibilities for regulation need to be divided. The main challenge lies in the different responsibilities of the public and private sectors, which makes it difficult to regulate private actors despite the kinds of far-reaching impacts they have on the fabric of public life (see Box 5.2 for an interesting description of this problem). Public organizations are required to treat citizens equally, while the assumptions are much looser in the private sector. Furthermore, the public sector is the higher authority in society and must step in to regulate the private sector's use of ICT.

Like the issue of centralized and diffuse regulation, public and private regulation touches on questions of how to regulate through multiple actors. The economic purpose of private companies poses particular problems for gamesmanship opportunities. Companies have a primary responsibility to protect their shareholders and customers. These incentives can often align well with the goals of public regulation, but economic incentives can sometimes conflict. Centralized regulation of the private sector aims to create rules that are resistant to gamesmanship. However, diffuse regulation is often needed, recognizing the limits of government control and the necessity for private companies to take public responsibility for themselves.

*Internal and external regulation.* Internal regulation refers to the regulation of activities within the public information manager's own organization whereas external regulation refers to the regulation of other organizations, groups or individuals. Internal regulation is primarily the

## Box 5.2: Facebook and regulation

Following a series of high-profile cases where Facebook breached the privacy and good faith of its users, as well as a growing sense of public concern about the sharing of dangerous or hurtful information which led to a subpoena by a United States congressional committee, the social media giant Facebook launched a series of initiatives aimed at restoring users' trust.

In 2019, it launched 'Community Standards', which was an articulation of values – authenticity, dignity, privacy and safety – that users were expected to (voluntarily) adhere to when using the site.[1] This statement was followed shortly by an announcement that a long process of internal deliberation and gathering of public feedback had led to the creation of an independent Facebook Oversight Board. Facebook reserved the right to remove material posted by users that undermined the Community Standards. But the creation of the Board meant that anyone whose material was removed could lodge an appeal. If the appeal is successful, the Board is bound to restore the material.

In a world of complex social media information and misinformation sharing, Facebook CEO Mark Zuckerberg had long expressed reluctance to curtail Facebook's commitment to free speech. But by launching the Oversight Board, Facebook is committing itself to a kind of self-regulation that had been recommended to social media companies by human rights advocates and international governance bodies such as the Council of Europe.[2]

area of responsibility of human resources managers. However, ICT such as wearables, video, apps and smart monitoring devices give public managers potentially considerably stronger capacity to support and improve the performance of their staff. Problems of digital regulation apply widely at the employee level. Human capacity to understand employees, motivate them,

---

[1] The letter written by Facebook CEO Mark Zuckerberg announcing the board can be found here: https://about.fb.com/wp-content/uploads/2019/09/letter-from-mark-zuckerberg-on-oversight-board-charter.pdf.

[2] See, for example, the blog 'Some reflections on the announced Facebook Oversight Board', https://cmpf.eui.eu/some-reflections-on-the-announced-facebook-oversight-board/#_ftn4 and the recommendation adopted by the Council of Europe, https://rm.coe.int/1680790e14.

support them and fairly reward them is vital. Managers have to be careful about how conscious or unconscious biases may be built into algorithms used to assess employee performance or hire new employees, and there are a host of other legitimacy challenges that managers face (see Box 5.3). They should also be cognizant that gamesmanship may occur from employees when they see that regulations are increasingly automated and thus have weaknesses and loopholes to be exploited. This is known as *organizational cheating* (Bohte and Meier 2000).

---

## Box 5.3: Workplace surveillance

A specific form of internal regulation in each and every organization is workplace surveillance. Workplace surveillance certainly predates digital technology, and is in some ways a natural mode for business organizations which are built upon a hierarchy whereby a small group of managers control other employees. So, the greater ease of use and normalization of geolocated devices, building access identification, project management software and electronic databases can also lead to greater workplace surveillance.

A range of technologies comprise a repertoire of 'bossware' that is increasingly available to HR managers (Tursunbayeva et al. 2021). According to Ball (2010) workplace surveillance includes the following kinds of organizational activities:

- Output, keystrokes, telephone call content
- Use of resources
- Communications contents: email and web monitoring
- Location: cards, pagers, CCTV (closed-circuit television), GPS (global positioning system), RFID (radio-frequency identification)

These are entirely normal activities that organizations undertake every day with their employees. Ball's point is that they all require managers to think in new ways about how employee data will be used. But there are also other activities that take a more aggressive approach to employee data that need much more attention from managers and regulators:

- Mystery shoppers, counter employee theft
- Psychometric testing, drug testing, biometrics
- Lie detector tests

- Predisposition to health risk, genetic testing, pregnancy testing
- Data mining, headhunting, e-recruitment

In one example, supermarket chain Tesco has been using wearable technologies to monitor employee performance and to remind them of tasks in order to reduce the number of staff necessary to manage a shopping aisle (James 2013). For government, the responsibility to manage employee data is more complex because of their role as an upholder of law and rights. Government has a double role in workplace surveillance: it needs to organize its own workplace surveillance in an effective and legitimate manner and also needs to check whether other organizations do this correctly.

*Source:* Ball (2010)

# Algorithmic regulation

A new, high-tech perspective on regulation has emerged in the last few years, largely through the work of the scholar Karen Yeung. According to Yeung (2018), regulatory efforts that function through automatic computer programmes, which sift through people's data and make decisions about them, are a new type of regulation that she calls 'algorithmic regulation'. Public managers use algorithmic regulation if they use technologies that are programmed with algorithmic decision-making systems to produce a desired regulatory effect.

While algorithmic regulation is largely a matter of how public managers can regulate *through* ICT, they may also need to regulate private companies' uses of algorithmic regulation if the decision outputs of those tools cross legal or ethical lines (more on regulation of technologies in the section on 'Politics of regulation'). Yeung stresses that relatively simple cybernetic systems can evolve into learning systems through the introduction of machine-learning algorithms. This is primarily a rational perspective of regulatory processes based on the following three functions of algorithm-based regulatory systems: monitoring, decision-making and intervening. Under the rational perspective, inputs and outputs are rationally controlled by public managers through a step-by-step process. All three functions are available through the use of modern ICT as follows:

- *Monitoring.* Monitoring entails the observations of relevant behaviour as a basis for regulatory measures aimed at correcting or punishing deviant behaviour. Surveillance structures such as speed cameras as well as the analysis of web data and the collection of data from telephones to track the presence of people are examples of the use of ICT to strength the monitorial capacity of regulators.

- *Decision-making.* Decision-making refers to the processing of information to check whether it is in line with (legal) norms and to decide whether an intervention is needed. A key technology here is big data analytics which enables regulators to process surveillance data and combine this with data from other sources to detect deviant behaviour. Algorithms provide the support for decision-making on the basis of all this data.
- *Intervening.* Intervening refers to the measures that are taken to enforce compliant behaviour. Traditional forms of intervening include police action and fining. New ICT may be used for automated fining on the basis of automated number plate recognition but in an online environment it may also include direct action through, for example, warnings that appear on a user's screen when s/he views illegal material.

Algorithmic regulation is based on a cybernetic system (for an example of this see Box 5.4). As shown in Figure 5.1, cybernetics of regulation follows how a signalling process between a decision system and its environment represents a loop so that programmed sensors (information from the environment such as electronic transactions by citizens) and effectors (the programmed rules for processing the transactions) produce the desired effects (regulation). A computer algorithm can be trained to read signals, which are the data that are regularly fed to the computer programme. The

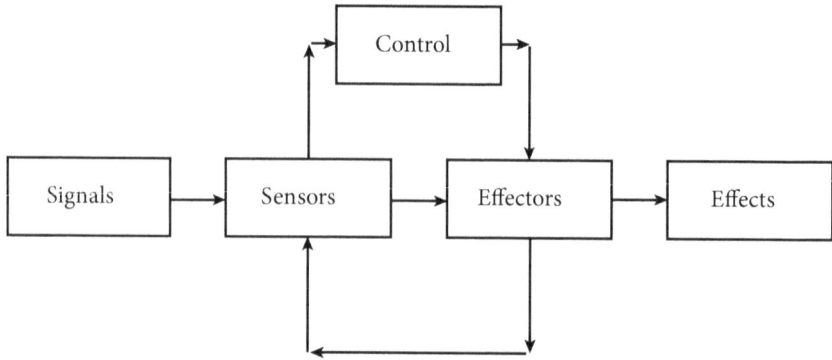

**Figure 5.1** Basic cybernetic system for regulation.

## Box 5.4: Speeding control

The regulation of speeding on highways in the Netherlands is a key example of a high-tech regulatory system. Certain highways are fully controlled, and no unobserved forms of speeding can take place. This means that each form of speeding results in a traffic fine. This high-tech system makes use of a range of different technologies:

- There are fixed cameras at regular intervals on highways to continuously observe traffic
- These cameras are connected to software that measures the speed and calculates the average speed of all passing cars in order to assess whether speeding has occurred
- If cars are speeding, the licence plate is read to identify the speeder and image recognition software is used to read the registration number
- The registration number is combined with information from the registry to identify the speeder
- The home address of the speeder is retrieved from the registry and a fine is posted to them
- The administrative system checks whether the fine has been paid and follow-up action is taken if the speeder does not pay

Similar systems have been adapted by countries around the world to regulate traffic and to ensure compliance to traffic rules. For more on the operation and management of automated traffic systems, see Carnis (2007).

algorithm has a kind of sensory system or 'intelligence' that is the decision-making rules. Following this, there are effectors, which are the types of decision that are made. An effector could be something such as deciding what type of social benefit a family will receive or what kind of performance score and employee will be awarded. The algorithm rationally learns from this and processes and evolves further to optimize regulation.

Modern forms of regulation in general, and algorithmic regulation more specifically, have been heavily criticized for the bias they may contain and also for their lack of transparency – flaws which require a redesign to correct any mistakes. Rationality can give the appearance of neutrality in the way that the algorithms make decisions. The shortcomings, however, can also be understood from another perspective as resulting from the power position of those steering the developments of ICT and algorithms for regulation. The dominant idea in all these forms of regulation is surveillance. Information technologies can be used to obtain better information about the behaviour of others as a basis for regulation. A metaphor that is frequently used to describe how information, surveillance and behaviour are connected is the 'panopticon', which is a circular building structure initially proposed for prison management by Jeremy Bentham in the eighteenth century. The panopticon, because of the 360° view afforded to any person standing at the centre, gives plenty of information on which to base any interventions in the environment. Such ideas about surveillance have a lot in common with the idea of the Big Brother state, which became a significant cultural trope after George Orwell's novel *Nineteen Eighty-Four*. While the panopticon was originally concerned with prison design, the idea offers a useful image of how governments could operate in an everyday sense so that they have as much information as possible to make decisions about policy and administration.

The parallel of the panopticon and the modern state with ICT such as sensors, cameras and drones at their disposal means that public managers have crucial ethical dilemmas to resolve about how they employ data about their own employees or citizens. By the same token, public managers need to be vigilant about the way that private companies use such data and how they need to be regulated (see Box 5.4 for how these dilemmas can play out in an area such as policing). Many scholars have highlighted the ways that algorithmic regulation is dangerous. David Lyon (2003) argued that government attempts to pay very close attention to citizen data enable governments to extend the reach of their bureaucratic systems to sifting and sorting data in ways that can be unfairly burdensome on very specific groups in society that have been traditionally marginalized such as low socio-economic groups and ethnic and racial minorities. Tackling the other side of the regulation of private companies, scholars such as Ball and Snider (2013) focus on the role of technology companies as leaders in surveillance practices. Internet companies, online marketplaces and advertising companies have economic incentives for collecting as much data about people as possible. While governments do not have access to as much data as such companies, they are responsible for data privacy policies and public service contracting that give companies quite a lot of influence in what kinds of services and choices are available to citizens, as well as what happens to their personal data.

## Box 5.5: Legitimacy of police algorithms

While proponents of police algorithms highlight their contributions to the effectiveness and efficiency of the police, critics claim that these systems may result in all kinds of adverse effects such as privacy breaches and bias towards certain groups. In a more general sense, these algorithms can be viewed as instruments that strengthen the police's capacity to act but their usage also demands great responsibility. In many ways, these algorithms should be regarded in the same way as police weapons: they can be used if required but need to be embedded firmly in legal and organizational frameworks to ensure their legitimate use.

The principles of value-sensitivity and transparency can form important starting points for their legitimate use. Value-sensitivity refers to the significant consideration and weighing up of the various values that are (directly or indirectly) being influenced by the use of the algorithm such as equal treatment, efficiency, bias, etc. Transparency refers to the accessibility and justification of their usage which opens up the opportunity for accountability.

*Source:* Meijer and Grimmelikhuijsen (2021)

# Politics of regulation

The regulation of private companies that use sensitive data analytics tools to market their products is an increasing problem for SPIM. However, regulation has always been a political matter. Now that companies are using advanced technologies, political challenges have become more complex and, from the strategic point of view of the public manager, the question of how regulation will affect behaviour is increasingly intricate. The effects on citizens and society are wide-reaching and difficult to determine. Biases of algorithms may be highly subtle, politically contentious and difficult to detect due to lack of transparency. Further, companies have ways that they can use algorithmic systems to circumvent or frustrate efforts at regulation. According to Bamberger (2010), new forms of ICT regulation raise new types of political and governance challenges. Bamberger identifies four main problems:

1 *Problems of translation.* This relates to whether complex decision-making about who gets regulated and how can really be encoded into

and executed by computer software. Regulations have serious practical and political consequences, and the question is whether this can be left to an algorithm.

2 *Systemic effects.* These kinds of effects take place in the decision-making system of which public managers are a part. They may not be intended effects, but they are still powerful and can change the system in terms of what kinds of habits, norms or biases are built into the general institutional machinery of government.

3 *Cognitive bias in decision-making.* Humans have cognitive biases, so, if they design the regulatory instruments using code that is hardwired into automated decision-making, these biases could also become hardwired.

4 *Opportunities for gamesmanship.* Individuals and companies for whom the regulations are meant can alter their behaviour so as to 'work the system'. Algorithmic decision-making has the advantage of being impartial and consistent, but for the same reason it makes it possible to understand exactly what goes into the regulatory decision and thus to predict how the decision-making will work.

The scale of the challenge for public managers in translating a complex regulatory process into an ICT-driven process was shown by the scholars Martin Lodge and Karl Wegrich (2015) who carried out analysis and interviews of a large national initiative in the United Kingdom to review government regulations with the help of citizens. The so-called 'Red Tape Challenge' launched by the then prime minister David Cameron had a worthy goal: to reduce the unnecessary burden of regulations on businesses and citizens. But, by the end of the public crowdsourcing process, it had become clear that participants were largely supportive of the original regulations. Participants were supportive of removing some of the regulations, but they also wanted to strengthen regulations in other areas. This was quite the opposite outcome from what Cameron's Conservative government was seeking, which was to win political support by tackling over-regulated government.

From a political perspective, regulation is a system of power. A variety of technologies is used to force citizens and companies to behave according to certain rules. A key question for public managers to ask themselves is regarding the legitimacy of these regulatory systems. Yeung (2017) argues that the legal and normative basis of regulatory systems can be very obscure when such systems are designed and implemented through computer programmes based on algorithms. The reason for this is that, while traditional regulations are designed through a statutory legal process overseen by elected officials, algorithmic regulations are designed by computer programmers. For public managers, these regulatory programmes appear to be a purely technical matter at first, as they rely on making sure that the monitoring, deciding and intervening are done in a way that is secure against malfunction or security breaches.

But systemic influences from ICT-driven regulations can be very powerful indeed. Take, for example, algorithms that award schools with funding-dependent performance scores.[3] These systems where decisions with financial impact are algorithmically programmed raise the question of how such regulatory decision-making should be regulated. Very often, the algorithms used to design these regulatory decisions are a 'black box', i.e. lacking transparency. The public – even those who are directly affected by the regulatory decisions – cannot easily see what the logic and design parameters are of the algorithm. Moreover, public managers will often find that, if the algorithm has been designed by a private contractor for the government, then information about the algorithm may not be accessible even if they demand it.

In addition to the systemic effects that require good strategic understanding from public managers, Bamberger's political approach to regulation also considers the non-rational or instinctive cognitive processing traits that humans often have. This has profound consequences for areas in Bamberger's framework such as cognitive bias. Understanding of such bias requires psychological insights by managers about themselves as well as other people. It is a kind of psychological knowledge that managers may find takes a long time to learn and develop through experience. Some kinds of bias are deeply, historically embedded in society, and algorithms can encode such biases into decision-making systems when programming their technologies. This is a difficult area for regulation given the political importance of protecting groups who are victims of bias as well as the difficulty of opening the black box to identify algorithmically encoded bias. Through the implementation of laws and ethical principles, public managers can encourage individuals and organizations to comport themselves in a law-abiding fashion. The threat of punishment and the promise of rewards is another important tool in the SPIM toolbox. In addition to recognizing their legal and ethical responsibilities, companies are highly aware that there is a risk of being fined, getting a criminal record or simply being publicly shamed for breaking the rules.

---

[3] A notable case was a teacher in the Washington, DC school system who lost her job due to poor assessments given by an algorithm when personal evaluations told a different story: https://www.washingtonpost.com/blogs/answer-sheet/post/firing-of-dc-teacher-reveals-flaws-in-value-added-evaluation/2012/03/07/gIQAtmlGxR_blog.html.

Finally, regulations are vulnerable to gaming by both individual citizens and companies. That is, while regulations are set up with rational design choices to achieve regulatory goals as efficiently and fairly as possible, they are also a political game whereby decision-makers from different sectors (government, but also business and the civil society sector) decide how and what to regulate, and the subjects of the regulations strategize on how to maximize their self-interest; complying only to the degree necessary to protect their interests. Public managers need to be aware that, due to their powerful status, self-interested corporations may exert a disproportionate influence on what gets regulated in the first place (Yackee and Yackee 2006). Understanding how and why people try to game systems is key to public managers' abilities to prevent it or to channel it in ways that are beneficial.

# Two approaches to regulatory legitimacy

The politics of regulation is certain to be a challenge that public managers will face. Bamberger's arguments show just how difficult this growing challenge can be. Legal approaches such as the European Union's 'General Data Protection Regulation' have given managers new tools to check the misuse of people's private data (Kaminski 2019). Public managers may seek legal assistance for the application of such frameworks. However, there are also managerial approaches that they could use. According to Van der Wal (2017), new leadership challenges for public managers entail novel approaches that often diverge from traditional top-down approaches. Public managers need to explore ways to work horizontally with diverse stakeholders, and often stakeholders that are outside of the traditional structure of authority. This situation is especially pertinent for regulatory legitimacy involving algorithmic systems. We present two prominent approaches: public participation and regulatory networks.

## Public participation

As regulatory processes become more complex and regulatory tools more diverse and digitalized, it is increasingly important for public managers to understand the ways that citizens and civil society organizations can contribute their experience and expertise to the regulatory process. The scholar Cary Coglianese (2004) argues that technology can make regulations more effective and legitimate by accomplishing two things simultaneously: agency management of regulations and public involvement with regulations. This approach has been implemented in the United States with the website regulations.gov (see more in Box 5.6). Public participation provides alternative viewpoints on regulatory proposals, new ideas and expertise, and enhances the legitimacy of the regulatory process.

## Box 5.6: Regulations.gov: inviting comments on regulatory changes

In the United States, since the early 2000s, the website regulations. gov has been used by the federal government as a platform for government agencies, citizens, civil society organizations and businesses for publishing, collaborating, tracking and developing new federal regulations.

Any proposed regulatory change must go through a public consultation process if the impact of the change is expected to significantly affect existing budgetary, legal or administrative arrangements. The public can send their comments on a proposed regulation by post or via a website called regulations.gov. Using regulations.gov, citizens can sign up to receive automated alerts for proposed regulations from particular agencies or on specific policy topics. Citizens can post a comment, read other comments and receive updates on the subsequent review and revisions process of the regulation. Businesses are also allowed to submit comments, which means that new regulations receive input from a wide range of points of view. At the end of the process, agencies must report back to the public on how they responded to the comments; what ideas were adopted or rejected and what changes were made in the final regulation as a result.

Some scholars have argued that the comments process delivers feedback of a low quality which is a waste of valuable government time and resources. But supporters point out that regulations.gov regularly receives thousands of public comments, which are taken seriously by agencies. It is a tool for legitimacy and effectiveness in the regulatory decision-making process (Coglianese 2004).

Despite the value of public participation, it can also present challenges for public managers. Finding a balance between participation and effectiveness of regulation is a major puzzle. How, for example, can public managers move with swiftness to develop a regulatory approach to a health emergency such as Covid-19 while also consulting the public? Emergencies of this kind are likely to be affected by poor understanding and even deliberate misrepresentation of the facts (disinformation). In the context of the Coronavirus pandemic, public health experts from a range of different research organizations such as the World Health Organization, the Harvard Global Health Institute and the GovLab raised the alarm about the dangerous effects of false information being spread on the internet. The United Nations Secretary General, António Guterres, referred to it as a 'pandemic of misinformation'.[4] Thus, while public participation may help public managers to improve their regulations, there is no replacement for evidence-informed advice from scientific and expert institutions.

# Regulatory networks

Another strategic tool available for public managers is regulatory networks. Dutil and Williams (2017) argue that regulatory networks composed of the companies and public organizations with access to data and information are necessary for public managers to address capacity shortfalls when it comes to regulatory challenges. Regulatory networks are a difficult thing to manage, and require a light-touch, collaborative approach. To be successful, regulatory networks need to be adaptable to the constantly changing (and novel) problems that new technologies create as well as finding clever ways to address existing regulatory problems. Both learning ability and the role of public participation will also be necessary according to Dutil and Williams. Grobosky (2013, 117) calls this the 'democratization of technology'.

Networks can take many different forms, from informal gatherings of organizations that emerge for a particular policy initiative to more formal networks that are established in law. Similar approaches could be taken for regulatory networks. Formal regulatory networks can be seen in public policy problems that have affected societies for a longer time, for example environmental regulation networks. The Chesapeake Bay Program on the

---

[4] See António Guterres on the importance of press freedom during the Covid-19 pandemic: https://news.un.org/en/story/2020/05/1063152.

east coast of the United States involves management and regulation of one of the largest estuary fishing, wildlife and recreation areas in the country. Partners include city governments, universities, nonprofit organizations, advocacy groups, businesses and trade unions. The network in general works to support the ecosystem of the Bay, and it runs a central data hub where trends can be modelled, and maps are generated showing changes in important indicators over time. By sharing this information, the regulation of the Bay draws from a common pool of information that is open and trusted.

We can come back to the case of the Coronavirus pandemic for an interesting example of the regulatory network approach that was recently adopted by the World Health Organization (WHO). The WHO launched a network with social media companies to report and publish misinformation in the Stop the Spread campaign.[5] In this case, social media companies, governments and the WHO worked together to regulate the spread of false epidemiological information regarding Covid-19. Public managers need to have a good sense of political savvy to develop networks with organizations such as social media companies that have their own interests in how and where information should be shared. The benefit of this kind of approach is that, with the help of a good open data platform, it can be a relatively simple, self-organizing collaborative programme. However, in related work on environmental network governance, Mills and Koliba (2015) warned that self-organizing networks rely on clear process agreements. If a market-oriented regulation regime is the main form of accountability in the network, then the network may lose effectiveness at critical moments, when the economic interests of the market pull participants in different directions.

# Ethical issues

As highlighted in previous chapters, SPIM is characterized in part by an awareness of the interconnections between technological developments and the growing acuteness of ethical issues around the adoption and employment of these technologies. The area of regulation – touching as it does upon matters of free will, behavioural control and distribution of

---

[5] For more on the Stop the Spread campaign, see https://www.who.int/campaigns/connecting-the-world-to-combat-coronavirus/how-to-report-misinformation-online.

public goods – is no less an important area of ethical deliberation for public managers. Regulation through algorithms has many risks because of the kinds of (often unintended) impact they can have on people. The problem is that algorithms are highly complex and their influence on individuals and organizations can be equally complex. Though algorithms may be a legitimate tool of regulation for SPIM, public managers need to be aware of the risk. Box 5.7 covers six such risks as conceptualized by Andrews (2019), for which we provide examples from different countries in each category.

## Box 5.7: Ethical risks of algorithms

*Selection error.* When algorithms make mistakes that can lead to the wrong person or thing being picked out for special treatment.

Example: The Correctional Offender Management Profiling for Alternative Sanctions (COMPAS) used in some states in the USA is designed to inform courts about the likelihood that a criminal defendant will commit further crime in the future. Studies have shown that COMPAS makes as many or sometimes more errors than a human.[6]

*Law-breaking.* When algorithms are cleverly used to evade legal requirements or norms.

Example: In 2015 the car manufacturer, Volkswagen AG, admitted that it had installed millions of diesel vehicles in the United States with software that would allow emissions information to be underreported to regulators.[7]

*Manipulation or gaming.* When individuals who know how an algorithm works change their behaviour to make the most of the algorithm for their personal benefit.

Example: The view counter algorithm on YouTube allows viewers and advertisers to see how much a video is being watched. Some companies have exploited this feature by writing their own algorithms that will add fake views to the counter.[8]

---

[6] See Dressel and Farid (2018).
[7] See Greenemeier (2015).
[8] See Keller (2018).

*Algorithmic propaganda.* When algorithms are used to undermine or promote political values by manipulating information.

Example: Cyber propaganda has become a widespread part of cyber warfare. The political damage created through cyber propaganda has alarmed governments around the world.[9]

*Brand contamination.* When micro-targeting in the form of personalized adverts is used to influence consumer behaviour.

Example: The now-defunct company Cambridge Analytica used political advertising to influence elections in many countries around the world including Kenya and Nigeria where videos and newspaper adverts were placed to discredit political opponents.[10]

*Algorithmic unknowns.* When the repercussions of algorithmic systems are beyond our control because of the enormous complexity of their programming steps and learning loops.

Example: One serious algorithmic unknown is the impact of AI on the jobs market. Some analysts predict huge displacement of the human labour force while others paint a more complex economic picture with different effects on different sectors and improvements in quality of life.[11]

According to Harrison (2017) there are six main ethical areas where efforts to strengthen regulatory excellence should be focused: transparency, clear rationales, commitment to evaluation, procedural fairness, honesty and neutrality.

- *Can complex regulatory decision-making processes be made transparent?* Absolute transparency of regulatory decision-making is almost an organizational impossibility. The key thing for achieving transparency is that successes and failures can be accounted for and that the right public audience is found to see what is going on. Freedom of information requesting procedures should be robust, effective and user-friendly to allow those interested to get the information they

---

[9] See Sanovich (2017).
[10] See Ekdale and Tully (2020).
[11] See Rainie and Anderson (2017).

need. Further, regular publishing of clear data on successes and failures should be mandatory.

- *How can the rationales for regulation be made clear and understandable to other stakeholders?* As the rational and political dimensions of regulation demonstrate, there is a tension in regulatory work between positive questions that concern objective facts and goals on the one hand and, on the other, normative questions concerning what people value. Scientists are the archetypal rationalists and they inhabit a world of facts. Similarly, political officials are self-evidently the archetypal politicians and they inhabit a world of values. Regulation is a human construct, and both facts and values are needed. Regulatory problems occur if facts and values are conflated. Thus, an independent process for developing regulations is an important step towards keeping the two spheres clear.

- *What types of evaluation and public reporting are necessary?* Two areas of reporting are necessary to maintain public examination and monitoring: assessment of the efficiency of regulations and assessment of compliance by private actors (citizens and companies). Creating a system of periodic review at the start of a regulatory decision-making process prevents your organization from shying away from the possibility to criticism.

- *How can procedural fairness in the development of regulations be helped?* This refers to the ability of the public to enter a process similar to one of those from regulations.gov described above. A broad range of stakeholders should be able to share their opinions of the regulations. Public managers should also strive to find a good balance between substantive and procedural goals of regulations.

- *What should be done to protect the principle of honesty in regulations?* Public managers should not support production or communication of false information. This may sound intuitive, but, in practice, the line between positive framing of message control and falsehood is constantly shifting due to organizational conflict. Information is sometimes unclear, but it may also be in the vital interests of society to be informed. For these reasons, having an internal peer review mechanism with many eyes is important to ensure that a spirit of clarity and honesty runs through the decision-making. This is especially true with matters that are scientifically novel or unclear for citizens or when the matter is politically charged.

- *How to remain neutral while negotiating the political complexity of regulations.* Neutrality is a fundamental value of bureaucratic decision-making. Regulatory decision-making should treat all similar cases equally. A regulation should be 'blind' to political matters that may potentially incentivize treating some people differently than others. Greater embeddedness of ICT is positive for neutral decision-making, but this strength for neutrality should not lead to public managers being complacent about the institutional and political embeddedness of their technology. The neutrality strength of regulation in the ICT sphere can be protected through democratic governance. Democratic governance or the creation of accountable boards to supervise regulations prevents institutionalized bias affecting regulatory decision-making.

# Conclusions

Regulation is a key function of public management. The public information manager has traditionally played a small role in regulation, but the growth of information and use of ICT for regulatory purposes have changed this dramatically. Careful understanding of the regulatory process, knowledge about the technologies that constitute new kinds of algorithmic regulation and sensitivity to the wider impacts of regulation are vital to SPIM. Now, ICT are key to implementing new kinds of regulations, often of all automated kinds aimed at nudging or shaping behaviour. There are also emerging opportunities and challenges from the increased role that technology companies play in using technologies with such far-reaching social and political implications that public managers also need new approaches to regulating the private sector.

The benefits of using ICT for regulation are impressive, and, from a strategic perspective, there is much that can be achieved to improve the efficiency and effectiveness of regulations. However, algorithmic regulation relies on a high degree of surveillance both by public and private organizations. We explored this dimension through a political lens and identified ethical problems related to accountability and bias. Ethical frameworks focusing on transparency, clear rationales, commitment to evaluation, procedural fairness, honesty and neutrality can go some way to addressing these concerns.

At the beginning of this chapter, we posed five key questions to be answered:

- *How do ICT influence different areas of regulatory work for public managers?* There are different spheres where regulation takes place (centralized and decentralized, private and public, internal and external). Clearly some of these areas are somewhat in tension and public managers should consider each area separately and consider the unique challenges that need to be addressed.
- *How does algorithmic regulation raise the risk of surveillance by governments and businesses?* We used a cybernetic perspective to show how computerized decision-making systems are integrated closely with environmental signals in ways that require very careful attention to citizen behaviour. Inevitably this heightens the occurrence of surveillance and attendant concerns about data privacy.
- *What politically contentious areas of ICT-driven regulation should public managers address?* We illustrated four main political challenges using Bamberger's ideas on translation, bias, systemic risk and gamesmanship. Translation problems occur when traditional regulatory domains are turned into ICT-based forms of regulation. Cognitive bias is a dangerous problem because ordinary human biases such as perceptions about the value of different demographic groups in society can become affected. Systemic risk grows as different political actors can be inadvertently affected by algorithmic regulation. Finally, gamesmanship can be used by citizens and companies to exploit their knowledge of how regulatory rules work to manipulate the system for their own interests. This requires careful design choices by managers.
- *What measures should be put in place to ensure that regulatory approaches are legitimate in the eyes of citizens?* As regulations increasingly have systemic impacts or are influenced by potential for bias, citizens need (and want) to play a greater role in giving their input on regulation. Models such as the US website regulations.gov provide a traditional template for this. In addition, sensitive areas such as transparency and fairness need to be carefully addressed by a SPIM approach.
- *What are the main ethical areas to address when public managers use ICT for regulation?* Six areas were highlighted: transparency, clear rationales, commitment to evaluation, procedural fairness, honesty and neutrality. These areas are more important for ICT-driven

kinds of regulation because they rely heavily on the use of citizens' data. It is therefore important that they are explicitly handled, given due transparency and understood through both the rational and political lens.

# KEY LESSONS FROM CHAPTER 5

- The growth of ICT has meant that there is a twofold challenge that public managers need to be aware of: regulation of and by technology.
- The starting point for SPIM is to identify what the object of regulation is (e.g. internal decisions, companies, diffuse impacts on society, etc.) and decide how to manage possible trade-offs between these.
- A key tool available to public managers is algorithmic systems, which can be used to monitor and collect information needed to make regulatory decisions, or be used to execute automated decisions to nudge companies or citizens.
- A cybernetic system provides a basic template for planning the kinds of design steps that are needed for algorithmic regulation.
- Critically, algorithmic tools can also be used to invade people's privacy and influence their behaviour without their permission. SPIM requires recognizing and finding ways to address such harmful influences of algorithms.
- The capacity for algorithm-based regulation requires careful approaches to transparency and accountability. Two tools available to public managers are public participation in design of algorithms and regulatory networks.
- Public participation may sometimes be helpful to improve the legitimacy of algorithms that may have an influence on society.
- Regulatory networks are an important tool for SPIM because they encourage better communication and compliance between regulators and the organizations being regulated.
- The confluence of regulation and ICT highlights the need for ethical awareness in several key areas such as equal treatment, transparency and clear communication about the goals of regulation.

# 6

# Managing the risks of information and technology

*Strategic public information management (SPIM) requires both awareness of the risks of ICT and the skills to manage them. This chapter argues that the risks of information technologies cannot be adequately addressed with traditional risk management tools only. The traditional risk management tools correspond with the rational analysis of risks but throughout this book we have shown that multiple perspectives need to be applied simultaneously. Public managers need to address three ICT-related risks in particular: 1) man–machine interaction; 2) underlying power dynamics shaping ICT; and 3) cultural biases. In this chapter, we provide conceptual and practical tools that enable public managers to develop a full understanding of risks and risk management in the realm of information technologies. The chapter ends by providing a framework for resilient SPIM.*

## Introduction

The use of ICT has introduced new risks and organizational accidents. Information systems can, for example, be hacked. Systems may become unstable or fail. Confidential documents or personal data may be leaked. Newspapers frequently publish horror stories about all the things that have gone wrong with ICT in public organizations. One could even wonder whether the benefits of ICT outweigh the risks. The answer is relatively simple. Not using new technologies to improve government organizations, policies and services also produces serious risks. Moreover, new technologies can improve risk management and support greater safety in and around organizations.

Risks are thus part and parcel of ICT and should also be part and parcel of SPIM (see Box 6.1). The risks cannot be avoided so it is a better approach for public managers to develop some form of risk management. This chapter provides a framework for a risk management approach to the risks of ICT and information systems. The risk idiom and risk management tools have penetrated all corners of the public sector: from policymaking in the realm of migration to food safety regulation, to name a few. As this chapter demonstrates, the use of information systems has been both a driving force and a focus of risk management. In this light, this chapter addresses the following questions:

- What risks arise if ICT are introduced in public organizations?
- How can these risks be managed and what tools are available for risk management in the hyper-connected context of ICT?
- What human, cultural and political drivers should be taken into account in preparing and implementing ICT risk management strategies?
- How can ICT be leveraged to improve risk assessment and risk management?

## Box 6.1: With or without ICT: both risky

Imagine a public organization responsible for building and maintaining roads and other public infrastructure. This organization operates a regular drawbridge over a canal in order to regulate the traffic on the canal. It has always worked with mechanical systems to lift the bridge in case a ship wants to pass. These mechanical systems were operated by a bridge master, but are becoming increasingly replaced by ICT and devices that enable remote control. In the smart age, the construction of the bridge requires numerous sensing technologies in order to prevent remote-controlled lifting of the bridge when there are still cars or people on it. If the public organization adopts these sensing technologies it becomes vulnerable to the risk of hacking or failing technology. If the organization decides not to adopt the new sensing technologies it also takes a risk because the old-fashioned way of checking a bridge before lifting it includes the risk of overlooking pedestrians still on the bridge by the operator that presses the lift button.

We build on the risk management literature and begin by exploring the technological background of the current focus on risks and risk management. We continue by discussing risk management from the four perspectives and highlight that managing risks not only demands a clear set of systems and protocols but also a perspective on managing man–machine interaction, an eye for the political trade-offs and an understanding of both the cultural foundations of risk and the cultural barriers to risk management. In the final section, we provide key lessons for resilient SPIM.

# Societal background of technologically triggered risks

Risks are as old as society itself but risk management started attracting widespread scholarly attention in the 1980s. At least two interrelated developments have triggered scholars and public managers to focus on risk: the introduction of large-scale technologies and the disasters produced by these technologies have raised the awareness of the possible impact of new technologies. Technology has always produced risks and accidents but the industrial revolution amplified these risks to a historically unprecedented scale. Large-scale accidents such as that in the Chernobyl nuclear plant and the growing awareness of the ecological disaster caused by the industrial society inspired Ulrich Beck to develop his thesis of a risk society (Beck 1992). Beck's key argument is that 'while in classical industrial society the "logic" of wealth production dominates the "logic" of risk production, in the risk society this relationship is reversed'. Risks have come 'out of the closet and achieve a central importance in social and political debates' instead of being just side effects of production (Beck 1992, 12–13). Building upon ideas that disasters are increasingly man-made it appears that risks are produced by modernity itself (see also Turner and Pidgeon 1978). Beck argues that the risks of post-industrial societies differ from the classical industrial risks.

> At the center lie the risks and consequences of modernization, which are revealed as irreversible threats to the life of plants, animals, and human beings. Unlike the factory-related occupational hazards of the nineteenth and the first half of the twentieth centuries, these can no longer be limited to certain localities or groups, but rather exhibit a tendency to globalization which spans production and reproduction as much as national borders, and

in this sense brings into being supra-national and non-class-specific global hazards with a new type of social and political dynamism.

(Beck 1992, 13)

It should come as no surprise that, because of ICT, political institutions, business and citizens are increasingly preoccupied with risks. Technological developments have further increased the relevance of risks but the new ICT also require further reframing of Beck's now-thirty-year-old thesis.

# Rational analysis of risks

The co-evolution of technological and cultural developments has thus produced a risk culture; or even a culture of precaution (Pieterman 2008). Let us first address what a rational analysis of ICT-risks looks like: how does the public manager as an 'engineer' approach the risks of information systems, large-scale computer networks and artificial intelligence (AI)? From the perspective of rational analysis, public information managers start with defining the technologies that cause risks. This requires a separation of the different types of technologies and the risks of introducing these technologies. Each type of risk can then be addressed with traditional risk management tools that enable public managers to identify the probability and the impact of a risk as well as to take measures in order to mitigate any high-impact risks. In this perspective, the types of risks outlined in Table 6.1 need to be identified and mitigated.

Information technologies increasingly take over decision-making in public agencies (as outlined in Chapter 4). Today, decisions on policy development, policy implementation and enforcement, and even policy evaluation, are outsourced to computers. Ever since the 1970s, computers have taken over decision-making processes in the public sector (e.g. Bovens and Zouridis 2002). Initially, only simple administrative decisions were made by computers such as the calculation of a welfare benefit or a traffic fine. During the 1980s and 1990s, sophisticated algorithms were developed for policy implementation in many realms. Nowadays, implementing public policies is unimaginable without computers also making decisions. Computers not only guide aviation traffic and aviation safety but ICT also play a major role in the allocation of police resources, health policy resources and sometimes even in promoting citizenship.

**Table 6.1** Rational analysis of risks of information management.

| New risks | Computerized decision-making | Data and big data | Networks |
|---|---|---|---|
| Error | Example: software errors in a system for welfare benefits | Example: traffic safety policies are grounded in invalid data | Example: network flaws show discrepancies between cases as presented to the public prosecutor and the judge |
| Failure | Example: a system for air traffic handling breaks down | Example: a patient information system breaks down in a hospital | Example: communication networks break down and emergency calls cannot be made |
| Interdependencies | Example: automated missile systems respond to automated detection systems | Example: data collected for population statistics are used for child-care benefits | Example: vulnerabilities in network software diffuse malware and spyware |

## Box 6.2: The social credit system in China

The government of the People's Republic of China (PRC) first initiated regional trials of its social credit system in 2009, which was scheduled to be fully implemented in 2020. In 2011 the Chinese prime minister Jiabao introduced the programme officially. The social credit system connects with the financial credit rating system but broadens its scope to the social behaviour of its citizens, and works with both rewards and punishments. People and businesses can be blacklisted or whitelisted based on their behaviour. Since behaviour should be objectively established, the Chinese government relies on ICT for both mass surveillance and algorithms that register and process the behaviour that may trigger either blacklisting or whitelisting.

*Source: Guardian* (2018)

## Box 6.3: CAS and Predpol

Police organizations around the world experiment with algorithms and AI to support predictive policing. From the perspective of risk management, the Crime Anticipation System (CAS) in the city of Amsterdam is interesting. It has been developed in order to predict crime and it is based on the Predpol software used by the Los Angeles police in the US and several other US police departments (Perry 2013). CAS informationally partitioned the city of Amsterdam in square parts of 125 by 125 metres. Based upon crime statistics and other data on inhabitants and known suspects, CAS enables the police to produce heat maps. These heat maps indicate the probability of crime, in particular burglary and robbery. The system thus offers both an efficient and effective use of police resources. The Amsterdam police claims that it prevents 40–60 per cent of the robberies. Research impels some modesty since it appears that these reductions can also be related to other causes (Willems and Doeleman 2014).

Whereas the initial algorithms in the 1980s and 1990s were quite simple and static, current algorithms are built on machine learning and AI. Algorithms and AI are already widespread in industry such as chemical plants and aviation. Operational and managerial decisions in public organizations also increasingly rely on algorithms (see Box 6.3).

The digitization of data is a second type of technology that public managers need to identify. Smart algorithms and AI are fed with massive collections of digitally recorded data. In the digital era, collecting and processing data have been compared with the work of mining and refining fossil fuels during the industrial era (Mayer-Schönberger and Cukier 2013). Many interfaces and new sensing techniques translate the images, sounds, smells and any other signals of humans, animals, nature or machines into data in order to record them, exchange them and process them digitally. The larger the amount of data, the more aggregate patterns can be derived from the data. Big data analysis techniques also enable managers to produce personalized information (e.g. Doppelgänger research; see Stephens-Davitowitz 2017). Commercial data brokers have expanded and become players on a global economic data market. Personal data are continuously gathered, traded and processed for commercial reasons (Goodman 2015; Zuboff 2019). The Cambridge Analytica scandal shows that even political parties buy and produce information on individual voters from commercial data brokers.

> ## Box 6.4: The Cambridge Analytica scandal
>
> A consultancy firm in the UK, Cambridge Analytica collected and analyzed the data of millions of Facebook users for political advertising. Cambridge Analytica used the data to support political campaigns, among others the 2016 campaign of Donald Trump for the US presidency. Facebook had initially organized an informed consent process for the use of the app This Is Your Digital Life. However, the app not only collected the data of the users that consented but also that of their Facebook friends who had not consented. This triggered a scandal because of the possible effects on the US elections. In 2018 Cambridge Analytica filed for bankruptcy.
>
> This story first broke in the *Guardian* in March 2018: https://www.theguardian.com/news/2018/mar/17/cambridge-analytica-facebook-influence-us-election

In the digital era, computer-made decisions and data collection and processing are not isolated processes but intensely connected by networks, usually via the internet. This connection adds a particular dynamic to the risks of computer-made decisions and big data because both humans and computers respond to each other, which in turn generates new data. Networks thus add a layer of complexity because of the reflexivity of the processes. Computerized systems that support drivers of cars may learn from the decisions taken by these drivers to correct the algorithm. A pre-set algorithm may thus become very complex when drivers all around the world may affect the algorithm with their decisions (for example, a decision to stop for something that was not previously recognized by the system as an object).

From the perspective of rational analysis, a strategic public information manager views these technologies as both producing new risks as well as providing new opportunities for risk management.

## New risks

As with any use of technological devices, ICT and digital networks can break down or fall out. The causes for breakdown of ICT may be diverse, ranging from cybersabotage and hacks to technical causes. Apart from cybersabotage, the stream of continuous changes, updates, patches and new connections between systems creates a type of complexity that is difficult to handle.

The usual risk assessment and risk management tools cannot deal with the complexity of large-scale information systems in public organizations, such as hospitals or tax authorities. Some public organizations simultaneously run hundreds or even thousands of different applications developed by many different ICT providers, supported by just as many different service agreements. Some applications may be twenty or thirty years old, while other applications are brand new and have been developed on modern platforms. So, any ICT failure or breakdown will probably involve many different providers and many different interconnected systems. Ageing adds another layer of complexity. Applications developed in the 1980s may run alongside new applications developed almost thirty years later. The enormous speed with which both hardware and software change does not align with the gradually developed and hard-changed routines and practices of many public organizations. Therefore, a serious risk resulting from this complexity and volatility is breakdown or failure of information systems and information networks (see Box 6.5).

## Box 6.5: Cyber disruption and breakdown in Dutch hospitals

The Dutch Safety Board (DSB 2020) has investigated the risks of breakdown of information systems in three hospitals. It appears that hospitals to a large extent depend on information technologies that provide and process patient information. Even old-fashioned telephones may be operated on the computer network, so an information systems breakdown affects all modes of communication. The DSB claims that the breakdown of information systems in hospitals is not rare, and systems can take hours if not days to be restored. Even in hospitals that have invested in redundant systems (in one hospital both the storage servers and the application servers were redundant), these breakdowns still appear and may endanger the safety of the patients. Some hospitals even had to close wards because of the breakdown of the information system. The DSB concludes that the risk of information systems that break down should be addressed by top-level hospital management. Simulating the collapse of information systems generates knowledge on the dependencies and shows what processes are actually affected if an information system stops working. In one case, the laboratory that analyzes blood samples proved to be a key process affected by a breakdown. Since the sheer complexity of the interconnected information systems in hospitals does not allow for traditional mitigation strategies, the DSB recommends to just accept the risk of a breakdown of information systems and focus on managing the implications (DSB 2020).

Next to the breakdown of ICT, the corruption of data can be seen as a new risk. Since many public organizations are continuously attacked by hackers who attempt to steal or corrupt data this seems a likely scenario (e.g. Goodman 2015). Large-scale successful data hacks have been observed on big platforms like LinkedIn and Facebook but hackers also were successful in breaking into commercial businesses such as British Airlines, as well as government systems. Hacking may aim to steal personal data but corrupting government data may become an interesting future crime and it is certainly a risk that should be taken into account (Goodman 2015). Backup versions may provide effective solutions for the problem of corrupted data but these only work if the government agency is aware of the hack and the corruption of its data (see Box 6.6).

## Box 6.6: Christmas hack of Maastricht University (the Netherlands)

On 23 December 2020, Maastricht University in the Netherlands was hit by a serious cyberattack (see https://www.maastrichtuniversity.nl/um-cyber-attack-symposium-%E2%80%93-lessons-learnt). Almost all its systems were hit by ransomware and the university more or less faced a breakdown of its activities. It could no longer be reached by email, neither staff nor students had access to the university and the key systems were unavailable. Because of the Christmas holidays, the impact of the cyberattack on teaching and research was limited. All systems went offline for a couple of weeks. After a couple of tense weeks for the university's management and ICT staff, the university could restart most of its operations on 6 January. According to the university's independent newspaper, the university paid several hundreds of thousands of euros in ransom money to have the hackers release the systems.

Information systems also cause new risks because they produce new causes for organizational failure and organizational accidents. Since both people and things increasingly become smart and connected to the internet, all major economic sectors will be confronted with new causes for accidents or systems failure. So, what are the new causes of risks produced by information systems? In at least two ways, digitalization entails new causes for familiar risks: deliberate human action aimed at corrupting or sabotaging ICT is the first risk that should be mentioned. Human action can be directed at manipulating the algorithms, the data or the network connections in order to cause a breakdown of ICT systems or erratic decision-making. A tighter coupling between ICT systems can cause accidents because of interfering ICT systems. Hacking government systems may be perceived by some as ethical or innocent but it can have a profound impact and may corrupt government data on which real government decisions are based (see Box 6.7).

## Box 6.7: The DigiNotar example in the Netherlands

In 2012, the Dutch Safety Board (DSB) published a report on an ICT-related accident. DigiNotar was a digital spin-off of the Dutch notarial profession. Since traditional notary services provide legal certainty for parties involved in a transaction, the notarial profession decided that the same type of services could be offered in a digital environment. Using asymmetrical techniques for encryption (in a public key infrastructure digital environment), DigiNotar issued digital certificates that authenticate the link between a public key and the identity of the corresponding private key. After some explorative hacking in June 2011, a real digital burglary in the protected part of the DigiNotar network followed on 1 July 2011. As the DSB report shows, the hack allowed the generation of false digital certificates from 1 July to 20 July. Since the private business of DigiNotar was associated with the Dutch government's public key infrastructure the hack allowed the production of digital certificates authorized by government. The DSB's investigation showed that the lack of managerial attention for the risks involved with the government's public key infrastructure was one of the main causes of this incident. The research also showed highly different managerial practices with regard to information security in

Dutch government organizations. Organizations primarily aimed at processing information for decision-making such as the large-scale bureaucracies that produce decisions on traffic fines or welfare benefits are more focused on information security than policy-driven organizations. The DSB also concluded that digital security is better guaranteed in processes and organizational chains that are tightly regulated by law (DSB 2012).

Next to deliberate human action, the second risk is that the design of information systems can be flawed if the systems are not updated regularly (see Box 6.8). These flaws may cause breakdown, corrupt data or risky network connections. In the end, any information system will show some vulnerabilities but some systems are more susceptible than others. For example, redundant systems in which both data storage and applications are copied are less vulnerable than systems that are not redundant.

## Box 6.8: Updating systems in the Dutch water management sector

The Dutch sector of water management very much relies on ICT to manage and operate its dams and sluices. The General Audit Office (2018) has analyzed the cyber security policies of the ICT for operating the dams and sluices. These information systems were developed in the 1980s and 1990s when cyber security was in its infancy. The original standalone systems have also been connected with large-scale computer networks and the internet. The vulnerabilities have increased but the cyber security policies did not grow proportionally. The General Audit Office managed to obtain physical access to the operations and also to connect a laptop. Although this was detected by the system, it appeared that in other cases measures to detect intruders had not been implemented. Apart from the passwords that were written on small notes attached to the screen and other vulnerabilities in the human organization around the ICT, it appeared that the ageing systems are weak if they are not systematically updated.

*Source:* General Audit Office (2018)

# New opportunities

The perspective of rational analysis reveals that information technology not only creates new risks but also enables new opportunities for risk management strategies. A number of these opportunities for risk management should be mentioned.

1   *Data-driven risk assessment* is already quite common in many public agencies. Risk management has been one of the first applications of big data in the public sector. Big data analysis can be used to detect fraud or crime risks as Box 6.3 on CAS and Predpol illustrates. If a regular house in a residential area is inhabited by a professional hairdresser and the use of water exceeds the average use of a regular household, it is likely that there is an illegal hairdressing salon that could expect a visit by the tax authority. If someone receives welfare benefits according to the tax authority's administration but also owns an expensive car according to the car registration administration, there may be a risk that the person has an illegal source of income. By combining more and more of the data from various public organizations, anomalies spring up that point at risks. As the examples show, fraud can be detected but there are many other applications of big data for risk management. New sensing techniques enable continuous monitoring of the quality of the water and air around a particular industrial plant in order to detect if and when risks arise. The 100 per cent check at Schiphol Amsterdam airport in the Netherlands is an example of the use of data analysis to detect drug trafficking. The data of all passengers of flights from particular destinations to Schiphol Amsterdam airport are analyzed based on a risk model with a number of indicators. If a threshold of the red flags shows up the passenger attracts extra attention and checks. The more red flags pop up, the more intensive the check. This way, data analysis enables new strategies for risk management and a rationalization of law enforcement resources.

2   *Continuous monitoring and quick response algorithms* provide a second opportunity for risk management. Connected with data-driven risk management techniques are the ICT-based algorithms used for risk management. These algorithms allow large-scale processing of individual situations (see Box 6.9).

## Box 6.9: Algorithmic decision-making by tax authorities

The Dutch tax authorities use algorithms for both the assessment of the tax applications of small and medium-sized businesses and private persons (Van Eck 2018). Some of the necessary data are extracted from the tax application while the rest of the information is collected via automated links with the information systems of partner organizations (public and private, such as banks and employers). The algorithm then assesses the individual situation based on programmed decision rules. The decision rules include standard calculations (a certain amount of taxable income goes along with a certain amount of taxes to be paid) but also the range that is allowed (for example the range of deductible costs given a certain turnover of a small or medium-sized business). The rules on the boundaries of tolerance are used as an algorithmic risk management system because if the tax application exceeds the pre-programmed range the application will be rejected from the automated system and handled by a tax officer.

3   *Digital defences and buffers.* Information systems produce new risks but the technology also enables public organizations to create new defences and buffers. As argued by Reason (1997, 2), 'all organizational accidents entail the breaching of the barriers and safeguards that separate damaging and injurious hazards from vulnerable people or assets – collectively termed "losses"'. These barriers and safeguards are referred to as defences while other accident researchers emphasize the need for buffers (e.g. Perrow 1999). Decision-making systems, big data applications and digital networks can be designed as organizational defences. In order to use digitization as an organization defence, both the socio-technical system and the information systems should be designed as such. As Clearfield and Tilcsik (2018) show, such a design requires simplifying ICT systems, increasing the transparency of the linkages and also adding slack to these systems.

As argued, the rational analysis highlights new risks, new causes of risks and new risk management techniques. However, this rational focus only results in a limited understanding of these risks, causes and the new strategies for risk management. Table 6.2 examines the different kinds of

**Table 6.2** Four frames applied to risk awareness and risk actions.

| | Awareness | Action |
|---|---|---|
| Rational analysis | Public managers should: 1) map the new risks of ICT breakdown and corruption of data, and 2) understand new causes for risks involved with digitalization (cybercrime and cybersabotage as well as vulnerable ICT systems) | Managers can address and mitigate the risks and the causes involved with digitalization. Use ICT for data driven, risk management, continuous monitoring and response, and digital defences and buffers |
| Human perspective | Managers should be aware of the social embeddedness of ICT and information systems and the biases involved (over-reliance and information system parochialism). They should also carefully analyze the risks involved with over-reliance and system parochialism | Public managers should deliberately include psychologists, behavioural experts and other outsiders in the processes of ICT development |
| Politics of risk management | Managers should be able to deploy a political perspective to reveal the hidden ideologies, values and political conflict in ICT and the way ICT transform politics | Public managers should use political assessment tools and organize different political perspectives and interests around the development and use of ICT |
| Risk culture | Managers should know how shared values shape the framing of risk, risk aversion and the preferences for risk management strategies. In particular public managers can counter these biases by pertinently asking questions on worst-case scenarios | Managers should deliberately research and compare how different cultures and organizations assess and deal with the risks involved with the use of ICT in order to detect how cultures produce risks and how worst-case scenarios can be envisioned |

risk awareness and action that follow from the aforementioned new risks and new opportunities.

Clearly the first strategy of detecting, addressing and mitigating the risks involved with information systems enables public managers to avoid risks or the impact of accidents and failure. As such, dealing with risk does not suffice to organize informational resilience. Resilience also demands a particular design of information systems to make them less vulnerable (e.g. redundancy of applications and storage). Even though this is primarily the domain and work of technology specialists, public managers can be both a check on engineering resilience and a barrier to it (e.g. De Bruijne, Boin and Van Eeten 2010). From an organization perspective, resilience not only refers to less vulnerability but also the organization being better able to bounce back after an incident. The strategies described in this chapter contribute to this ability. In his book *The Safety Anarchist*, Sidney Dekker (2017) adds a lesson for public managers who want to avoid organizational accidents and failure: if they want to improve the resilience of their organizations, public managers should build on the creativity and innovation of their frontline workers instead of relying on rules and compliance based on risk management strategies. This warning again highlights the importance of the four different perspectives on SPIM. As the next sections argue, a rational analysis can only be effective if the manager also takes other perspectives into account.

# Human perspective on risks

As we have seen throughout this book, ICT and public information are intrinsically connected with humans and their particularities. If the human side of ICT and information management is overlooked, a major risk for SPIM will ensue. As Polanyi (1958) argued, personal, tacit or background knowledge plays a major role in any professional judgment and interpretation of what is usually referred to as objective information. The human side of information was revealed quite early in the ICT-revolution which took place at the end of the nineteenth century and the start of the new millennium. The examples mentioned by Brown and Duguid (2000) may be dated to the 1990s and be derived from business (Xerox), but they clearly show how information is embedded in human and social experiences. Brown and Duguid noticed an increasing tendency to redefine things as information: 'Books are portrayed as information containers, libraries as information warehouses, universities as information providers, and learning as information absorption. Organizations are depicted as information coordinators, meetings as information consolidators, talk as information exchange, markets as information-driven stimulus and response' (2000, 21). This type of reductionism overlooks the human dimension both included in and underlying these phenomena. In order to avoid reductionism this book adopts a socio-technical approach (as explained in Chapter 1).

The introduction of information systems based on the misunderstanding that information can be detached from human judgment is thus destined to fail. Brown and Duguid (2000, 99–109) illustrate their proposition with the example of one of their Xerox PARC colleagues (Julian Orr). He studied the work of the Xerox technical representatives ('reps') who service and repair the company's copiers at customers' sites. Their work is critical to client satisfaction and the success of the company. The repair work they do may be difficult but the process is simple and familiar. Customers facing problems with their copiers called the customer service centre which then notified the reps. They would then go to the customer's site and fix the problem after which they cleared the call with the service centre. Even though the reps' work was independent from each other they got together on their own time for breakfast, lunch, coffee or at the end of the day. The reps also used the clear call with the customer service centre to share their experiences with the operators. Even though the operators' job was to direct the reps to the customers who faced problems with their copiers, the operators learned from these clear calls. As a result, the reps, the operators and the specialists that were sometimes needed for very complex problems developed a collective pool of knowledge on how to diagnose and fix problems with copiers. Since copiers are constructed mechanically and equipped with pre-programmed software it seemed logical to develop an expert system to help the operators. An expert system would better guide the operators to support the reps and help customers to solve some problems themselves instead of directing a rep to them. It appeared that this idea was based on the misunderstanding that information can be meaningfully detached from humans. While a top-down logical analysis of problems with copiers may seem an appropriate solution, it overlooks the tacit collective knowledge of the reps, the operators and the specialists. The research carried out by Julian Orr shifted Xerox's attempts to improve the processes from top-down expert systems for the operators, to systems reinforcing the internal ties, collaboration, storytelling and improvisation. The rational approach was thus replaced by a focus on humans and their interaction.

Thus any strategic public information manager who wants to avoid risks better start with putting public information in a human, social and professional perspective. Otherwise, man–machine interaction will be the first and most important risk s/he will face. As experiments with self-driving cars show, humans do make mistakes but they are generally better than ICT in being able to quickly interpret what they observe and act upon a correct interpretation. Computer scientists Pearl and Mackenzie (2018) even suggest that instead of aiming to mimic the human brain with algorithms we should first try to make computers as intelligent as a three-year-old child. They refer to this challenge as the mini Turing test. Tasks that require complex interpretation of ill-structured data should thus be attributed to groups of professionals who are able to meaningfully interact with each other. But a sole focus on humans and their professionalism does not suffice for SPIM. Effective SPIM also requires that tasks that can better be attributed to computers are shifted from professionals to computers. Tasks that require calculation, structured decision-making and discerning patterns in massive amounts of data can better be carried out by computers.

Effective SPIM is concerned with man–machine interaction. If professional humans perform complex, interpretative and out-of-the-box activities and they are supported by perfect computers the interaction between man and machine may be ineffective. Many ICT failures in public organizations can be explained by the lack of alignment between the work of the professionals and the support by computers (see Brown and Duguid 2000; Ciborra 2002). Policy decisions are not only the products of computerized algorithms or AI no matter how sophisticated these may become. It is not the level of sophistication that is pertinent but the misunderstanding of the nature of policy work. SPIM that facilitates policymaking thus builds on the professionalism of policymakers but it also enables or even forces the policymakers to use the data, the patterns and correlations, the algorithms and the networking capacity in such a way that they produce better policies. SPIM is thus not merely a technical matter but a socio-technical one also.

Managing the risks of information systems thus also entails managing human biases and their occurrence in the realm of SPIM. What human biases may occur in public organizations with regard to the risks of information systems? At least two should be taken into account: the first is the over-reliance on technologies that occurs in public organizations. Since information processing is the core business of many public organizations, the use of information systems to replace human information processing seems logical if not inevitable. The limitations of technologies as information processing devices can easily be overlooked or ignored. Software developers and IT consultants emphasize the advantages of these technologies and usually present them as the best solution that contributes both to the efficiency and the reliability of decision-making.

Both with regard to the *type* of decisions and to the decision-making *context*, technologies have limitations that are easily overlooked. Information systems usually only perform better if the information and the decisions are well structured. Ill-structured information and complex decisions require at least human intervention if not human judgment. So, in order to use technologies either the decision-making context and the information should be structured or human backup should be provided. Technological over-reliance in public organizations may cause continuing incidents and crises as the case of the Dutch tax authority shows (see Box 6.10).

## Box 6.10: The Dutch tax authority and its over-reliance on ICT

The Dutch tax authority is stuffed with ICT (Van Eck 2018; Zouridis and Leijtens 2018). The authority uses ICT to both levy and collect many taxes. The administration of taxes on car ownership and the income tax of individuals is almost completely automated. Corporate taxes are predominantly levied by ICT. While individuals complete their applications online via the system of the tax authority, corporations can upload their administrations in order to fulfil their duties. Since all processes of levying and collecting taxes strongly if not solely rely on ICT, the organization is fully blended with information systems. ICT have enabled large-scale processing of tax applications and the management of the organization does not seem to be able to imagine any operation outside the information systems. Because of the standardization and massive standard operations inherently connected with ICT the organization is not only unable to deal with complex tax problems but it can no longer even detect these problems. Almost all incidents and problems associated with the tax authority nowadays push the limits of ICT. Many types of fraud remain undetected and unaddressed while citizens with complex tax situations are dealt with by information systems that cannot cope with the complexity of their situation. Hence the top management of the tax authority is confronted with a continuous stream of incidents and public and political outrage that can only be attributed to its own over-reliance on ICT and the information system parochialism embedded in the ICT.

This example also shows a second human bias that should be taken into account by managers: the literature on public organizations has extensively shown organizational parochialism (see, for example, Wilson 1989). Organizational parochialism refers to the human inclination to define problems and situations primarily from the perspective of their profession or organization. If a person steals something from a pharmacy a police officer may see criminal behaviour, a psychiatrist may see mentally disturbed behaviour, a social worker may see a person in need of social support and a lawyer may see the police violence during the arrest. Organization members tend to identify their perspectives and values with the tasks and values of their organization, hence organizational parochialism. Information systems add a new layer of information system parochialism. Once an information system is put into effect, public managers will be inclined to define the environment of the organization according to the information system.

Again, the case of the Dutch tax authority provides a worrisome example here. It has become quite difficult for the managers of this authority to observe the environment of the organization beyond the information system. Some problems are simply not observed because these are not reflected in the information system. While the owners of cars registered in the Netherlands automatically receive the request to pay for the motor vehicle taxes, the owners of cars registered in other countries are not seen by the tax authority even though these owners may have lived in the Netherlands for many years and used the roads.

Managers should be aware of these biases. Next to the calculated rational analysis, risk management strategies from the perspective of the 'coach' with a focus on man–machine interaction also teach some new strategies for risk management. First of all, man–machine interaction and the biases of technological over-reliance and information system parochialism should be included in the design process of the information systems. The design cannot be merely left to software developers and data specialists – it is a major responsibility of the public manager himself. Second, man–machine interaction should be included in the development of policies and regulations. Instead of separating the development of policies and regulation from the development information systems, both should be co-developed taking into account man–machine interaction and the biases mentioned above. The need to address these biases does not end with the completion of the information systems and the policies. While man–machine interaction should be embedded in the design of both policies and information systems it should also guide public managers in the stage of operation. Again the case of the Dutch tax authority provides an illustration.

# Politics of risk management

The alleged power-free and technocratic nature of information technology has been broadly exposed and unmasked ever since the first technological tools were developed thousands of years ago (for an overview see Van der Pot 1994). Information systems may be presented as technocratic solutions that merely contribute to the efficiency of organizations but they also embody values and transform organizational routines (e.g. Winner 1993). In at least three ways information systems and ICT can be infused with politics. The most obvious and well-documented pathway from politics to ICT and information systems runs through the data on which models and algorithms are based.

## Box 6.11: The Allegheny algorithm

Eubanks (2017) uses the Allegheny Family Screening Tool (AFST) to illustrate how politics is embedded in the design of an algorithm. This tool has been developed to forecast child abuse and neglect and it is used by the Allegheny County Office of Children, Youth and Families (CYF). The variables used to design a system that predicts the risks of child abuse and neglect look familiar. According to the algorithm, children under five are at the highest risk of neglect and abuse and parent hostility toward CYF investigators indicates high-risk behaviour. But Eubanks questions the technocratic nature of both the outcome indicators and the predictive variables. Child abuse and child-maltreatment-related fatalities and near fatalities in Allegheny County is too low to construct 'a statistically meaningful model' (Eubanks 2017, 143). One of the variables is whether the report is substantiated by CYF caseworkers. According to Eubanks, substantiation is an 'imprecise metric: it simply means that CYF believes there is enough evidence that a child may be harmed to accept a family for services'. Eubanks (143–4) concludes:

> Though it would be best to use a more direct measure the AFST uses two related variables – called proxies – as stand-ins for child maltreatment. The first proxy is community re-referral, when a call to the hotline about a child was initially screened out, but CYF receives another call on the same child within two years. The second proxy is child placement, when a call to the hotline

about a child is screened in and results in the child being placed in foster care within two years.

The predictive variables in AFST are based on a regression analysis that showed 131 factors that predict child harm. Taken together these factors produce a predictive model that performs 'halfway between a coin toss and perfect prediction' (76 per cent). While the predictive model may be challenged because of its accuracy the outcome variables or proxies also display design choices that mirror social and political values.

The example of the 'Allegheny algorithm' (see Box 6.11) shows how seemingly innocent and objective data are the result of a politically constructed reality. The predictive variables may have been derived from the data by using standard and widely accepted regression techniques but the data themselves are not apolitical. The construction of the data mirrors political goals, power and even ideology. The same applies to the design of the algorithmic models or the design of the information system. As with the design of a sculpture, a painting or a book the design of information systems reflects choice. What variables are included in the system and what decision rules should be applied? These design choices may be made explicitly or result from deliberation between competing interests but the design choices may also be hidden behind seemingly neutral categories. So politics by design is the net result of these design choices. Any design of an information system should thus be critically analyzed by public managers from a political perspective. As argued by Hendriks and Zouridis (1999), the choice for a particular design or even a particular technology should be approached with the question 'cui bono?' (who benefits?). O'Neill (2016) refers to the algorithmic models produced by data scientists as Weapons of Math Destruction (WMD). She claims that a 'model's blind spots reflect the judgments and priorities of its creators' (O'Neil 2016, 21). Even despite their 'reputation for impartiality', the models 'reflect goals and ideology' (see Box 6.12).

So both the data and the design of the information system mirror politics and can be regarded as the outcomes of political choice and political conflict. But the link between politics and information systems is more complex and nuanced. Information systems do not only mirror politics, they also transform politics by their very nature. In 1989 Zuboff showed that technologies do not only replace administrative and information processed but they inherently add a layer of 'informating capacity'. The

## Box 6.12: The LSI-R case as described by O'Neill

Both in the US and in the Netherlands, research shows that ethnic or racial background matters for the penalty criminals are sentenced with (e.g. Epp, Maynard-Moody and Haider-Merkel 2014; Wermink et al. 2015). Apparently implicit or even unconscious considerations drive police officers, public prosecutors and judges to choose different penalties if confronted with black criminals or criminals with a different ethnic background. Since computerized models are unprejudiced and neutral we may expect these differences to disappear if computerized models are used for sentencing. O'Neill sketches the LSI-R, or Level of Service Inventory Revised, a recidivism model that should help judges to make better and more neutral judgments. She shows that the questionnaire is based on implicit assumptions that discriminate between people with different backgrounds.

> Ask a criminal who grew up in comfortable suburbs about 'the first time you were ever involved with the police,' and he might not have a single incident to report other than the one that brought him to prison. Young black males, by contrast, are likely to have been stopped by police dozens of times, even when they've done nothing wrong.
>
> (O'Neill 2016, 25)

Thousands of inmates have completed a LSI-R questionnaire since it was introduced in 1995. The results have been analyzed by statisticians to correlate the factors with recidivism and distinguish between factors that highly determine recidivism and factors that do not correlate at all. In some US states (O'Neill mentions Idaho and Colorado), judges use these scores to guide their sentencing. By uncritically using the so-called neutral model the judges either are not aware of the politics embedded in the model or they adhere to it. Either way the very design of the model displays political choice, value and power.

actions and transactions are not only carried out by the new technologies but the technologies always also register the actions and transactions (Zuboff 1989). Today we would probably refer to the 'informing capacity' as the registration and use of metadata. Because of the 'informing capacity' the introduction and use of information systems transform and reshuffle power and political structures as Zuboff shows. The transformation of power and politics is neither random nor does the technology simply reinforce existing power structures. According to Zuboff (2019) the transformation can be labelled as 'surveillance capitalism'.

The transformation referred to as surveillance capitalism is enabled by the already mentioned 'informating capacity' of information systems and ICT. Since the information systems do not only accommodate transactions and communication but also register data on transactions and communication, the use of these technologies has given rise to a new set of values. Zuboff (2019, 8) describes these values as follows: 'Surveillance capitalism unilaterally claims human experience as free raw material for translation into behavioral data. Although some of these data are applied to product or service improvement, the rest are declared as a proprietary behavioral surplus, fed into advanced manufacturing processes known as "machine intelligence," and fabricated into prediction products that anticipate what you will do now, soon, and later.'

The trend towards surveillance capitalism implies that the information systems not only mirror politics but also reshuffle politics. Again Zuboff (2019, 8) comments:

> Competitive pressures produced this shift, in which automated machine processes not only know our behavior but also shape our behavior at scale. With this reorientation from knowledge to power, it is no longer enough to automate information flows about us; the goal is now to automate us. (…) In this way, surveillance capitalism births a new species of power that I call instrumentarianism. Instrumentarian power knows and shapes human behavior toward other ends. Instead of armaments and armies, it works its will through the automated medium of an increasingly ubiquitous computational architecture of "smart" networked devices, things, and spaces.

As a 'mediator' a public manager is capable of distilling the power, political goals and political ideology embedded in the information system through its design, data and inherent 'informating capacity'. In this role, the manager focuses on who is exposed to what risk, who holds the power to address a risk and in particular how power shapes the design of risk and risk management. The awareness of how politics is embedded in informational risk management and the ability to connect power, ideology and conflict with informational risk management shows how public managers can and should also act as 'mediators'.

# Risks and organizational culture

From the perspective of rational analysis, risks appear as the formula 'probability times impact'. A manager foresees risks and calculates the probability and the impact. As argued above, this perspective should be complemented with attention for man–machine interactions – the human aspect – and attention for power relations because risks also reveal human error and political values and conflict. In order to understand the risks surrounding information systems a final perspective should be added. The strategic public information manager should also be able to perceive risks from the perspective of the cultural roots and nature of risks as well as the cultural tools to deal with risks and the cultural barriers that hamper risk management.

Not too long ago, risks were considered as an inevitable product of either nature or technology. Natural disasters such as flooding, earthquakes, hurricanes and volcanos threaten the lives and property of humans and should thus be regarded as risks. Large-scale complex technologies such as chemical plants, nuclear plants, aviation and shipping also cause risks for life and limb. The sources of these risks are seen as exogenous from the perspective of the people involved and the risks can be identified. Turner and Pidgeon (1978) have redefined the concept of risk by showing how disasters are man-made. Risks are not exogenous to how we organize our lives, our societies and our production but they are inherently connected with the social and economic order. Tierney (2014) takes this shift even further by showing how social order produces risk. The risks of information systems are not exogenous to a social order but they are both the product of the social and information order and are embedded in the very architecture of the information systems.

Strategic public information managers should not only be aware of how the given social and informational order produce risk, they should also be able to assess, mitigate and address these risks. In this role, awareness cannot be limited to the root causes of risk because the very nature of risks is also cultural. People differ with regard to what they see as risk and the extent to which they are willing to accept risks. While for some, racing a Formula 1 car may sound exciting, others will consider it to be too risky. Some people are willing to accept the risks of nuclear energy while others believe that the risks should be completely avoided. Values not only guide the acceptance of a risk (the degree to which people are risk averse) but also how a risk is defined. Some people consider the risks of smoking and drinking alcohol to be part of the responsibility of the individual. Other people believe that the risks of smoking and drinking should be seen as societal. The values that guide both the risk aversion and risk perception may be individual values but at the level of groups and even societies some remarkable patterns have been found.

It appears that shared values at least partially explain risk aversion, risk perception and the framing of risks as well as the preferences on how to deal with risks. Both Douglas and Wildavsky (1982) and Hood, Rothstein and Baldwin (2001) have used group-grid theory (cultural theory) as a framework to understand how risks are perceived and managed. Risks are seen as collective constructs guided by value sets that can be ordered with cultural theory that identifies four different world views.

Hood, Rothstein and Baldwin (2001) use cultural theory to show how these world views or different cultures produce different risk perceptions, risk attitudes and preferences for the type of risk management strategies. They distinguish the following world views:

- The *fatalist* emphasizes the unpredictability and unmanageability of hazards and unintended policy effects. Government cannot anticipate these risks and only needs to respond properly after the event.
- The *hierarchist* focuses on the role of experts in forecasting and managing risks. Government needs to engage expert committees to develop anticipative whole-society solutions.
- The *individualist* highlights market and individual choice processes. Government needs to support and develop markets and underpin informed choice, perhaps supplemented by community information asymmetry reduction measures.
- The *egalitarian* emphasizes community participation in decision-making. Government needs to support and develop popular participation and stimulate local participatory institutions, forums and citizen juries.

These cultural biases partially coincide with the public manager roles we distinguished earlier in this book. Whereas the rational perspective shows some elective affinity with either the hierarchist and individualist world views, the human or cultural perspective may produce egalitarian biases. At the same time, the perspectives we use throughout this book are quite different from the cultural biases as mapped by Hood, Rothstein and Baldwin (2001) and highlight managerial issues rather than societal world views.

Whatever the risk perception and preferred strategy of risk management, there may be cultural barriers to dealing with the risks of ICT and information systems in the first place. In the realm of risk management, the cognitive biases that hamper risk detection and risk management have been lucidly summarized by Meyer and Kunreuther (2017; see also Kahneman 2012). They reduce the extensive literature to six human biases that explain why humans underprepare for disasters and organizational accidents (see Box 6.13).

## Box 6.13: Cognitive human biases towards risk

Meyer and Kunreuther (2017) suggest six biases:

1. The Myopia Bias, which refers to the human tendency to focus on the short-term rather than the long-term implications of particular actions. This bias explains why people do not invest in protective measures that can be taken now but will bring benefits in a more distant future.
2. The Amnesia Bias, which 'causes attitudes toward protection to become increasingly lax with time'. Even though on a cognitive level people do not forget tragedy and accidents the 'hedonic impact of past losses, the acute sense of tragedy that one feels when seeing one's house destroyed, or the fear one feels in the immediate wake of a terrorist attack' are quickly forgotten (23–4).
3. The Optimism Bias, the 'tendency to believe that we are more immune to others to bad outcomes' (42), makes people underestimate the risks to which they are subjected.
4. The Inertia Bias. According to Meyer and Kunreuther '(w)e tend to be highly inertial in our thinking, preferring to stay with the status quo rather than follow new paths of action, and to look for defaults that free us from the labors of difficult, deliberative (…) thinking' (50).
5. The Simplification Bias, which involves the 'tendency to make decisions based on the consideration of only a small subset of cues', 'can have harmful effects on preparedness that go beyond ignoring probability information' (56).
6. The Herding Bias. Although Meyer and Kunreuther acknowledge the possibility of crowds, the human instinct 'to follow the herd goes awry' when it is 'used in an information vacuum – when in fact, the collective crowd is no better informed than the least informed of its individual members' (61–2).

These psychological and cultural biases hamper effective risk management. Moreover, Cerulo (2006) has found a more fundamental cultural barrier for taking risks into account. She shows how positive asymmetry explains why cultural practices push aside the worst case or scenario. Cerulo defines positive asymmetry as the cultural mechanism in which the 'best is continually defined as the most immediate and familiar dimension of quality. In contrast, the worst is distanced and blurred, perhaps completely blocked by images of perfection and excellence' (12). Culturally, groups tend to highlight a positive view of the future and blur or even block the worst scenarios. 'A trio of practices (…) both initiate and sustain positive asymmetry: "eclipsing", "clouding" and "recasting." Eclipsing practices render the worst people, places, objects, and events invisible. Clouding practices keep the worst vaguely defined. And recasting practices redefine the worst as something positive and good' (14). Obviously in any culture the opposite – negative asymmetry – also occurs but these practices are usually regarded as 'instances of cultural deviance' (15).

# Conclusions

As this chapter shows, the introduction of new technologies for information management includes new risks and new causes for organizational accidents and failure. In order to improve the informational resilience of their organizations public managers should set up a system of informational risk management that entails at least two strategies. First, a systematic analysis of the new risks caused by information systems enables public managers to map, address and mitigate these risks. The building blocks for the analysis and for the types of measures are provided by this chapter. These include a typology of new risks and new strategies for risk management. The different perspectives also show that mapping, addressing and mitigating the risks involved with information systems is not enough. Man–machine interaction and human error, the politics that guide the development and use of ICT and data, and both the cultural production of risk and the cultural barriers that hamper risk detection and risk management should also be taken into account.

This chapter started with a number of questions on risks and risk management in the realm of SPIM:

- *What risks arise if ICT are introduced in public organizations?* Information systems can be hacked by malicious individuals. Such systems also have inherent technical vulnerabilities, and the risks of such vulnerabilities increase as the scale and interdependency of the systems increase. Big data and networked forms of ICT frequently managed through algorithms introduce many types of ethical and technical risks. As such risks cannot be entirely avoided, risk management is needed to introduce and maintain acceptable levels of risk.

- *How can these risks be managed and what tools are available for risk management in the hyper-connected context of ICT?* There are many possible ways that new risks can be managed. New opportunities for risk management paradoxically often rely on the same kinds of techniques that are also risk related such as using big data for techniques such as prediction and automated detection systems. Other public management frames such as the 'human' or 'cultural' can help too. For example, by consulting psychologists and behavioural experts or assessment of organizational risk cultures.

- *What human, cultural and political drivers should be taken into account if ICT risk management strategies are prepared and implemented?* Important human drivers include information sharing through in-person interaction and collaboration, man–machine architectures and limitations to human reasoning and cognitive processing. Important cultural drivers include perceptions of risk based on cultural background and different cultural values such as individualist and egalitarian approaches. Important political drivers include political ideology and the information and knowledge structures that shape political power.

- *How can ICT also be used for risk assessment and risk management?* Public managers can use ICT for data-driven types of risk management. Well-designed systems for continuous monitoring and decision-making can help to manage risks, especially those related to cybersecurity. Additionally, public managers should use political and organizational assessment tools to support their use of ICT.

# KEY LESSONS FROM CHAPTER 6

- The opportunities for ICT to improve the performance and quality of public organizations inherently also create risks for public organizations that should always be taken into account.

- Risk management in the realm of ICT differs from traditional risk management because of the complexity and global mutual interdependencies embedded in ICT. New tools for risk management can be used for risk management in the realm of ICT.
- Managing the risks of ICT always involves man–machine interaction, hence the need for a multidimensional risk management approach based on the perspectives elaborated in this book (the rational, political, human and cultural perspective).
- ICT can also be used to support risk management as illustrated by many examples in this chapter.

# 7

# Managing information in a political environment

*Public managers are a formal part of a political system of government and therefore face quite different political environments compared to their counterparts in the private sector. Public organizations are an integral part of an institutionalized political decision-making process and are legally bound to help implement democratically reached policy decisions. This has important consequences for the kinds of political environments that shape strategic public information management (SPIM). In this chapter, we explore how public managers can approach political management by taking on board strategic and normative factors of operating within a political system with specific democratic processes and key political stakeholders such as citizens and public interest groups.*

## Introduction

Politics is an inevitability for public organizations. But politics can also cause problems for public managers, and the decisions made by public managers can contribute to political crises. Take, for instance, the nightmarish case of the roll out of the website for the Affordable Care Act (ACA) in the United States, healthcare.gov, which crashed numerous times at critical moments in its implementation and became a symbol of a political fight over the legitimacy of the new healthcare law. The political stripe of some states determined how they adopted the law, and evidence has subsequently shown that individuals from one political party were statistically more likely to use the website for purchasing insurance options (Lerman, Sadin and Trachtman 2017). Despite the major costs of the ICT infrastructure needed to roll out the ACA, subsequent actions by politicians succeeded in undermining the policy by attacking it and refusing to implement it (Anthopoulos, Reddick, Giannakidou and Mavridis 2016).

Other problems faced by public managers in the politicization of public information – such as the media choosing to focus on sensationalist information rather than that most relevant for policies – are much more common. These kinds of political phenomena are difficult to solve in societies where the press and open public debate play important but sometimes obfuscating roles in the public information ecosystem. Further, given the value of political neutrality in the bureaucracy, proactive engagement in political events is a complex and delicate matter for public managers. And yet, though complex, strategic intervention in this sphere is necessary. According to van der Wal, writing about multistakeholder engagement for public managers in the twenty-first century, 'Managing an unpredictable landscape of stakeholders – and one that is constantly changing in terms of prominence, allegiance, and stance towards policies, programs, and objectives – will be a key demand of public managers in the 21st century' (2017, 67). Public managers can strategically anticipate the influence of politics and act in ways that can mitigate some of the negative effects.

What precisely these challenges entail for public managers has long been studied by scholars, and it continues to be a question that divides opinion. Broadly, there are two different types of answer to this question: *normative* and *strategic* answers. Normative answers concern the expectations of what managers can do in their capacity as representatives of the democratically supported authority of the state. In particular, managing the affairs of government involves making decisions that influence the users of public services (citizens) and the people with the final say on such services (elected officials). In contrast, strategic answers concern the practical function that public managers have in managing services and having as their goal implementation as efficiently and effectively as possible.

Both normative and strategic constraints affect SPIM. The 'strategic' in SPIM depends on a good understanding of public values goals and the ways to realize them in practice. Just as the political challenges of the public sector are both normative and strategic in nature, information use in the public sector can also address questions of both strategic and normative sorts. Information is a valuable, utilitarian good. Simultaneously, information has a powerful bearing on decisions that governments make regarding right and wrong, justice and injustice, value and waste, etc. Public managers have strategic political questions to consider because public organizations have a normative responsibility to govern and an instrumental responsibility to deliver on public resources supplied by taxpayers.

In this chapter we address the following questions:

- What are the important characteristics of a political system, and what do these entail for strategic management of public information?
- What political knowledge and skills do public managers need to get the most value out of data?
- What are the main strategic information management questions impacting/shaping relationships with different political actors?
- What are the key strategic opportunities for public information usage in a political system?
- What are the key normative challenges for public information in a political system?

To answer these, we start by describing the key characteristics of a political system, its influence on public information systems and the relevance of these characteristics for SPIM. We will explain what role different political actors play and how this influences SPIM. Each of these spheres of activity raise different kinds of questions about what public managers should do and how, which we set out with practical examples on strategic and normative challenges of politics for public managers. We conclude by looking at how public managers can steer their organizations towards a politically intelligent form of SPIM.

# Public information and the political system

Public information management is built on a political system. By the same token, public information is politically contentious because it can be misused (as well as responsibly used) to accomplish political ends within the given political system of institutions, constitutions and laws. Public information is necessary, but always a product of a political system at the same time. Public managers must nevertheless contend with this fact and continue to manage public information in ways that still achieve important public sector goals. Scholars have divergent views on the primary function of information in political systems (see Box 7.1 for a brief discussion of the main areas of divergence).

## Box 7.1: Modernist and post-modernist theories of public information

Information certainly plays a powerful role in governing the political sphere. But scholars differ widely on the theory of how political information fits together with political organization and political behaviour. Two divergent views can be seen in the difference between modernist and post-modernist views on public information.

*Modernists*, in the tradition of nineteenth-century liberals Jeremy Bentham (1748–1832) and John Stuart Mill (1806–1873), see information as a tool of enlightenment and liberation. According to this view, the wide availability of information about what government does is critical to civilized society. Only by providing facts and information that people can use to reason independently about social and political matters is it possible for society to achieve its democratic ideals. As information enables political behaviour, decisions about what information to make available to the public is an inherently political matter.

*Post-modernists*, in stark contrast, turn the view of modernists on its head and argue that – far from being democratic and egalitarian – the enlightenment perspective signifies a biased view of knowledge according to a particular position of power or class in society. Truth is socially constructed and there is no possibility of information providing unmediated access to reality. The sociologist Michel Foucault (1926–1984) argued that the fundamental purpose of public information is to continue power interests in society that are aimed at internalizing discipline on themselves and imposing self-surveillance to keep individuals under control.

Today, many approaches to public information combine some elements of both modernist and post-modernist views. Other approaches sit more distinctly within one view or the other.[1]

The quality of public information ecosystems is heavily dependent on the kind of political system in which it exists. Though we focus primarily in this book on public information management in democratic political systems, the other side of the politics-administration coin is the experience faced

---

[1] For example, see Williamson and Fung (2004) for a modern perspective. For a post-modern perspective, see Ferlie and McGivern (2014).

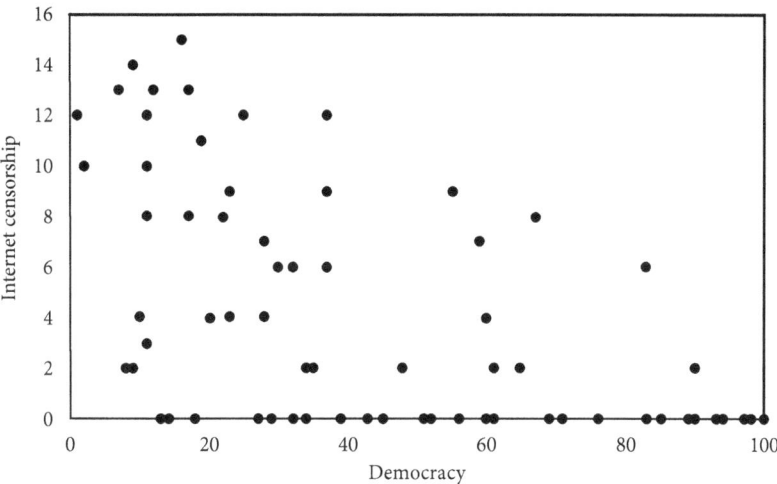

**Figure 7.1** Correlation of internet censorship and democracy level in seventy countries.

by public managers in non-democratic countries where the barriers to effective and legitimate use of public information are much more attenuated. According to the non-governmental organization Freedom House, twenty-one out of the seventy countries surveyed across the world have serious problems with obstacles to access, limits on internet content and violations of user rights, and therefore are classed as *not free* when it comes to internet adoption and its uses in society. As shown in Figure 7.1, where each dot represents a country, there is a negative correlation of the degree of internet censorship to the level of democracy shown in a country. The correlation is far from perfect. Some countries have quite a poor level of democracy and simultaneously low internet censorship, which is probably because internet censorship relies on some characteristics that many undemocratic states do not have such as technological infrastructure and wide commercial uptake of internet technologies among the population. However, almost all of the highly censoring countries are countries that have a low democracy score.[2]

Figure 7.1 communicates a strong message that politics influences public information. Public managers work in many different kinds of political systems, some with strong democracy and others with weak democracy. Sometimes public managers face so much corruption it is difficult to

---

[2] Internet censorship is measured using data on seventy-four countries from the Open Net Institute available from https://opennet.net. The 'Democracy' measures are taken from Freedom House Freedom in the World Report, available from https://freedomhouse.org/countries/freedom-world/scores.

exercise discretion when choosing new programmes and policies. However, from the view of SPIM, we have to assume that a public manager has at least enough freedom and licence to act with a degree of independence within a political system that grants him or her the ability to pursue managerial goals with a stable set of expectations for what will happen as a result. To this end, it will help to describe the kinds of political actors that public managers deal with in SPIM.

We begin by providing a structural description of the political system. Public managers must contend with several fixtures that are a regular feature of their institutional environment. This is the political structure in which public managers work, and which constrains the kinds of opportunities and challenges they encounter. Public managers need to be aware of their political context just as they need to be aware of the structure, processes and priorities of their own departments. Without this, they cannot work to their full potential. The especially challenging difference, however, between their own departments and the political system is that the latter is larger and more complex, and public managers typically only glimpse or control the small parts of it that affect their daily work.

To better understand and manage the political dimensions of SPIM, it helps to identify the main types of political actors in the political system. Below, we identify four main types and explain what kinds of practical uses they find in information produced by and circulated in the public sphere: 1) elected public officials, 2) ministers, 3) citizens and 4) interest groups. Politics arise in the relationships between the actors.

## Elected public officials

Elected public officials are the politicians who receive their professional mandate and tenure through elections and who normally represent the political interests of a specific geographic region. Elected public officials can represent their voters at the local, regional and national level. They can also become senior executive officers of governmental departments responsible for spending public money. Elected public officials hold extensive powers in shaping strategic use of public information. Public administrators – the non-elected public officials who carry out the orders of elected public officials – know that bad administrative performance is more likely to attract the attention of media and political opposition than good performance. As a result, institutionalized procedures ensure that the bureaucracy has sufficient autonomy and distance that act as a buffer against reputational damage.

From a public information manager's perspective, the bad news here is that public officials are often not incentivized to address erroneous performance results because this directs public attention to their own performance and affects their chances of getting re-elected. In fact, research shows that the provision of performance information makes politicians more likely to attribute negative performance results to bureaucratic leaders (Nielsen and Moynihan 2017). Blame games using public information may often, therefore, hamper real efforts to improve the kinds of services and processes on which public managers are focused. On a more positive note, political competition can help politicians be more compliant with information managers. Research has shown that higher levels of competition between political parties, rather than domination by one party, can improve governance decisions around public information by leading politicians to be more accommodating to sharing information with the public (Berliner 2014). Governments with strong political competition tend to have better public information management systems, evidenced by higher compliance with information requests from citizens, among other things (Berliner 2014).

# Ministers

Ministerial heads are the individuals working in public organizations that are appointed to the executive lead of public service departments such as education, cleaning, security, administration, etc. All these positions will involve some degree of information management. Ministers are active consumers of information because they rely on good data to perform their work and they communicate with elected public officials and end users of services, public and economic actors. Ministers also have many different political interests in information. A principal interest is that they seek to use information in a way that will boost their chances of getting better performance reviews, and, ultimately, more financial resources for their departments.

In seeking this goal, ministerial heads may undercut the very services for which they are responsible. For example, extensive studies have shown that schools and hospitals systematically cut administrative and legal corners and proactively shape the rules around reporting of institutional performance in ways that will make their performance appear better than it really is (e.g. Bohte and Meier 2000). If public service providers can influence public information in the way that suits them, then information may not be harnessed for better public management. Herbert Simon (2013) called this 'satisficing': where individuals make do with the easiest route to meeting targets rather than attempting better, but more costly, actions.

Public managers need to be able to tell the difference between efficient management of information and satisficing. The former is about getting as much value as possible out of information, while the latter is about doing as little as possible to 'get the job done'. Satisficing may sometimes appear necessary if working under unusual levels of political pressure and prioritization. But it helps for public managers to recognize it in political actors and manage information in ways that make choices and incentives clear (Stevens 2019).

## Citizens

Citizens are individuals who are granted legal rights consistent with being a free person living within a given sovereign territory. Citizenship comes with rights and responsibilities regarding how the person must be treated by the government (such as having rights to a fair trial in the case of being accused of a crime or to vote in an election), and how they should themselves behave (such as treating other citizens lawfully and being loyal to the political entity of which they are a part).

Citizens are often directly or indirectly the drivers of political uses of public information by elected public officials or public administrators. It is important for public managers to be aware of these channels. For example, elected public officials may actively seek data to share publicly that shows policy results citizens will like. How politicians react to policy results is heavily influenced by the political power and social construction of the recipients/subjects that support the policy (Weaver 2014). Public administrators may also be politically motivated to influence how public decisions will be made by actively representing citizen preferences for policies and public spending (Hyytinen et al. 2018).

## Interest groups

Interest groups are groups of individuals or organizations formed either as companies or non-governmental organizations that try to influence public policy decisions. Interest groups have long been recognized as possessing tremendous ability to influence public policy. So-called 'pluralist' theories of democracy (Kingdon and Thurber 1984) have given interest groups a key role as power brokers and information mediators.

Like citizens, interest groups sit outside of formal governmental structures. They do not vote in political elections but they can still influence voting behaviour through support for policy issues. Further, interest groups can play a critical part in SPIM because they often have considerable technical expertise and specialist knowledge about public policy. Interest groups sometimes hire professional lobbyists to represent their interests by using sophisticated strategies to influence the policy agenda. Agenda-setting processes in this sense are both formal and informal, and interest groups can influence both types of processes. In such cases, understanding the political interests of lobbyists is essential for public managers. Lobbyist communication campaigns can persuade policymakers of the need for a specific policy direction to be undertaken. Formally, institutional processes managed by information experts and enshrined in law, such as open comments periods on new regulations, are also ways that interest groups can mobilize. Evidence suggests that public managers do channel these efforts for the development of new regulations especially if the interest groups have significant financial power (Haeder and Yackee 2015).

# Key questions in the politics of SPIM

Below we describe the key questions for public managers that arise from the political consequences of different relationships between political actors, there are both strategic and normative types of questions. Not all possible dyads are shown, but for the sake of extracting the most relevant learning points for public managers, the questions focus on dyads in which at least one of the partners is the public organization represented by the public information manager.

*Are information platforms available to allow elected public officials and citizens to make informed decisions?* Many platforms are created in the public sector. These provide a wealth of information, but the information needs a venue for sorting and sifting. Public media needs careful attention by policymakers to address problems of misinformation and long-term development of reputational capital.

*How can information and data be shared by elected public officials and interest groups?* Interest groups often have a wealth of information that public officials can use for policymaking. But information sharing needs to be done in a transparent and accountable way with the possibility for other groups such as citizens and public service providers to monitor.

*What kinds of information is needed from citizens in order to coproduce services with public service providers?* Service usage statistics provide useful insights into citizen preferences, but opinion feedback and service 'reviews' are also essential.

*How can information be given fair and equal consideration by public administrators?* Open government approaches enable swift and transparent information sharing. However, public managers should be careful about laissez-faire approaches that lend political advantages to more powerful groups.

*How can accurate performance information be shared between elected officials and public service providers?* Public organizations should rely on a system-wide performance measurement system that makes comparisons across departments possible and that provides incentives for performance improvements.

*Are political incentives for sharing of critical information aligned between different public service providers?* Alignment is needed to create a level playing field between agencies. Agency information sharing and collaboration avoids information silos.

*Does the symbolic value of information unfairly bias public officials or citizens?* Information about citizens or public officials can be misinterpreted if it conflicts with well-established narratives about how citizens and officials behave. Understanding of information bias is an important skill for public managers.

*Is information sharing transparent and is communication sufficient to avoid costly blame strategies between public officials and interest groups?* Blame games become more likely when information is unclear or ambiguous. Opening up channels of communication between public officials and interest groups may help to develop narratives to which all actors have access.

*Does public service information unfairly discriminate against any group of citizens?* As information access becomes wider, intermediary platforms depending on algorithms sorting information are increasing. Increased checks are needed to ensure that algorithms do not inadvertently favour specific kinds of citizens.

*Does the sharing of data and information avoid communication barriers between public officials and interest groups?* Communication barriers or barriers in understanding largely come down to what information groups value most. Public officials and interest groups can have widely differing values. Nonprofit interest groups are likely to sympathize most strongly with values of public officials. Relationship building is at the root of good communication.

*Is performance information sharing between public officials and service providers structured in such a way that goals can be mutually understood and assessed?* As data becomes a more valuable resource, public officials need to make sure that clear contracting agreements and legal norms are adhered to.

*Are institutional cultures and norms between public service providers aligned for data sharing and systems integration?* Government departments have different kinds of data. They often have different systems for organizing data. Typically, governments need to mandate collaborative data sharing initiatives that establish procedures and standards across agencies.

How can public managers adequately address these normative and strategic questions within the political constraints of their work? How can they better manage public information in a political context? In the following two sections, we discuss strategic opportunities for understanding and working with different political actors and therein managing public information more effectively. We also address several important normative challenges that arise from the political context of public information management.

# Strategic opportunities of public information

## Information intermediaries as a management resource

The old saying is that 'knowledge is power'. If information is raw material that awaits its handling and transformation into 'knowledge' then logically it follows that information is an extremely valuable resource. Information is sought after by individuals who exercise and maintain power. But, by the same token, information requires extensive management of skill and technique in order to be turned into knowledge that can be used for responsible power in government. Over time, public managers can form information networks with citizens or interest groups in governance networks. These go beyond the basic dyads of different actor–actor relationships and ensure that information management systems are aligned in such a way that they can achieve their managerial goals.

Strategic management capacity comes from the leverage and capacity an organization has within inter-institutional relationships with other stakeholders and organizations (Coremans and Meissner 2018). In modern government, many administrative tasks are outsourced, and principal among their tasks are coordination and communication of information by participating in networks and interacting with external stakeholders (Rabovsky 2014a). Finding and understanding performance information in such forms of networked organization is very challenging. In such an environment, information intermediaries of any kinds of political actor – other public administrators, elected officials or third parties – are critical to developing and maintaining intelligent network relationships.

Strategic information management involves not just the *what* and *how* of managing information, but also the *who*; that is, who among the political actors supplied the information and what are the consequences of knowledge for different stakeholders. Information is always sent or received by specific individuals who are holders of different kinds of power. For example, an immigrant (normally someone with weak power) may send a request for asylum to a home affairs department (normally a large department with lots of power). Similarly, who provides and receives the information influences how important or actionable that information is considered to be (Blom-Hansen et al. 2016). For example, addressing an asylum request concerns not just how much merit the request has, but the capacity the department has to agree to the request or to influence other parties that influence the decision. If capacity is limited, there is room for other considerations to be taken into account, and political considerations such as trying to co-opt powerful actors such as other political leaders or citizen opinion may make more headway.

## Managing institutional reputation

One big repercussion of the dynamics regarding open, and increasingly contested, information is that public managers need to be experts on how these flows influence the political perception of their own work as a form of reputation management. Some public managers may work in a communication or media liaisons capacity. Here, understanding the political sensitivity of information is highly important. In a study of 1,012 public managers from Australia, New Zealand and the United Kingdom, Hartley et al. (2015) found that political astuteness was a skill essential to the manager's abilities to bring an understanding of democratic politics and public values into their daily management. Similarly, according to Van der Wal (2017), at a time when public institutions face legitimacy challenges, public managers can use their expertise and central position within the information ecosystem to connect different stakeholders and build and maintain legitimacy.

Over time, the way that information from government is communicated to the public at large has powerful consequences, even shaping the fate of entire institutions. Bertelli and Sinclair (2015) found that attention from newspapers which is either supportive or in opposition to specific agencies influences long-term administrative decisions towards those agencies such as their economic support or their eventual defunding and termination. Of course, it would be unlikely that newspaper coverage over a single point in time for a specific event could ever be sufficient to persuade ministers to terminate an agency. However, the Bertelli and Sinclair research shows that political mediation by the media is very important for the fate of public organizations, and that the way that information is communicated has consequences in the long term. The type of media attention received by government contributes to important social and political discourses that ultimately begin to have an impact regardless of the 'facts' about how well the agency is performing.

Not only is the content of information about public organizations important, but also the regularity of that information. If political consequences are serious, this can have consequences for the ability of public manager's departments to do their work effectively. For instance, it has even been observed by researchers that the very *absence* of media discussion can have an impact on the information ecosystem of politics, albeit in a more disruptive way. According to a six-year longitudinal study of media attention on the topic of asylum and immigration, Boswell (2012) observed that if information is scarce then political attention is affected and occasional rises in attention can be disruptive because managing sudden increases in information is presumably more challenging than managing a predictable, steady supply of information.

Public managers should also be aware of the role that politicians play in this dynamic. Elected officials may behave in a similarly strategic political way to insulate bureaucracy from sharing policy information that can be used by opposition elected officials, or in blame games. According to principal-agent theory, public administrators are never really their own masters (Moe 1984). Rather they work at the beck and call of an endless series of superiors who are voted in and out of office every few years. This basic observation about the situation facing strategic calculations of principals and agents leads to a fascinating game played by both parties to use information in such a way as to gain an advantage over the other. On the agent side, public managers – under the strictly self-interested approach of principal-agent theory – use their information advantage gained from hands-on experience in the decision-making processes of government to keep politicians at arm's length or to influence key parties in ways that work to their interests. By the same token, public managers should be aware that, on the principal side, political superiors have certain powers to choose who their agents will be. They can also change policies or laws in the hope of influencing public administrators to change their behaviour.

The principal-agent perspective sometimes seems to imply that politicians and managers are enemies. Experience of public management in reality shows that this is not the case. However, principal-agent theory is still a powerful tool for public managers to understand what incentivizes political actors to act in ways that suit their own interests but may restrict or manipulate the information available to others. This latter example of strategic behaviour, which Reenock and Gerber (2007) have called 'design-induced political insulation', may lead to public information management losing sufficient public accountability, but it nevertheless plays a key role in how agencies plan their role as information mediators. Evidence suggests that this shift in skills is already taking place for public managers. The change in availability of information has ended the neutral expertise model of bureaucratic expertise. For example, public managers can strategically share information with contacts who can minimize transaction costs and maximize outreach and information (Leifeld and Schneider 2012). Change in availability of information also highlights the need for public managers to simultaneously engage in the other dyads. Information can be shared collectively by departmental agencies in order to pool information resources and create common information sharing standards and performance metrics that overcome proprietary information ownership and bureaucratic departmental silos. In some cases, new kinds of data management architectures are helping managers to do this more effectively. See, for example, the description of the Estonian X-tee in Box 7.2.

---

## Box 7.2: The Estonian X-tee

The Estonian X-tee (originally called the X-Road), launched in 2001, is an example of an entirely integrated data management system. The X-tee connects all departments and citizens in a single information highway where information is created and managed in a decentralized way by each public agency allowing information to be quickly shared by any user in the system. What is really remarkable about the X-tee is how it was born in a deliberate, planned approach to succeed the crumbling bureaucratic infrastructure after the end of the Soviet Union. Seeing the need to rapidly advance its capacities as a new state, the system was built virtually from scratch. Coupled with this unique political structure, Estonia, at the time of its independence, also had several technology universities and a decentralized system of government departmental computer centres.

*Source:* Kattel and Kalvet (2006)

---

# Engaging citizens and interest groups

In addition to information from experts, public managers rely on information that is already in the public sphere – generated by both experts and non-experts – and actively seek information to achieve their managerial tasks. This difficult position was worryingly highlighted by the role that government leaders took in countries around the world during the Covid-19 pandemic. Identifying the most important scientific and policy expertise on which to base a governmental response as well as communicating that effectively with the public became an urgent priority, though there was huge variability in how successfully it was done. According to Ansell, Sørensen and Torfing (2020, 952), in such turbulent times, 'the public sector must meet turbulence with robust strategies where creative and agile public organizations adapt to the emergence of new disruptive problems by building networks and partnerships with the private sector and civil society'.

Due to the digitalization of information and the rapid communication of information over the internet, citizens have become more aware of what goes on inside government. Performance feedback from citizens is increasingly available in the form of online service statistics that show how frequently citizens consume different kinds of services, from using public transport to paying to visit public cultural events. The task of coordinating other groups with important information has also grown in importance for their work. Interest groups (groups that are motivated by policy or political interests to get involved in government policy) often have good information resources and have taken on greater significance. Digitalization processes have also strengthened the position of interest groups in public policy. The reason for this, according to Bellamy (1996), is that the informatization of public services reinforces political pressures towards rationalization and cost-cutting by focusing on specific clients. Digitalization has rationalized information management in both front and back office systems for delivering public services.

Today, changes in the shape of information networks are increasingly rapid, which places more responsibility on managers to adapt and design their networks at speed. Crozier (2010) argues that the fact that information is an essential productive resource means that circulation of information – the flow-puts – have become more important than the information inputs and outputs of information management. There is increasing social complexity and reflexivity of knowledge. In this environment, dynamic and emergent configurations characterize communication events with no pre-set roles, and public managers play a critical role in shaping public information flows. As Crozier says, this is an 'open license to get things done'. As information mediators, public managers focus on understanding and controlling the flow-puts of information; understanding where it comes from and how it can be diverted to the right places.

Interest groups, particularly nonprofit groups that deliver some services such as education or health that are similar to public organizations, often have a very good understanding of what goods citizens need. They are therefore good data-sharing partners for public managers. Interest groups can sometimes be very powerful, but at other times they are quite small organizations with minor political and economic influence. In either case, interest groups often hold expert knowledge that public managers would like access to. To this end, public managers can use the information provided by interest groups but only if they consider what the interest groups seek in return as interest groups are by definition interested in achieving specific political goals and will not easily give up their informational advantages.

---

### Box 7.3: Hurricane Katrina

Hurricane Katrina in 2005 is a notorious example of how key emergency response efforts can be hampered by the failure to share important information.[3] Multiple organizations were involved in critical risk management and emergency rescue efforts before, during and after the hurricane landed on the southern coast of the Gulf of Mexico. Conflicting political loyalties meant that two major national agencies – the Federal Emergency Management Agency (FEMA) and the US Army Corps of Engineers – did not make the risks of flood planning clear to local authorities in cities that were affected by the hurricane such as New Orleans. The US President, George W. Bush, head of FEMA Michael Brown and the New Orleans mayor Ray Nagin were each anxious to demonstrate their leadership credentials, though the existing protocols for delegating leadership were based on guidance that was decades old and provided no basis for them to collaborate in a unitary fashion. Ultimately, local organizers and other groups such as the Red Cross became the conduits for collecting and sharing rescue information including arranging transport and identifying places where people could find shelter.

---

# Normative challenges of managing public information

## Management bias and neutrality

The American news show host and comedian Stephen Colbert famously said with tongue in cheek that 'reality has a well-known liberal bias' (Groeling 2013, p. 137). This claim has often been repeated by political progressives who see the tendency for socially liberal public policies to be more open to diverse viewpoints rather than fixed according to traditional moral norms, as political conservatives tend to believe. Conservatives in turn often accuse liberals of lacking simple common sense and aspiring to wishy-washy social goals rather than sticking to facts. It is thus clear that where information bias

---

[3] See Garnett and Kouzmin (2009) for an extensive review of the Katrina catastrophe from a communication perspective.

begins and neutrality ends is a highly politically contested problem. How we should strategically use public information is itself a political question. Research has shown that political opinion influences how public officials use information. For example, the political ideology of university presidents is a factor that determines whether or not they embrace performance measurement as a public information tool (Rabovsky 2014b).

Cognitive psychology has taught public managers that human beings are incurably biased in the ways that they acquire, process and act upon information. Human beings are not robots that can process information in a detached way. Rather, information always has repercussions for how it can satisfy human needs and desires. This calls for a certain amount of self-scrutiny by public managers. Understanding the natural way that the mind processes information is therefore key for public managers, both for understanding their own biases and those of others. Bias can be pervasive in areas of government that are supposed to be rooted to detached scientific reasoning. Even something as important as forecasting economic trends in order to plan public spending by national governments is prone to bias as public agencies will change the optimism of their economic forecasts if they anticipate reputation damage from failing to meet their forecasts (Krause and Corder 2007).

This matter of bias becomes especially important if public managers are developing automated decision-making systems that may have bias programmed into their algorithms (Busuioc 2021). Scholars such as Karen Yeung (2017) and Rob Kitchin (2014) have warned that algorithms in the public sector are being used to sort through information and make public service decisions that automate human biases. This can exacerbate the digital divide and lead to biases in the way that public organizations such as police or tax authorities make interventions in investigations or auditing. Scholars therefore warn that some forms of algorithmic decision-making should not be used if they are likely to attenuate areas of political or social unfairness. At the least, public managers need to think carefully when they decide to use such systems. Other research suggests that the role for public managers goes beyond the decision to select certain kinds of performance tools to decisions about how exactly to use the tools after their adoption (Yang 2008; Van der Wal 2017).

Bias in public management systems has also been observed in performance measurement regimes. A management tool such as performance measurement may seem to be politically neutral, but its use may actually be partially dependent on an agency's political leaning with agencies that are closer to the right of the political spectrum being most likely to use performance information systems (Lavertu and Moynihan 2012). At the top, ministers in a government agency are typically appointed by the political party in power, and the symbolic value of adopting a particular type of information management strategy, such as performance measurement, can have profound consequences on the kinds of leadership used across government.

In this respect, agency leaders signal what kinds of general political and cultural values they will put at the centre of their regime. Indeed, symbolic battles are at the root of public information management strategies that at first glance may seem merely technical matters. Neutral interpretations of laws are supposed to be carried out according to bureaucratic principles that, on the surface, appear to be simple execution of the law, while in fact, bureaucratic discretion can easily influence outcomes based on small tweaks that do not appear to be politically motivated. That is until closer attention is paid. For example, in the accessibility and duration of the public regulation comments process lies significant space for political discretion (Balla 2015).

# Social media and misinformation

Public managers today have to navigate the complex environment created by viral news, personality politics and social media spin (see Box 7.4 for an example). Information has social and political potential; its tendency to be manipulated, misunderstood and weaponized has real world consequences for institutional and leader reputations, financial behaviour, political movements and the legitimacy of scientific and medical evidence. Due to this power of information, the SPIM sphere and the media are intricately interconnected. The crossing over of these spheres reveals that there is an information ecosystem where the public information that is often produced in public organizations meets with the public information that is disseminated, analyzed and discussed in the media.

In some countries, governments take an aggressive approach to managing social media, but even in less repressive contexts, the question of how information is presented and framed for public consumption remains vital (for an example of repressive use of social media, see Box 7.5). Public managers thus face a normative challenge of how to adapt to the social media era while taking responsibility for how information could be perceived and consumed in the public sphere.

## Box 7.4: Micro-targeting and fake news

In 2016, long-held assumptions about how public information and deliberation should influence democratic politics were thrown into doubt by surprise results from two major political events: the election of Donald Trump as President of the United States, and the United Kingdom's referendum on membership of the European Union that resulted in Brexit. In the wake of those events, it emerged that cleverly placed adverts and even fake social media posts created by malicious bots and web crawlers heavily affected the decisions of voters. Tech companies regularly use micro-targeting to personalize adverts for social media users. But the aim of these political algorithm-based tools was to shape public opinion in favour of specific policy choices or political leaders. Further these campaigns were often found to be orchestrated by countries against other countries. Facebook, the most popular social media platform worldwide, is particularly vulnerable to misinformation campaigns of this kind. Facebook's CEO, Mark Zuckerberg, was summoned to give evidence to the United States Congress. Social media companies are now expected to take proactive measures to prevent dangerous misinformation campaigns. The role of micro-targeting campaigns in the Brexit referendum was fascinatingly portrayed in the HBO television series, *Brexit: The Uncivil War*.

## Box 7.5: Social media and surveillance

In the Islamic Republic of Iran, freedom of speech is heavily curtailed. In 2009 in the wake of pro-democracy protests, the Iranian government was widely reported to be monitoring social media pages of citizens in hopes of catching people the government suspected of stoking the unrest and criticism. Supporters of all sides of the political spectrum relied heavily on social media to promote their political party, but the Iranian establishment feared that social media would lead to too much negative commentary about the political system and embolden dissidents. The journalist Yevgeny Morozov has called this approach to monitoring social media, 'open intelligence gathering' because it is relatively easy for the government to spy on what people publish on social media.

*Sources:* Grossman (2009); Morozov (2011)

These normative challenges are difficult for public managers to manage because they concern commercial social media platforms over which they have little control. When using social media, public managers should understand political values and know how to weigh the symbolic value of information in addition to the factual accuracy of the information. Misinformation is information that has been shared with the intended aim to present it as accurate, when in fact it is not. But symbolic value appeals to the human meanings that are embedded in information beyond its factual or scientific value. What really matters from a symbolic point of view is how the information is *perceived*; what the information means to different individuals and groups based on how the information adds or subtracts to psychological or moral values regarding political identity or cultural values.

# Transparency and accountability

A well-functioning democracy relies on a well-informed citizenry. Education of citizens through sharing of public information is critical for detecting credibility of information sources when assessing accountability of politicians (Weitz-Shapiro and Winters 2017). Transparency is the process of making information availability meet the needs of specific institutional and political actors (Heimstädt and Dobusch 2018). Indeed, freedom of information users tend to have political purposes in mind when they seek information (Michener and Worthy 2018). Rationally, then, information about decisions made by government should be widely available and accessible for citizens. In fact, while this may seem an appropriate principle for public managers to follow, the problem is that it is often not in the self-interest of elected public officials to make all information available to onlookers who are potentially highly critical. Public managers may frequently find themselves, therefore, caught between a rock and a hard place.

Another problem with transparency is that it can negatively affect public trust and satisfaction. In the book *Democracy's Double-Edged Sword: How internet use changes citizens' views of their government*, Bailard (2014) collected international data on internet use and citizen attitudes such as trust. After analyzing her data, Bailard draws a startling conclusion: rather than helping democracy as some have claimed, ICT development has dual effects: in countries with political problems of corruption and poor rule of law, the internet, by revealing and spreading more information about corruption, seems to make citizens less satisfied and more distrustful of the government.

Of course, dissatisfaction with corruption is a good thing especially if it can prompt government reform. But the result may also be a blame game; or rather, a game of hide and seek between public officials and external information users (citizens) who negotiate what kinds of information should be shared, and when. Public managers find themselves in the middle of this game with important decisions to make in regard to what information they can make available and how. The example from the United Kingdom's open data programme illustrates this well in Box 7.6. Decisions about transparency are political, and decision-makers may decide to strategically control the release of types of information to lessen the impact of negative consequences as well as boost the possibility of positive consequences.

---

## Box 7.6: The risks of transparency

The scholar Benjamin Worthy (2015) has studied closely some of the perverse effects that politicization can have on transparency initiatives such as open data. Worthy studied the evolution and growth of the open data movement in the United Kingdom, a country ranked by the Open Data Barometer as a world leader on open data for many years.[4] Worthy described the impact of open data initiatives on the UK government as 'complex, unpredictable, and political'. Local government councils in England were required to publish information on their spending in a public data repository in line with the hope of policymakers that this would prompt members of the public to examine the data and encourage a better culture of accountability in the councils. However, other kinds of unexpected political problems occurred as a result. Councils had some leeway to decide what kinds of data to share and how to present it in the most favourable light. The users of the data were also representative of a narrow segment of society, which posed the question of how democratic the influences of the open data would be on the council's actions and spending policies.

*Source:* Worthy (2015)

---

[4] The Open Data Barometer ranks countries annually on their ability to use and employ open data, https://opendatabarometer.org.

# Conclusions

In this chapter, we positioned public information management within the realm of politics, with contestation of public information for political gain by various actors being a pressing issue. Public managers need to learn to navigate their political environment by using the right skills to deal strategically with the influence of politicized information, because it highlights how public information is never politically neutral; there will always be a political context to information, and there will also be political consequences to the management of information.

There are two primary types of issues that pertain to political SPIM – normative and strategic – and both of these matter profoundly to the skill set the public managers should avail themselves of as they negotiate and function within networked relationships between political actors. At the beginning of the chapter, we posed the following questions, which we can now use to summarize the key points of the chapter:

- *What are the important characteristics of a political system, and what do these entail for strategic management of public information?* In democratic political systems there are key institutions such as elected political assemblies, civil society and the free press. Four key actors are elected public officials, public administrators, citizens and interest groups. Each group can, instrumentally, add value to information. Further, normative questions relating to political implications are different for each. By identifying the kinds of political relationships or dyads involved, public managers can ask salient political questions that prepare them for the kinds of expectations the actors will have. Managers certainly need not agree with these expectations, but awareness of them can prevent misunderstanding.
- *What political knowledge and skills do public managers need to get the most value out of information?* Public managers are better placed to use information strategically if they understand the political system of which they are part. In today's collaborative, networking approach to governance, communication, mediation, cultural sensitivity and relationship-building skills are highly important. Public managers have more opportunity today to delegate to other actors such as other public service personnel, contractors or citizens, and to strategically co-manage technologies as well as the public norms, and values involved in the use of technologies.

- *What are the main strategic information management questions for relationships with different political actors?* Depending on the relationship dyad, public managers have different sets of questions. These questions concern the kinds of information that can be shared and the sorts of values or norms that belong to that particular dyad. Interest groups can also increasingly become instrumental supporters of the engineer. Interest groups are increasingly specialized as political representatives that have expert knowledge and technologies that can help public managers to do their work. But there are risks that come with this role for interest groups given their ability to strongly affect the shape that information policy takes.
- *What are the key strategic opportunities for public information in a political system?* We discussed four key opportunities: 1) information as a critical resource; 2) information ecosystems and cycles; 3) public managers as information mediators; and 4) the role of interest groups. Public managers are strategically well placed to mediate and use information as a critical resource that can be shared with critical actors in the ecosystem.
- *What are the key normative challenges for public information in a political system?* We discuss three key challenges: 1) management bias and neutrality; 2) e-participation and citizen and media relations; and 3) transparency and accountability. As public managers are strategically placed to manage information that influences each of these normative areas, it is their responsibility to address this challenge by drawing attention to bias, wisely managing e-participation opportunities for citizens and ensuring that decision-making processes are transparent and accountable.

# KEY LESSONS FROM CHAPTER 7

- Information can be a highly politicized matter and it therefore behoves public managers to understand how it can be used by different kinds of political actors.
- Understanding the role of citizens, public administrators, public officials and interests groups is critical to SPIM because it helps public managers to be sensitive to the perspectives and interests of different political actors and their role within a political system.

- The complex data ecosystems of public management rely on information intermediaries. Intermediaries such as the media and research organizations are important for public managers to work with.
- Understanding politics relies on understanding the highly symbolic value that information can have. This can impact institutional reputation, which influences how public managers do their work.
- The value of information resources in political systems can lead to data and information being misrepresented or misinterpreted. In this environment, neutrality and clear communication are vital.
- SPIM will increasingly rely on an approach of 'politically intelligent information'. Important properties of such an approach are building staff skills and capacity for managing information, understanding the close connection between information management and public values, and building the right relationships with different actors in the political system.

# 8

# Strategic public information management as innovation challenge

*This concluding chapter stresses that strategic public information management (SPIM) requires a continuous effort from public managers since changes in technology and society are ongoing. SPIM is never finished; it always needs to be updated. We discuss how public managers can take steps towards more strategic public information management by focusing on their organization's innovative capacities. We also emphasize that this requires a new type of public manager who is aware of the key role of information and technology and is able to steer the organization through processes of continuous change. Managing this ongoing organizational transformation is the key task for public managers in an information age.*

## Introduction

The overarching message of this book is that public managers need to respond in a strategic way to the continuous changes in technology and society. In their responses, they need to recognize new responsibilities and the kinds of managerial dexterity that are needed for not only surviving but also for driving their organizations towards excellence in all areas from policymaking and regulation through to politics and citizen engagement. We have broken down the major spheres of the challenge by each chapter, and have given practical suggestions, case examples and frameworks to guide public managers. However, any reader of this book who is engaged in the daily activity of developing their own organization may rightly wonder what they can do to prepare their own management style and the capacity of their organizations to effectively deal with the *process* of change. This question is one of innovation, the capacity to continuously reshape the organization, and it is this capacity that forms the final focus of this book.

In this chapter, we highlight that SPIM requires a continuous focus on organizational transformation. We present public sector innovation frameworks which managers can use to move forward step by step. We also take a more critical view of the digital innovations that public managers are tasked with handling and consider the negative impacts they could have on the public sector. These risks need to be balanced with the positive aspects, and we make recommendations for how SPIM can make the best of this situation. We will keep this overarching goal in mind, but will also go further and offer practical suggestions. This chapter is concerned with delving into *how* innovative approaches built around SPIM are produced and sustained, and what managers can do to make SPIM an integral part of the information management process.

In brief, we answer the question from managers seeking to go from information to innovation: *'how can we get there?'*. We also set this question within a scholarly context and examine how researchers can support practitioners by building on the concept of SPIM. In particular, the following questions will be addressed:

- What risks or negative impacts can result from the wrong kinds of innovation?
- What are the different capacities of managers and who should be involved in the different phases of a process of innovation?
- How can public managers take a strategic, long-term approach to creating innovative organizations which will not just meet the current innovation demands but keep on doing so in the future?

This chapter begins by arguing that innovation is of key importance to SPIM in view of the continuous changes in technology and society and it also stresses that these processes of innovation are not without risk. Subsequently, a model of five phases of innovation is used to identify the key capacities of public managers. We continue to argue that the requirements for public managers go beyond a set of capacities: new public managers who are able to continuously innovate the organization and adapt it to ongoing changes are needed for the information age. We end the chapter, and the book, by emphasizing that SPIM is never finished: it requires continuous innovation.

# Key importance of innovation for SPIM

By 'innovation for strategic public information management' we mean new approaches used to integrate the rapidly evolving digital tools that collect, organize, analyze, present and reuse information. Innovation in information management is about how organizations seek to adopt and capitalize on new technologies and associated management processes. Each period in the history of government has had notable innovations in this sense. We have already introduced the major types of technological innovation that interest public managers in today's world: *software for project management* for delivery of services such as building public infrastructure or piloting a new public service; *desktop programmes* for design of communication or legal materials such as new laws, service advisory posters, websites, etc.; *mobile devices* that can be carried by public officials to enable work tasks such as smart monitors to track activities of, say, security personnel or back office staff; and *internet-enabled big data platforms* for integrating data and digital tools from multiple locations such as cloud technology for storing data, wikis for sharing website features and smart tools for automated processing.[1]

Technology changes are expeditious, and a recurring worry of managers in organizations – both public and private – is that they will somehow fail to get where they need to be to keep up with the latest technology. Causes of this worry are many, ranging from cultural concerns such as being too static and inward-looking, not being young and hip enough or having an outmoded organizational culture, to the more technical such as insufficient information about competitors, failing to hire staff with the right skills and falling foul of legal or financial rules and regulations, or perhaps fundamentally just not being able to afford the latest and best technology. Other managers would – with some justification – put these matters of innovation progress down to falling into the right bit of luck or stumbling across an innovative idea accidentally.

Without a strategic approach to innovative uses of technology and information management, processes will not just remain stultified but may

---

[1] For further information on current ICT trends, see gsa.gov/technology for United States General Services Administration (GSA) information technology services. It has a detailed listing of the kinds of ICT that government regularly seek from technology providers.

actually result in unintended and harmful consequences. Innovation is highly prized in organizations, but it should not be viewed as an unalloyed good with only positive effects. According to Meijer and De Jong (2019), managing innovation risks means that public managers are forced to make strategic choices about the types of public values to promote such as transparency, efficiency, security and rule of law. For example, the risk of unforeseen security risks means that information needs to be tightly secured. This might serve public values of efficiency (saving money that might be lost through cybercrime) and security, but, simultaneously, the value of transparency will be negatively impacted if the information needs to be hidden behind secure infrastructure.

Risks of innovation are amplified because of the fast rate of technology change today. According to Schilling (2015), rapid technology change creates uncertainty and opportunity, and networks and collaboration are needed to turn this into innovations. The arrival of the internet and its impact on organizations has led to a large technology shock that has increased the need for organizations to develop business alliances and partnerships (Schilling 2015). In reality, one of the main pressures that managers face in the public sector is that innovative technologies or the processes involved in managing them are contracted out to the private sector precisely because of a lack of specialist skills within existing human resources to deal with the risks. The possibility of things going wrong through mismanagement is high when technology change is rapid and public organizations exist within complex interorganizational and intersectoral networks (see Box 8.1 for an insight into Shoshana Zuboff's theory of the dangers of creeping private control of technology innovations).

In a nutshell, what is new and empowering is not necessarily good for public managers. One of the recurring themes of this book is that information management is a complex business, and it requires a high level of vigilance by public managers. This vigilance has major impacts for the way that innovation is managed because public managers must address novel ways to manage risk and avoid major crises and negative impacts of technology.

Once organizations adopt a technology, we tend to assume that most of the hard work has been done. But whether managers actually use innovations in the right way when their organizations adopt them is not a foregone conclusion (Lee 2008). There are many different kinds of negative effects. A whole range of dangers need to be strategically dealt with by

## Box 8.1: A new age of information capitalism?

According to Shoshana Zuboff (2019) in her book *The Age of Surveillance Capitalism*, the omnipresence of rich information sources has led to a type of innovation model that exploits personal and individual experiences that technology users share through the internet. This is a kind of predatory model that is highly lucrative and which technology companies pursue without many legal or moral checks on their power. Zuboff calls this model 'The Dispossession Cycle', and it consists of four stages: incursion, habituation, adaptation and redirection. Incursion involves organizations finding sources of information that technology users view indifferently as a kind of surplus that they have no need for. Critically, incursion involves a kind of pseudo legal appropriation where the data becomes 'theirs' because they are the ones that have obtained it and have the technological wherewithal to use it. Habituation involves the 'combination of agreement, helplessness, and resignation' (140) shown by the original owners of the personal data, and the dependencies that result from the role of tech companies as providers of technology platforms, devices and other products. Adaptation refers to the clever way that tech companies amend their practices to fit in with legal and regulative frameworks set up by governments.

public managers. Meijer et al. (2019) carried out a comprehensive literature review and consulted a range of experts on their views of innovation risks. The research resulted in a taxonomy of the dark sides of innovation. There are ten categories of perverse effects that can follow innovation processes if public managers are not careful. Indeed, even when they are aware of these challenges, dealing with them can be an altogether different matter. The ten perverse effects are:

1 *Lack of stability.* Constant or regular changes in technologies and practices can prevent organizations from developing a regular system of processes and functions. Organizations need this to create uniformity and coherence for organizational members and users of products and services.

2 *Illegal practices.* Some innovations push up against the boundaries of existing legal precepts and rules. As a result, rules may become broken either because they offer individuals the wrong incentives or because they open up legal loopholes that were previously not noticed. Privacy laws have become particularly affected in this way.

3 *Corruption.* Innovations can increase corruption by opening up new gateways for illegal interference or by opening up lucrative opportunities for individuals to exploit.

4 *Waste of public money.* The attraction of a new innovation may lead public managers to adopt it without careful planning. In such cases, public money can become wasted either because of mismanagement or because the innovation was no better than existing approaches.

5 *Absence of democratic control.* Many technological innovations, particularly those such as artificial intelligence (AI) and big data, give extraordinary powers to businesses to shape political process that circumvent traditional processes of democratic control by 'the people'.

6 *Damage to local initiatives.* One of the main benefits of ICT innovations such as mobile apps or news media is that they reach a greater number of people at greater speed. But while this is beneficial in some respects, it may lead to democratic efforts at a smaller, local level being crowded out.

7 *Disruption of power balance.* In the age of the internet, the famous saying 'knowledge is power' has taken on greater urgency. ICT innovations have created a new landscape to political power in a way that is often unpredictable.

8 *Undesirability according to many actors.* Some innovations, such as biometric systems or surveillance, are often strongly opposed by a significant number of relevant stakeholders. This happens because the innovations are perceived as potentially harmful or disruptive.

9 *Technocratic dominance in public processes.* As ICT innovations increasingly enter into every area of our lives, there is a risk that machine-based processes will displace traditional (human) public processes.

10 *Unforeseen security risks.* Rapid technological innovation has multiplied the ICT platforms used for everyday tasks. There are countless points of remote contact between individuals and government. These need to be made secure from criminal interference, but doing so is hard to do without some vulnerabilities.

The need to strategically manage these risks becomes more acute as perception of positive and negative effects of innovation will also be a subjective matter which the various stakeholders in information systems will view differently. As we have seen from De Vries, Tummers and Bekkers (2018), it is quite likely that some organizational members will view the effects of an innovation very differently from others because of the variation in interests and priorities that come with different organizational positions. Initially, the qualities of usefulness and experience are important in determining employee adoption of a new innovation, but after a while use becomes routine and the usefulness becomes less important. Routinization can introduce negative effects of their own, too, if employees become complacent or miss opportunities to check and improve their systems (Antòn, Camarero and San José 2014).

# Required capacities for public innovation

So what do public managers need to do to ensure successful innovation can occur in their organizations? We can break down public innovation to continuously re-adjust SPIM into five distinct phases, following the approach of Meijer (2015): 1) idea generation, 2) idea selection, 3) idea testing, 4) idea promotion and 5) idea roll-out. These phases can be used to identify the capacities that are needed to realize public innovation. We have summarized the main SPIM capacities of each phase in Table 8.1 on page 204.

## Phase 1: Required capacities for idea generation

The problem at the centre of idea generation concerns the level of involvement from citizens. Higher levels of ICT sophistication are highly variable in government (Nasi, Frosini and Cristofoli 2011). According to Thompson (1965), you can actually compare organizational sophistication in this way to an individual person's capacity for creativity and sophistication. Certain practices and habits can go a long way to enhancing this capacity to generate fresh ideas as they can for an individual. It involves the public information manager having a good knowledge of what ingredients help with innovativeness and organizational change. These ingredients of creativity diverge significantly from many traditional ways of understanding government organizations. Today, managers tend to use *flexibility* and *professionalism* rather than what Thompson (1965) called duty-based roles, departmentalization and parochialism, which discourage freedom and innovation.

Research has found, for example, that the idea to adopt social media by managers is determined not by unilateral leadership decisions but by an interplay of individual and organizational factors, organizational culture and formal guidance on using social media (Fusi and Feeney 2018). Managers cannot rely only on internal organizational talent to be technically matched to every single possible new technology innovation. Rather, SPIM is a profoundly collective process, and that is why cultivating external relationships is such a key managerial activity (Lusch and Nambisan 2015). Research shows that external pressure from citizens and non-governmental organizations plays a critical role in encouraging public managers to innovate (Wang and Feeney 2016). Technologies may be helpful for public managers to cultivate such relationships. For example, relationships can be fostered through service platforms that make exchange of information more efficient and more dense/diverse. Such network resources also enable value co-creation that helps to integrate the resources needed for organizational change.

There is another reason for public managers to act in this way: citizens and NGOs often have stronger exposure to the latest technologies and ideas and can therefore act as a kind of support or advisory mechanism to idea generation in government agencies. Citizens and NGOs at the grassroots can act as advocates for specific policies or programmes and use their role as representatives of service users to build legitimacy for those policies or programmes. Hackathons can be a good way of harnessing this knowledge, as illustrated in Box 8.2. Indeed, empirical evidence also shows that external pressures such as seeking legitimacy from peer organizations and external demands from citizens are more important than internal bureaucratic politics in e-government innovation (Jun and Weare 2010).

> ## Box 8.2: A hackathon to improve urban mobility policies/ideas/thinking in the Netherlands
>
> Hackathons are competitions where participants attempt to 'hack' an element of governmental operations such as a specific service delivery programme, computer software or policy statute thereby testing new ideas that can improve what currently exists. Hackathons normally grant privileged access to rules, internal documentation, data or code that make hacking a genuinely innovative task with practical consequences for what happens next. In 2018, the city of Zwolle organized a hackathon to solicit ideas for improving the economic mobility of young people as they progress from education into careers. Multidisciplinary teams were organized comprising government, business, educationalists and students to develop innovative digital programmes which addressed the persistent gap of information and opportunities that often make the transition from university to the workplace difficult, confusing and ineffective both for students and industry.

# Phase 2: Required capacities for idea selection

The main challenge at the centre of idea selection is balancing dynamic decision-making with organizational structure. According to Tolbert, Mossberger and McNeal (2008), putting in place the right decision-making architecture is vital for long-term planning in innovation. A decision-making architecture or governance system determines the quality of organizational decision-making in deciding between alternative kinds of technological innovations to pursue.

Having interviewed hundreds of public managers about management innovation in local government in the United States, Tolbert and colleagues found that institutional capacity (presence of IT board, CIO and intergovernmental architecture) and reform orientation are important, and wealth and education are important at later stages. Public managers may not of course have the means to easily adjust their wealth and education level, but institutional capacity and reform orientation among colleagues can be developed.

Today, one of the most important SPIM capacities in management decision architectures for the selection of new ideas is *open innovation*. According to Westergren and Holmström (2012), 'adoption of the open innovation model is grounded in developing organizational environments that are conducive to innovation, including expertise in creating a culture for knowledge sharing, building a trustful environment, and a resourceful use of IT'. Open innovation relies on the crowd: the collective wisdom and input of as many organizational members as possible rather than decision-making by a few people in formal positions (for an example of open innovation, see Box 8.3).

## Box 8.3: The Digital Services Playbook

The Digital Services Playbook is an open source digital services and software development platform developed by the United States department of Organization Management and Budget (OMB). The initiative was an idea of Barack Obama's White House team and the federal agency, 18F. Like other non-governmental open source platforms such as Github, the Digital Playbook is a user-oriented approach to innovation. However, in this case it is focused on the improvement of governmental services that will assist collaboration between governmental agencies and participation of citizens and civil society organizations. The guidance in the Playbook revolves around thirteen 'plays', which are practical pieces of wisdom for developing collaboration innovative projects. The plays cover all areas involved in turning an innovative idea into a new service, such as 'understand what people need', 'build the service using agile and iterative practices' and 'structure budgets and contracts to support delivery'. Despite advocating an open and non-proprietary approach to developing government services, the Digital Services Playbook has continued to be a useful tool for government agencies. The organization that created the Playbook, 18F, has grown in size since its founding in 2014 and continues to have an important impact on digital services innovation in the federal government.

We would argue that many of the most effective strategies for public managers may not be specific policy interventions designed to bring about change through rational design of systems per se, but rather the development of relationship building practices. These may be more difficult for managers to create from scratch, but managers can nevertheless shape such factors using collaborative practices. In idea selection, relationship building is particularly important for SPIM for another reason. According to Homburg, Dijkshoorn and Thaens (2014), human factors (as much as structural ones) contribute twice as much as technological opportunity and rational cost-benefit considerations. Their theory suggests that environmental factors such as citizen expectations, peer rivalry and national programmes must be shaped by managers in a process of framing before they are turned into organizational innovations. Such framing activities involve: 1) active engagement with other organizations and stakeholders, 2) championing support for organizational efficacy and image and 3) channelling communication and building organizational narratives that bind the participants together.

# Phase 3: Required capacities for idea testing

The challenge for public managers working at the stage of idea testing is deciding on the required level of expert knowledge. While public managers cannot collect as much data about citizens to the same degree as their counterpart in a private technology company such as Microsoft or Google, they still have possibilities with regard to administrative data that is collected from citizens.

Quinn (1992, 120) points out that, while public organizations do not face the same competitive pressures as the private sector, they must, like companies, seek ways to maximize their capacity to change and innovate. He suggests that 'A truly maintainable competitive edge usually derives from developing depth in skill sets, experience factors, innovative capacities, know-how, market understanding, databases, or information-distribution systems—all service activities—others cannot duplicate or exceed.' Public managers can take advantage of these core competencies for SPIM and develop them up-stream as well as down-stream in the development of new information-based innovations such as machine learning tools, filtering systems and cloud computing.

In all aspects of SPIM, it is critical for public information managers to get planning right by building a good evidence base. This may call for them to draw from a wider societal pool of knowledge in different phases of innovation (see Box 8.4). The public information manager can play a role here as a fact collector and causal theorist. If you look at statistical agencies, for example, where information technology is vital to their core function, collection of facts for information discipline, security and risk analysis have been found to be vital information technology innovation (Habermann 2010). Decision-making discipline needs to be even higher in such agencies because of the level of expertise now needed for software production as well as the need to accomplish objectives collectively because they do not have individual expertise. A further area of concern for public managers here is that security breaches can badly damage reputations of agencies, and risk analysis calls for service level agreements with other agencies that may have security vulnerabilities affecting statistical data.

## Box 8.4: Communication approaches in different innovation phases

*Citizen participation.* For the individually focused innovations at an early stage of conception, information management for citizen participation is important because the innovations are about direct contact with citizens who have an interest in how the ideas initially take shape in the early conceptualization phases.

*Mission building.* For collectively focused innovation at an early stage of conception, information management for mission building is the most important focus because innovation ideas should ideally emerge from an organization that is driven by a common sense of mission.

*Citizen feedback.* For individual focused innovations at the later stage of innovation implementation, information management of citizen feedback is important. Here, like citizen participation at the conceptualization phase, direct interaction with citizens is important and this citizen connection is vital for keeping an eye on how well the implementation is carried out.

*Organizational communication.* For collectively focused innovations at the later stage of innovation implementation, information management of organizational communication is important. Here, as in the case of mission building, the embeddedness of innovation processes in the larger organization is vital, but, unlike building a mission, the focus is on ensuring implementation is carried out with organizational members all being integrated, accommodated and informed.

One of the fundamental problems with strategic approaches to innovation is that it is often unclear whether managers actually go on to effectively use an innovation when their organizations adopt it. The hottest new technology is no more beneficial than a rock if it is not useful (Lee 2008). During the Covid-19 pandemic, for example, governments struggled to find the best way to use virus-tracking apps. Policymakers were not sure how to use the tool for public health policies as the success of the tool largely depended on the willingness of people to be tracked, and there were ongoing concerns about the personal privacy implications of the apps (Moon 2020). Therefore, for public managers, finding evidence of what employees will find useful, communicating with them and offering training are very important. According to Moynihan and Lavertu (2012), cognitive biases lie behind many of the decisions to adopt new technologies, and evidence should be patiently built and clearly communicated by managers before making decisions.

## Box 8.5: Can computers out-innovate humans? AI and innovation

Artificial intelligence comes in many forms: automated traffic signals, economic prediction, personalized service broadcasts and many other applications which can help public organizations perform better. As the sophistication of these tools grows, policymakers are starting to consider the possibility that an increasing number of traditional administrative or operational professions will be displaced. The United States National Bureau of Economic Research (NBER) calculated that most science fields have experienced a 50–100 per cent increase in the application of robotics, deep learning and symbolic systems to innovation research. Further the NBER believes that the next phase of global business growth will be driven by competition for access to valuable 'big data' data sets and races to develop the most effective algorithms. The authors of the report 'The Impact of Artificial Intelligence on Innovation' argue that only data-sharing collaborations and greater transparency will provide the impetus for the benefits of these innovations to be shared broadly across the economy.

*Source:* Cockburn, Henderson and Stern (2019)

# Phase 4: Required capacities for idea promotion

The SPIM puzzle at the centre of idea promotion is where to focus attention and communication. Aside from personnel decisions, leadership – vision and communication – is key in shaping innovation. In a study of managers in the information technology innovation sphere, Hansen and Nørup (2017) found that a variety of leadership behaviours are important: initial support for the idea, directive leadership in adoption, participative approach to implementation and good vision and communication to adapt to local conditions. Successful public policy leaders are often good at retelling their story again and again in fresh ways to new audiences; a good lesson for public managers to learn so that they can take new innovative ideas where they go so the diffusion follows their career trajectories (Yi, Berry and Chen 2018).

Public managers can also promote new ideas in a bottom-up fashion to encourage a broad human resources approach at all organizational levels (an example of this can be seen in Box 8.6). In 2001, at a time when digital technology innovations were quickly accelerating, the scholar Sandford Borins collected data from all the major international innovation awards prizes in the public sector to find out what best practices the winners claimed were behind their successes (Borins 2001). Overwhelmingly, the innovations were put down to rational *planning*. Furthermore, the innovations frequently came directly from middle and frontline workers, not just senior managers. Borins's findings suggest a vital role for public managers in idea promotion.

However, rational planning is not all. Part of the problem with evaluating the success of an innovation is that perceptions of organizational position are relative. In other words, individuals at different levels of an organization will have a different perspective on the success of an innovation. Thus, individuals at the managerial level might perceive performance differently from those in the non-executive or administrative levels (De Vries, Tummers and Bekkers 2018). Of course, public managers cannot literally take the place of other organizational positions in order to see things from their perspective, but it helps to understand how things may be seen from different points of view. Organizational power shapes these kinds of perceptions because individuals in different positions have different preferences and interests in the way that technology operates.

> ## Box 8.6: Data ecosystem initiative in Italy
>
> In 2019 the Italian government launched a massive mapping project of governmental and non-governmental capacity in artificial intelligence. On the website https://ia.italia.it/en/ai-in-italy/, the government is building an open database of respondents to a survey of AI capacity and planning for the future. Users of the website can find open data and an interactive map to help locate other agencies and organizations with whom they can collaborate. The website was launched by a Task Force for Artificial Intelligence comprising government and private sector technology experts.

# Phase 5: Required capacities for idea roll-out

The main challenge for SPIM in idea roll-out is *organizational learning*. New organizational competencies are difficult to observe directly because organizations are so complex. Today, public management competencies are more dynamic (networked) rather than process oriented as before. According to Schuppan (2014), new 'socio-technical' 'meta-competencies' are needed in a networked organizational system. This means that employees need innovation training that looks beyond quick gains from new technologies to *how* the innovations should be rolled out in preparation for the next technological wave that will soon come along. Skill needs are changing all the time. *Reskilling* is the dominant trend where employees are able to flexibly adapt to change. Orellana (2015) sees holistic process or information systems ways of thinking as essential (see Box 8.7 for an example of why this can be important for innovative organizations). Technology automation can cause upskilling, deskilling or reskilling of personnel skills. If the level of automation is high, the best response to innovation is to focus management on understanding the full information system. On the other hand, if automation levels are low, then traditional task-based skills may remain the best area to focus on.

For Schuppan, technology innovation has placed demands on public managers to make their organizations more intelligent about the entire process chain of information that goes into rolling out a new public service or designing a new policy. Network models of implementation have both increased and decreased the range of employee competencies available to managers because the division of labour becomes both more specialist and more generalist. The scope of tasks increases thus requiring more specialization. At the same time, specialization can result in a certain amount of deskilling due to automation. One task that public managers can use here is job rotation so that employees become familiar with a broad range of skills needed for public information management. In particular, this requires knowing about the whole process chain, and the requirement for skills such as self-organization and self-reflection has increased.

## Box 8.7: The origins of i-labs

Innovation labs (or 'i-labs') come in many forms today. They are typically start-up companies which combine elements of think tanks, research laboratories and resource hubs. The funding structure of i-labs largely relies on public grants with smaller grants from private enterprises for high-risk projects relying on highly expert teams. Innovation labs are a twenty-first-century creation, but the idea has a much older pedigree than appears at first glance. The Skunkworks unit of the United States Air Force emerged in the 1950s and has since spawned a variety of innovation models based on small, bespoke, highly skilled teams working autonomously. The original Skunkworks produced technological breakthroughs such as the first fighter planes to go over 500 miles per hour. What made Skunkworks so original in concept was the independence of all the scientists, project managers and engineers. Other companies rushed to copy the model, but many Skunkworks initiatives resulted in expensive failures. Subsequent research revealed that, in addition to high-skilled experts and independence, successful Skunkworks organizations needed to possess something else: toleration in the rest of the organization for a nonconformist element within its structure.

**Table 8.1** Summary of innovation phases and required SPIM capacities.

| Innovation phase | Main SPIM capacities |
|---|---|
| Idea generation | Skills focused on flexibility and professionalism rather than siloed approach to departmental responsibilities and roles |
| | Public engagement and crowdsourcing skills |
| | Network management skills |
| Idea selection | Ability to visualize and design decision-making architectures |
| | Management of open innovation tools such as hackathons and crowdsourcing |
| | Idea communication and framing skills |
| Idea testing | Research and data analysis skills |
| | Collaborative research and knowledge sharing skills |
| | Knowledge of legal constraints |
| Idea promotion | Ability to construct narratives and tell stories |
| | Project management skills |
| | People management skills |
| Idea roll-out | Long-term vision |
| | Ethical and visionary leadership |

# A new public manager

The capacities needed for innovation present an overview of the new challenges public managers are facing in an information age. The need to continuously work on innovating the organization in response to technological and societal changes requires a new public manager. We would like to reflect here on the variety of demands that we have identified in this book. What portrait of the public manager emerges from the building blocks described in the previous chapters?

A first striking feature of the portrait is the ICT-mindedness of the public manager. Compared with the administrative clerk, the new public manager and the network-driven boundary-spanner, today's public manager certainly needs to be more ICT-minded. They are interested in understanding how information is collected and refined, how algorithms and automated processes work and what information and communication networks look like. They should be neither an IT engineer nor fashionably focused on the latest gadgets in their office and at home. Real ICT-minded public managers are still an exception in public organizations, even in highly automated environments such as large-scale bureaucracies. Many public managers rely on the CIO and the CISO to take care of the information systems without understanding the technologies themselves. While the CIO and the CISO take care of the nuts and bolts of the information systems, understanding the interplay of information systems and the human, financial, political and legal forces is a key responsibility of the public manager. They should understand both the crucial role of information systems in their public organization and the man–machine interaction that goes along with it. The interplay between the information systems and the other systems in public organizations largely determines the opportunities and threats hence the survival of the organization. While public management theory still limits the concept of boundary-spanning to organizational boundaries, we suggest public managers are socio-technic managers who manage the interplay between the information systems and man-made action in public organizations.

ICT-mindedness helps to understand the organizations you are in charge of, but it also supports you in developing the strategies to maintain the equilibrium between the public organization and its environment. As shown in several chapters of this book, information systems highlight the strengths and weaknesses of an organization. Information systems also lead the way for opportunities for innovation, better performance and high-quality public services and to the threats that precede failure and accidents. As an ICT-minded public manager you continuously monitor the alignment between the organization's information systems and the technological environment. Doing so may prevent ICT fiascos, which are often triggered by public managers without ICT-mindedness, making them easy prey for either a naïve belief in fashionable technologies or ICT consultants. ICT-mindedness allows public managers to separate the real opportunities from the fake ICT news even without being an engineer yourself. ICT-minded public managers reflect proactively by regularly implementing a SWOT analysis from the perspective of information systems (see Box 8.8).

ICT planning that follows a plan–do–act–evaluate cycle is part of your work and this cannot be left to support staff. Both the SWOT analysis and the ICT planning process involves the whole organization so as to include the social organization, financial planning, and so on. As our concept of SPIM shows, ICT planning and ICT SWOTS are not exclusively technically focused but should focus on the key responsibilities of the organization as a socio-technical system.

It should come as no surprise that our redefined portrait of the public manager also includes the roles we have distinguished. In our view the public manager of the future is able to simultaneously deploy the different perspectives and switch between the roles of the engineer, mediator, reverend and coach in

---

## Box 8.8: SWOT analysis in an information age

Take, for example, a regular policy department on health. A traditional SWOT analysis would probably look like this:

Strengths: well-trained staff; team spirit; well positioned in the organization and good connections with political leadership

Weaknesses: not well embedded in the policy field of health organizations; funding problems because of budget cuts

Opportunities: public health has become more important because of Covid-19; new management

Threats: will health be still important after the Covid-19 crisis?; new government has announced new budget cuts

What would the SWOT for this organization look like from the perspective of information systems?

Strengths: up-to-date information systems on both the supply and demand of the health care system; data scientists are available in the department

Weaknesses: the department lacks forecasting models and foresight tools to map future health challenges

Opportunities: rapid computerization of the health sector; patients are empowered by publicly available diagnostic tools; patients can increasingly be monitored outside the hospital

Threats: securing medical information of patients because of continued hack attempts and data leaks; ageing of information systems used by the department

---

order to manage ICT and information (Bolman and Deal 2017). If you limit yourself to either one of these roles you will not be able to achieve control of the information systems. The engineer who looks solely at information systems from this perspective may believe that s/he is in control but will be unaware of the politics embedded and surrounding his/her information systems. S/he will also be surprised in the instance of an ICT fiasco or organizational failure because s/he believed that the information system was perfect and failed to recognize the alignment of the information system with the human, social and political systems in public organizations. And s/he will wonder why their staff still does not accept the information system and thus bypass it informally. So, simultaneously deploying all four roles and switching between them is crucial to effectively manage information systems in public organizations.[2]

# Conclusions

This chapter highlights that effectively navigating the managerial challenges across societal, organizational, political and policymaking spheres becomes a matter of building capacity for change. At the beginning of this chapter, we asked '*how can we get there?*'. In order to make the path to SPIM clearer, we drew on several different existing frameworks of public sector innovation to establish a set of steps that public managers can follow and laid out key theoretical elements of a research agenda to refocus scholars' as well as managers' attention on the key issues. We can summarize our answers to the chapter questions thus:

- *What risks or negative impacts can result from the wrong kinds of innovation?* There are many possible risks, and we analyzed them using ten types put forward by Meijer et al. (2019). Innovation risk raises the vital importance for the public information manager to avoid the facile assumption that any new technology is advantageous and should be adopted. It also raises the question of how public managers deal with conflicts between different values. Public managers can support an organizational learning process by recognizing the weaknesses of the four roles and selecting the right role to counterbalance the weaknesses.
- *What are the different capacities of managers and who should be involved in the different phases of a process of innovation?* A variety of capacities for managers is presented such as public engagement and crowdsourcing skills and the ability to construct narratives and tell stories. A public information manager's innovation strategy can make use of our framework of innovation phases to pinpoint and prioritize the areas that need most attention. In each phase, there are key roles

---

[2] See Chapter 1 for more on Bolman and Deal's (2017) four roles.

for citizens. Citizen participation can make the most difference in the development of very specific initiatives with new technologies or processes, and citizen feedback can help with these initiatives later on when they are implemented and evaluated.

- *How can public managers take a strategic, long-term approach to creating innovative organizations that will not just meet the current innovation demands but keep on doing so in the future?* Using Meijer's (2015) framework (idea generation, idea selection, idea testing, idea promotion and idea roll-out), we focused on the linear phases of the innovation process. Our overarching point for public managers is that developing SPIM capacity for change is about looking beyond the immediate needs or technologies of the day (these are constantly changing), and instead focusing on building innovative capacity so that the long-term strategy is informed by key actors in the manager's environment. The job of the public information manager is to try to bring these phases into harmony with each other in such a way that innovation can occur.

We close this final chapter by highlighting how public managers can influence the capacity of their organizations to adopt, use and improve their SPIM capacities and that of their organizations. The SPIM approach to public information management should also encourage a research agenda focused on the kinds of concepts that are useful for understanding how public managers can work better. SPIM requires managing an ongoing process of change that managers should cultivate through leadership and planning. In cultivating SPIM, public managers foster exchange of information from the environment to citizens, businesses or NGOs. The information is harnessed for idea generation and selection and implementation of ideas. Once innovations have been used and implemented, evaluation and learning should take place. This final chapter stresses that managing these processes of innovation are crucial to strategic information management within an ongoing dynamic of technological change.

# KEY LESSONS FROM CHAPTER 8

- SPIM requires continuous innovation due to the ongoing processes of societal and technological change. The work is never done; the organization is in continuous flux.

- Innovation does not come without risks: there is a dark side to public innovation which needs to be avoided. These risks include corruption, lack of stability, absence of democratic control and several others.
- Innovation for SPIM requires a variety of capacities of public managers which can be related to the five phases of the innovation process (idea generation, idea selection, idea testing, idea promotion and idea roll-out).
- Managing innovation for SPIM not only requires capacities. A new type of public manager is needed for the information age who can make the connection between technology and organization on the basis of a sensitivity for technological change, a capacity to shift between different perspectives and the ability to connect environmental awareness to strategic information issues.

# References

Abdou, A. M. (2021) 'Good governance and COVID-19: The digital bureaucracy to response the pandemic (Singapore as a model)'. *Journal of Public Affairs*. https://doi.org/10.1002/pa.2656.

Algemene Rekenkamer (General Audit Office) (2018) *Digitale Dijkverzwaring: cybersecurity en vitale waterwerken (Digital dyke reinforcement: cybersecurity and vital waterworks)*. The Hague: Algemene Rekenkamer.

Andrews, L. (2019) 'Public administration, public leadership and the construction of public value in the age of the algorithm and "big data"'. *Public Administration*, 97(2), 296–310.

Ansell, C., Sørensen, E. and Torfing, J. (2020) 'The COVID-19 pandemic as a game changer for public administration and leadership? The need for robust governance responses to turbulent problems'. *Public Management Review*, 23(7), 949–60.

Anthopoulos, L., Reddick, C. G., Giannakidou, I. and Mavridis, N. (2016) 'Why e-government projects fail? An analysis of the Healthcare.gov website'. *Government Information Quarterly*, 33(1), 161–73.

Anton, C., Camarero, C. and San Jose, R. (2014) 'Public employee acceptance of new technological processes: The case of an internal call centre'. *Public Management Review*, 16(6), 852–75.

Bailard, C. S. (2014) *Democracy's Double-Edged Sword: How internet use changes citizens' views of their government*. Baltimore, MD: JHU Press.

Bala, S. J. (2015) 'Political control, bureaucratic discretion, and public commenting on agency regulations'. *Public Administration*, 93(2), 524–38.

Ball, K. (2010) 'Workplace surveillance: An overview'. *Labor History*, 51(1), 87–106.

Ball, K. and Snider, L. (2013) *The Surveillance–Industrial Complex: A political economy of surveillance*. London: Routledge.

Bamberger, K. A. (2010) 'Technologies of compliance: Risk and regulation in a digital age'. *Texas Law Review*, 88(4), 669–739.

Baumgartner, F. R. and Jones, B. D. (2015) *The Politics of Information: Problem definition and the course of public policy in America*. Chicago, IL: The University of Chicago Press.

Beck, U. (1992) *Risk Society: Towards a new modernity*. London: Sage.

Bekkers, V. and Homburg, V. (2007) 'The myths of e-government: Looking beyond the assumptions of a new and better government'. *The Information Society*, 23(5), 373–82.

Bekkers, V., Edwards, A. and de Kool, D. (2013) 'Social media monitoring: Responsive governance in the shadow of surveillance?'. *Government Information Quarterly*, 30(4), 335–42.

Bellamy, C. (1996) 'Transforming social security benefits administration for the twenty-first century: Towards one-stop services and the client group principle?'. *Public Administration*, 74(2), 159–79.

Beniger, J. (2009) *The Control Revolution: Technological and economic origins of the information society*. Cambridge: Harvard University Press.

Berliner, D. (2014) 'The political origins of transparency'. *The Journal of Politics*, 76(2), 479–91.

Bertelli, A. M. and Sinclair, J. A. (2015) 'Mass administrative reorganization, media attention, and the paradox of information'. *Public Administration Review*, 75(6), 855–66.

Blom-Hansen, J., Baekgaard, M. and Serritzlew, S. (2016) 'Shaping political preferences: Information effects in political-administrative systems'. *Local Government Studies*, 42(1), 119–38.

Bogaard, van den A. A., Lintsen, H. W., Veraart, F. C. A. and de Wit, O. (eds) (2008) *De Eeuw van de Computer: De geschiedenis van de informatietechnologie in Nederland*. Deventer: Kluwer.

Bohte, J. and Meier, K. J. (2000) 'Goal displacement: Assessing the motivation for organizational cheating'. *Public Administration Review*, 60(2), 173–82.

Bolman, L. G. and Deal, T. E. (2017) *Reframing Organizations*. San Francisco, CA: Jossey-Bass.

Borins, S. (2001) 'Public management innovation: Toward a global perspective'. *The American Review of Public Administration*, 31(1), 5–21.

Boswell, C. (2012) 'How information scarcity influences the policy agenda: Evidence from UK immigration policy'. *Governance*, 25(3), 367–89.

Bovaird, T. (2007) 'Beyond engagement and participation: User and community coproduction of public services'. *Public Administration Review*, 67(5), 846–60.

Bovens, M. A. P. and Zouridis, S. (2002) 'From street-level to system-level bureaucracies: How information and communication technology is transforming administrative discretion and constitutional control'. *Public Administration Review*, 62(2), 174–84.

Bovens, M. and Wille, A. (2017) *Diploma Democracy: The rise of political meritocracy*. Oxford: Oxford University Press.

Boyne, G. A. (2002) 'Public and private management: What's the difference?'. *Journal of Management Studies*, 39(1), 97–122.

Brown, J. S. and Duguid, P. (2000) *The Social Life of Information*. Boston, MA: Harvard Business School Press.

Busuioc, M. (2021) 'Accountable artificial intelligence: Holding algorithms to account'. *Public Administration Review*, 81(5), 825–36.

Carnis, L. (2007) 'The automated speed enforcement system in Great Britain: Between a technical revolution and administrative continuity'. *International Review of Administrative Sciences*, 73(4), 597–610.

Cavoukian, A. (2009) *Privacy by Design: The 7 foundational principles.* Information and privacy commissioner of Ontario. Durham, NC: Duke University Press.

Cerulo, K. A. (2006) *Never Saw It Coming: Cultural challenges to envisioning the worst.* Chicago, IL and London: University of Chicago Press.

Chan, Y. E., Huff, S. L., Barclay, D. W. and Copeland, D. G. (1997) 'Business strategic orientation, information systems strategic orientation, and strategic alignment'. *Information Systems Research*, 8(2), 125–50.

Cheeseman, N., Lynch, G. and Willis, J. (2018) 'Digital dilemmas: The unintended consequences of election technology'. *Democratization*, 25(8), 1397–418.

Cheng, H. Y., Li, S. Y. and Yang, C. H. (2020) 'Initial rapid and proactive response for the COVID-19 outbreak—Taiwan's experience'. *Journal of the Formosan Medical Association*, 119(4), 771.

Christensen, R. K. and Wright, B. E. (2011) 'The effects of public service motivation on job choice decisions: Disentangling the contributions of person-organization fit and person-job fit'. *Journal of Public Administration Research and Theory*, 21(4), 723–43.

Christensen, T. and Lægreid, P. (2007) 'The whole-of-government approach to public sector reform'. *Public Administration Review*, 67(6), 1059–66.

Ciborra, C. (2002) *The Labyrinths of Information: Challenging the wisdom of systems.* Oxford: Oxford University Press.

Clearfield, C. and Tilcsik, A. (2018) *Meltdown: Why our systems fail and what we can do about it.* New York, NY: Penguin Press.

Cockburn, I. M., Henderson, R. and Stern, S. (2019) 'The impact of Artificial Intelligence on innovation: An exploratory analysis'. In Goldfarb, A., Gans, J. and Agrawal, A. (eds), *The Economics of Artificial Intelligence: An agenda,* 115–46. Chicago, IL: University of Chicago Press.

Coglianese, C. (2004) 'Information technology and regulatory policy: New directions for digital government research'. *Social Science Computer Review*, 22(1), 85–91.

Coremans, E. and Meissner, K. L. (2018) 'Putting power into practice: Administrative and political capacity building in the European Parliament's Committee for International Trade'. *Public Administration*, 96(3), 561–77.

Crozier, M. P. (2010) 'Rethinking systems: Configurations of politics and policy in contemporary governance'. *Administration & Society*, 42(5), 504–25.

Dawes, S. S. and Janssen, M. (2013) 'Policy informatics: Addressing complex problems with rich data, computational tools, and stakeholder engagement'. *Proceedings of the 14th Annual International Conference on Digital Government Research*. ACM, 251–53.

Dayanada, S. and Burack, R. (2017) 'What two years of open data has done for Pittsburgh'. *Government Technology*, 16 November. https://www.govtech.com/data/what-two-years-of-open-data-has-done-for-pittsburgh.html.

De Bruijn, H., Ten Heuvelhof, E. and In 't Veld, R. (2010) *Process Management: Why project management fails in complex decision making processes*. Heidelberg: Springer Science & Business Media.

De Bruijne, M., A. Boin and Van Eeten, M. (2010) 'Resilience: Exploring the concept and its meanings'. In Comfort, L. K., Boin, A. and Demchak, C. C. (eds), *Designing Resilience: Preparing for extreme events*, 13–32. Pittsburgh, PA: University of Pittsburgh Press.

De Vries, H., Tummers, L. and Bekkers, V. (2018) 'A stakeholder perspective on public sector innovation: Why position matters'. *International Review of Administrative Sciences*, 84(2), 269–87.

Dekker, S. (2017) *The Safety Anarchist: Relying on human expertise and innovation, reducing bureaucracy and compliance*. London/New York: Routledge.

Dijstelbloem, H., Meijer, A. and Besters, M. (2011) 'The migration machine'. In Dijstelbloem, H. and Meijer, A. (eds), *Migration and the New Technological Borders of Europe*, 1–21. Houndmills: Palgrave Macmillan.

Dorsman, S. J., Groeneveld, S. M., Thaens, M. and Tummers, L. (2015) 'Bringing the "public" in public leadership: A theoretical exploration of the relations between publicness and leadership'. Rotterdam: unpublished.

Douglas, M. and Wildavsky, A. (1982) *Risk and Culture: An essay on the selection of technological and environmental dangers*. Berkeley, CA: University of California Press.

Dressel, J. and Farid, H. (2018) 'The accuracy, fairness, and limits of predicting recidivism'. *Science Advances*, 4(1). https://www.science.org/doi/pdf/10.1126/sciadv.aao5580.

DSB (2012) *Het DigiNotarincident: Waarom digitale veiligheid de bestuurstafel te weinig bereikt* [The DigiNotar incident: Why safety fails to attract enough attention from public administrators]. The Hague: Onderzoeksraad voor Veiligheid.

DSB (2020) Patiëntveiligheid bij ICT-uitval in ziekenhuizen [Patient safety in case of ICT failure in hospitals]. The Hague: Onderzoeksraad voor Veiligheid.

Dunleavy, P., Margetts, H., Tinkler, J. and Bastow, S. (2006) *Digital Era Governance: IT corporations, the state, and e-government.* Oxford: Oxford University Press.

Dutil, P. and Williams, J. (2017) 'Regulation governance in the digital era: A new research agenda'. *Canadian Public Administration*, 60(4), 562–80.

Ekdale, B. and Tully, M. (2020) 'How the Nigerian and Kenyan media handled Cambridge Analytica'. *The Conversation.* https://theconversation.com/how-the-nigerian-and-kenyan-media-handled-cambridge-analytica-128473.

ENISA (2014) *Privacy and Data Protection by Design: From policy to engineering.* Brussels: The European Union Agency for Cybersecurity.

Epp, C. R., Maynard-Moody, S. and Haider-Markel, D. (2014) *Pulled Over: How police stops define race and citizenship.* Chicago, IL and London: University of Chicago Press.

Eubanks, V. (2017) *Automating Inequality: How high-tech tools profile, police, and punish the poor.* New York, NY: Sint Martins Press.

Fabre, M. (2015) 'Use of social media for internal communication: A case study in a government organisation'. In Nepal, S., Paris, C. and Georgakopoulos, D. (eds), *Social Media for Government Services*, 51–74. Cham: Springer.

Feldman, M. S. and March, J. G. (1981) 'Information in organizations as signal and symbol'. *Administrative Science Quarterly*, 26(2), 171–86.

Ferlie, E. and McGivern, G. (2014) 'Bringing Anglo-governmentality into public management scholarship: The case of evidence-based medicine in UK health care'. *Journal of Public Administration Research and Theory*, 24(1), 59–83.

Fernandez D., Zaini, Z. and Hawa, A. (2017) 'The impacts of ERP systems on public sector organizations'. *Procedia Computer Science*, 111, 31–6.

Floridi, L. (2010) *Information: A very short introduction.* Oxford: Oxford University Press.

Fountain, J. E. (2001) 'Paradoxes of public sector customer service'. *Governance*, 14(1), 55–73.

Franzke, A. S., Muis, I. and Schäfer, M. T. (2021) 'Data Ethics Decision Aid (DEDA): A dialogical framework for ethical inquiry of AI and data projects in the Netherlands'. *Ethics and Information Technology*, 23(10), 1–17.

Fusi, F. and Feeney, M. K. (2017) 'Electronic monitoring in public organizations: Evidence from US local governments'. *Public Management Review*, 20(10), 1465–89.

Fusi, F. and Feeney, M. K. (2018) 'Social media in the workplace: Information exchange, productivity, or waste?'. *The American Review of Public Administration*, 48(5), 395–412.

Garnett, J. and Kouzmin, A. (2009) 'Crisis communication post Katrina: What are we learning?'. *Public Organization Review*, 9(4), 385.

Goodman, M. (2015) *Future Crimes: Inside the digital underground and the battle for our connected world*. New York, NY: Anchor Books.

Grabosky, P. (2013) 'Beyond responsive regulation: The expanding role of non-state actors in the regulatory process'. *Regulation & Governance*, 7(1), 114–23.

Greenemeier, L. (2015, September 22) 'What's behind VW's downfall and secretive emissions deals'. *Scientific American*. https://www.scientificamerican.com/article/what-s-behind-vw-s-downfall-and-secretive-emissions-deals/.

Grijpink, J. (2010) 'Chain analysis for large-scale communication systems'. *Journal of Chain-computerisation*, 1(1), 1–32.

Groeling, T. (2013) 'Media bias by the numbers: Challenges and opportunities in the empirical study of partisan news'. *Annual Review of Political Science*, 16, 129–51.

Grossman, L. (2009, June) 'Iran protests: Twitter, the medium of the movement'. *Time Magazine*. https://www.cc.gatech.edu/classes/AY2015/cs4001_summer/documents/Time-Iran-Twitter.pdf.

*Guardian* (2018, June), 'The great firewall of China: Xi Jinping's internet shutdown'. https://www.theguardian.com/news/2018/jun/29/the-great-firewall-of-china-xi-jinpings-internet-shutdown.

Gulledge Jr, T. R. and Sommer, R. A. (2002) 'Business process management: Public sector implications'. *Business Process Management Journal*, 8(4), 364–76.

Habermann, H. (2010) 'Future of innovation in the Federal Statistical System'. *The Annals of the American Academy of Political and Social Science*, 631(1), 194–203.

Habermas, J. (1984) *The Theory of Communicative Action*. Boston, MA: Beacon Press.

Haeder, S. F. and Yackee, S. W. (2015) 'Influence and the administrative process: Lobbying the US President's Office of Management and Budget'. *American Political Science Review*, 109(3), 507–22.

Hansen, M. B. and Nørup, I. (2017) 'Leading the implementation of ICT innovations'. *Public Administration Review*, 77(6), 851–60.

Harrison, K. (2017) 'Regulatory excellence and democratic accountability'. In Coglianese, C. (ed.), *Achieving Regulatory Excellence*, 56–71. Washington, DC: Brookings Institution Press.

Hartley, J., Alford, J., Hughes, O. and Yates, S. (2015) 'Public value and political astuteness in the work of public managers: The art of the possible'. *Public Administration*, 93(1), 195–211.

Heimstädt, M. and Dobusch, L. (2018) 'Politics of disclosure: Organizational transparency as multiactor negotiation'. *Public Administration Review*, 78(5), 727–38.

Hendriks, F. and Zouridis, S. (1999) 'Cultural biases and new media for the public domain: Cui bono?'. In Thompson, M., Grendstad, G. and Selle, P. (eds), *Cultural Theory as Political Science*, 121–37. London and New York, NY: Routledge.

Henninger, M. (2013) 'The value and challenges of public sector information'. *Cosmopolitan Civil Societies: An Interdisciplinary Journal*, 5(3), 75–95.

Ho, J. C. and Chen, H. (2018) 'Managing the disruptive and sustaining the disrupted: The case of Kodak and Fujifilm in the face of digital disruption'. *Review of Policy Research*, 35(3), 352–71.

Homburg, V. (1999) *The Political Economy of Information Management: A theoretical and empirical analysis of decision making regarding interorganizational information systems*. Capelle a/d Ijssel: Labyrint Publication.

Homburg, V., Dijkshoorn, A. and Thaens, M. (2014) 'Diffusion of personalised services among Dutch municipalities: Evolving channels of persuasion'. *Local Government Studies*, 40(3), 429–50.

Hood, C., Rothstein, H. and Baldwin, R. (2001) *The Government of Risk: Understanding risk regulation regimes*. Oxford: Oxford University Press.

Hoogerwerf, A. (1998) *Overheidsbeleid (Government policy)*, 6th edn. Alphen aan den Rijn: Samsom Tjeenk Willink.

Hoogwout, M. (2010) *De rationaliteit van de klantgerichte overheid. Een onderzoek naar de spanningen van het klantdenken bij gemeenten veroorzaakt en de manier waarop gemeenten daarmee omgaan* [The rationality of the customer-oriented government. A study into the tensions caused by customer thinking in municipalities and the way in which municipalities deal with this]. Nieuwegein: Uitgeverij Réunion.

Hu, Q. (2018) 'Preparing public managers for the digital era: Incorporating information management, use, and technology into public affairs graduate curricula'. *Public Management Review*, 20(5), 766–87.

Hyytinen, A., Meriläinen, J., Saarimaa, T., Toivanen, O. and Tukiainen, J. (2018) 'Public employees as politicians: Evidence from close elections'. *American Political Science Review*, 112(1), 68–81.

James, W. H. (2013, September) 'Wearables in the workplace'. *Harvard Business Review*. https://hbr.org/2013/09/wearables-in-the-workplace.

John, P. (1998) *Analysing Public Policy*. London: Continuum.

Johnston, E. W. (2015) 'Conceptualizing policy informatics'. In Johnston, E. W. (ed.), *Governance in the Information Era: Theory and practice of policy informatics*, 3–22. New York, NY: Routledge.

Jordan, S. (2018) 'Public organizations and regulations'. In *Global Encyclopedia of Public Administration, Public Policy, and Governance*, 5167–71. New York, NY: Springer.

Jun, K. N. and Weare, C. (2010) 'Institutional motivations in the adoption of innovations: The case of e-government'. *Journal of Public Administration Research and Theory*, 21(3), 495–519.

Kahneman, D. (2012) *Thinking, Fast and Slow*. New York, NY: Penguin Books.

Kaminski, M. E. (2019) 'The right to explanation, explained'. *Berkeley Technology Law Journal*, 34, 189–218.

Kattel, R. and Kalvet, T. (2006) *Knowledge-based Economy and ICT-related Education in Estonia: Overview of the current situation and challenges for the educational system*. Tallinn: PRAXIS.

Keller, M. H. (2018, August 11) 'The flourishing business of fake YouTube views'. *New York Times*. https://www.nytimes.com/interactive/2018/08/11/technology/youtube-fake-view-sellers.html.

Kelly, K. (1998) *New Rules for the New Economy: 10 radical strategies for a connected world*. New York, NY: Viking Penguin.

Kickert, W. J., Klijn, E. H. and Koppenjan, J. F. (eds) (1997) *Managing Complex Networks: Strategies for the public sector*. London: Sage.

Kingdon, J. (1984) *Agendas, Alternatives, and Public Policies*. New York, NY: Harper Collins.

Kingdon, J. W. and Thurber, J. A. (1984) *Agendas, Alternatives, and Public Policies*. Boston, MA: Little, Brown.

Kitchin, R. (2014) *The Data Revolution: Big data, open data, data infrastructures and their consequences*. London: Sage.

Kitchin, R. (2020) 'Civil liberties or public health, or civil liberties and public health? Using surveillance technologies to tackle the spread of COVID-19'. *Space and Polity*, 24(3), 362–81.

Kling, R. (ed.) (1996) *Computerization and Controversy: Value conflicts and social choices*. Burlington, MA: Morgan Kaufmann.

Koliba C. and Zia, A. (2015) 'Governance informatics: Using computer simulation models to deepen situational awareness and governance design considerations'. In Johnston, E. (eds), *Governance in the Information Era: Theory and practice of policy informatics*, 189–212. Cambridge, MA: MIT Press.

Krause, G. A. and Corder, J. K. (2007) 'Explaining bureaucratic optimism: Theory and evidence from US executive agency macroeconomic forecasts'. *American Political Science Review*, 101(1), 129–42.

Kuziemski, M. and Misuraca, G. (2020) 'AI governance in the public sector: Three tales from the frontiers of automated decision-making in democratic settings'. *Telecommunications Policy*, 44(6), Article 101976.

Larson, J., Mattu, S., Kirchner, L. and Angwin, J. (2016, May) 'How we analyzed the COMPAS recidivism algorithm'. *ProPublica Magazine*. https://www.propublica.org/article/how-we-analyzed-the-compas-recidivism-algorithm.

Laudon, K. C. and Laudon, J. P. (2000) *Management Information Systems*. New Jersey, NJ: Prentice Hall.

Lavertu, S. (2016) 'We all need help: "Big data" and the mismeasure of public administration'. *Public Administration Review*, 76(6), 864–72.

Lavertu, S. and Moynihan, D. P. (2012) 'Agency political ideology and reform implementation: Performance management in the Bush administration'. *Journal of Public Administration Research and Theory*, 23(3), 521–49.

Lavinsky, D. (2013, September) 'Executive dashboards: What they are and why every business needs one'. *Forbes*. https://www.forbes.com/sites/davelavinsky/2013/09/06/executive-dashboards-what-they-are-why-every-business-needs-one/#60f5502937d1.

Lee, J. (2008) 'Determinants of government bureaucrats' new PMIS adoption: The role of organizational power, IT capability, administrative role, and attitude'. *The American Review of Public Administration*, 38(2), 180–202.

Leifeld, P. and Schneider, V. (2012) 'Information exchange in policy networks'. *American Journal of Political Science*, 56(3), 731–44.

Lember, V., Brandsen, T. and Tõnurist, P. (2019) 'The potential impacts of digital technologies on co-production and co-creation'. *Public Management Review*, 21(11), 1665–86.

Lerman, A. E., Sadin, M. L. and Trachtman, S. (2017) 'Policy uptake as political behavior: Evidence from the Affordable Care Act'. *American Political Science Review*, 111(4), 755–70.

Linders, D. (2012) 'From e-government to we-government: Defining a typology for citizen coproduction in the age of social media'. *Government Information Quarterly*, 29(4), 446–54.

Liou, K. T. and Hu, Q. (2019) 'Technology development and public organization management'. *International Journal of Organization Theory and Behavior*, 22(2), 114–22.

Lodge, M. and Wegrich, K. (2015) 'Crowdsourcing and regulatory reviews: A new way of challenging red tape in British government?'. *Regulation and Governance*, 9(1), 30–46.

Lusch, R. F. and Nambisan, S. (2015) 'Service innovation: A service-dominant logic perspective'. *MIS Quarterly*, 39(1), 155–76.

Lyon, D. (2003) *Surveillance as Social Sorting: Privacy, risk, and digital discrimination*. Washington, DC: Psychology Press.

Mayer-Schönberger, V., and Cukier, K. (2013) *Big Data: A revolution that will transform how we live, work, and think*. Boston, MA: Houghton Mifflin Harcourt.

McGregor, D. (1960) *The Human Side of Enterprise*. New York, NY: McGrawHill.

Meijer, A. (2007) 'Publishing public performance results on the Internet: Do stakeholders use the Internet to hold Dutch public service organizations to account?'. *Government Information Quarterly*, 24(1), 165–85.

Meijer, A. (2008) 'E-mail in government: Not post-bureaucratic but late-bureaucratic organizations'. *Government Information Quarterly*, 25(3), 429–47.

Meijer, A. (2015) 'E-governance innovation: Barriers and strategies'. *Government Information Quarterly*, 32(2), 198–206.

Meijer, A. and De Jong, J. (2019) 'Managing value conflicts in public innovation: Ostrich, Chameleon, and Dolphin strategies'. *International Journal of Public Administration*, 43(11), 977–88.

Meijer, A. and Grimmelikhuijsen, S. (2021) 'Responsible and accountable algorithmization: How to generate citizen trust in governmental usage of algorithms'. In Peeters, R. and Schuilenburg, M. (eds), *The Algorithmic Society*, 67–86. London: Routledge.

Meijer, A. and Löfgren, K. (2015) 'The neglect of technology in theories of policy change'. *International Journal of Public Administration in the Digital Age (IJPADA)*, 2(1), 75–88.

Meijer, A. and Potjer, S. (2018) 'Citizen-generated open data: An explorative analysis of 25 cases'. *Government Information Quarterly*, 35(4), 613–21.

Meijer, A. and Thaens, M. (2010) 'Alignment 2.0: Strategic use of new internet technologies in government'. *Government Information Quarterly*, 27(2), 113–21.

Meijer, A. and Thaens, M. (2013) 'Social media strategies: Understanding the differences between North American police departments'. *Government Information Quarterly*, 30(4), 343–50.

Meijer, A. and Thaens, M. (2018) 'Quantified street: Smart governance of urban safety'. *Information Polity*, 23(1), 29–41.

Meijer, A. J. and Torenvlied, R. (2016) 'Social media and the new organization of government communications: An empirical analysis of Twitter usage by the Dutch police'. *The American Review of Public Administration*, 46(2), 143–61.

Meijer, A. and Van Berlo, D. (2014) *De Nieuwe Overheid* [The New Government]. Den Haag: Boom Lemma.

Meijer, A., Grimmelikhuijsen, S. and Brandsma, G. J. (2012) 'Communities of Public Service Support: Citizens engage in social learning in peer-to-peer networks'. *Government Information Quarterly*, 29(1), 21–9.

Mergel, I., Gong, Y. and Bertot, J. (2018) 'Agile government: Systematic literature review and future research'. *Government Information Quarterly*, 35(2), 291–98.

Meyer, R. and Kunreuther, H. (2017) *The Ostrich Paradox: Why we underprepare for disasters*. Philadelphia, PA: Wharton Digital Press.

Michener, G. and Worthy, B. (2018) 'The information-gathering matrix: A framework for conceptualizing the use of freedom of information laws'. *Administration & Society*, 50(4), 476–500.

Migration Research Hub (n.d.) 'Dashboard of indicators for measuring policy and institutional coherence for migration and development (PICMD)'. https://migrationresearch.com/item/dashboard-of-indicators-for-measuring-policy-and-institutional-coherence-for-migration-and-development-picmd/474350.

Mills, R. W. and Koliba, C. J. (2015) 'The challenge of accountability in complex regulatory networks: The case of the Deepwater Horizon oil spill'. *Regulation & Governance*, 9(1), 77–91.

Mintzberg, H. (1987) 'The Strategy Concept I: Five Ps for strategy'. *California Management Review*, 30(1), 11–24.

Mintzberg, H. (1992) *Structures in Fives*. Hoboken, NJ: Prentice Hall.

Moe, T. M. (1984) 'The new economics of organization'. *American Journal of Political Science*, 28(4), 739–77.

Moon, M. J. (2020) 'Fighting COVID-19 with agility, transparency, and participation: Wicked policy problems and new governance challenges'. *Public Administration Review*, 80(4), 651–56.

Morgan, G. (1986) *Images of Organization*, 1st edn. Thousand Oaks, CA: Sage.

Morozov, E. (2011) *The Net Delusion: How not to liberate the world*. London: Penguin.

Moynihan, D. P. and Lavertu, S. (2012) 'Cognitive biases in governing: Technology preferences in election administration'. *Public Administration Review*, 72(1), 68–77.

Nasi, G., Frosini, F. and Cristofoli, D. (2011) 'Online service provision: Are municipalities really innovative? The case of larger municipalities in Italy'. *Public Administration*, 89(3), 821–39.

Nielsen, P. A. and Moynihan, D. P. (2017) 'How do politicians attribute bureaucratic responsibility for performance? Negativity bias and interest group advocacy'. *Journal of Public Administration Research and Theory*, 27(2), 269–83.

Nograšek, J. and Vintar, M. (2014) 'E-government and organisational transformation of government: Black box revisited?'. *Government Information Quarterly*, 31(1), 108–18.

O'Neill, C. (2016) *Weapons of Math Destruction: How big data increases inequality and threatens democracy*. New York, NY: Penguin Books.

Orellana, E. B. (2015) 'Automating and informating: Roles to examine in technology's impact on performance'. Working Papers 15–17, Centro de Investigación, Universidad del Pacífico.

Palma, L. M., Vigil, M. A., Pereira, F. L. and Martina, J. E. (2019) 'Blockchain and smart contracts for higher education registry in Brazil'. *International Journal of Network Management*, 29(3), 1–21.

Pandey, S. K. and Wright, B. E. (2006) 'Connecting the dots in public management: Political environment, organizational goal ambiguity, and the public manager's role ambiguity'. *Journal of Public Administration Research and Theory*, 16(4), 511–32.

Pawson, R. (2006) *Evidence-based Policy: A realist perspective*. London: Sage.

Pearl, J. and D. Mackenzie (2018) *The Book of Why: The new science of cause and effect*. New York, NY: Basic Books.

Perrow, C. (1999) *Normal Accidents: Living with high-risk technologies*. Princeton, NJ: Princeton University Press.

Perry, J. L. (1997) 'Antecedents of public service motivation'. *Journal of Public Administration Research and Theory*, 7(2), 181–97.

Perry, W. L. (2013) *Predictive Policing: The role of crime forecasting in law enforcement operations*. Santa Monica, CA: Rand.

Pieterman, R. (2008) *De voorzorgcultuur: Streven naar veiligheid in een wereld vol risico en onzekerheid* [The culture of precaution]. The Hague: BJU.

Plesner, U., Justesen, L. and Glerup, C. (2018) 'The transformation of work in digitized public sector organizations'. *Journal of Organizational Change Management*, 31(5), 1176–90.

Polanyi, M. (1958) *Personal Knowledge: Towards a post-critical philosophy*. Chicago, IL: University of Chicago Press.

Quinn, J. B. (1992) 'The intelligent enterprise a new paradigm.' *Academy of Management Perspectives*, 6(4), 48–63.

Rabovsky, T. (2014a) 'Using data to manage for performance at public universities'. *Public Administration Review*, 74(2), 260–72.

Rabovsky, T. (2014b) 'Support for performance-based funding: The role of political ideology, performance, and dysfunctional information environments'. *Public Administration Review*, 74(6), 761–74.

Ragowsky, A. and Somers, T. M. (2002) 'Enterprise resource planning'. *Journal of Management Information Systems*, 19(1), 11–15.

Rainie, L. and Anderson, J. (2017) 'Code-dependent: Pros and cons of the algorithm age'. Pew Research Center. https://www.pewresearch.org/internet/2017/02/08/theme-6-unemployment-will-rise/.

Ratcliffe, J. H. (2016) *Intelligence-led Policing*. Abingdon, Oxford, and New York, NY: Routledge.

Rathenau Institute (2017) *Urgent Upgrade: Protect public values in our digitized society*. The Hague: Rathenau Institute.

Reason, J. (1997) *Managing the Risks of Organizational Accidents*. London and New York, NY: Routledge.

Reenock, C. M. and Gerber, B. J. (2007) 'Political insulation, information exchange, and interest group access to the bureaucracy'. *Journal of Public Administration Research and Theory*, 18(3), 415–40.

Rezaee, Z., Ford, W. and Elam, R. (2000) 'Real-time accounting systems'. *Internal Auditor*, 57(2), 62–7.

Roman, A. V., Van Wart, M., Wang, X., Liu, C., Kim, S. and McCarthy, A. (2019) 'Defining e-leadership as competence in ICT-mediated communications: An exploratory assessment'. *Public Administration Review*, 79(6), 853–66.

Rooks, G., Matzat, U. and Sadowski, B. (2017) 'An empirical test of stage models of e-government development: Evidence from Dutch municipalities'. *The Information Society*, 33(4), 215–25.

Sanovich, S. (2017) 'Computational propaganda in Russia: The origins of digital misinformation'. Working Paper No. 2017.3. Oxford Internet Institute, Oxford University. https://demtech.oii.ox.ac.uk/wp-content/uploads/sites/89/2017/06/Comprop-Russia.pdf.

Schechner, S. (2017, December) 'Meet your new boss: An algorithm'. https://www.wsj.com/articles/meet-your-new-boss-an-algorithm-1512910800.

Schellong, A. (2005) 'CRM in the public sector: Towards a conceptual research framework'. In *Proceedings of the 2005 National Conference on Digital Government Research*, 326–32. Digital Government Society of North America.

Schilling, M. A. (2015) 'Technology shocks, technological collaboration, and innovation outcomes'. *Organization Science*, 26(3), 668–86.

Schmidt, C. (2016) *Agile Software Development Teams: The impact of agile development on team performance*. Heidelberg, New York, Dordrecht, London: Springer.

Scholl, H. J. and Bolívar, M. P. R. (2019) 'Mapping potential impact areas of Blockchain use in the public sector'. *Information Polity*, 24(4), 359–78.

Schuilenburg, M. and Peeters, R. (eds) (2020) *The Algorithmic Society: Technology, power, and knowledge*. London: Routledge.

Schuppan, T. (2009) 'E-Government in developing countries: Experiences from sub-Saharan Africa'. *Government Information Quarterly*, 26(1), 118–27.

Schuppan, T. (2014, January) 'E-government at work level: Skilling or de-skilling?'. In 2014 47th Hawaii International Conference on System Sciences, 1927–1934. IEEE.

Shin, D. (2019) 'Toward fair, accountable, and transparent algorithms: Case studies on algorithm initiatives in Korea and China'. *Javnost-The Public*, 26(3), 274–90.

Shirky, C. (2008) *Here Comes Everybody: The power of organizing without organizations*. London: Penguin.

Simon, H. A. (1947) *Administrative Behavior: A study of decision-making processes in administrative organization*, 1st edn. New York, NY: Macmillan.

Simon, H. A. (2013) *Administrative Behavior*. New York, NY: Simon & Schuster.

Stephens-Davitowitz, S. (2017) *Everybody Lies: Big data, new data, and what the internet can tell us about who we really are*. New York, NY: HarperCollins.

Stevens, D. (2019) 'Satisficing in political decision making'. In Thompson, W. H. (ed.), *Oxford Research Encyclopedia of Politics*. Oxford: Oxford University Press. https://doi.org/10.1093/acrefore/9780190228637.013.1020.

Stone, D. A. (1997) *Policy Paradox: The art of political decision making*. New York, NY: WW Norton.

Styrin, E., Mossberger, K. and Zhulin, A. (2021) 'Government as a platform: Intergovernmental participation for public services in the Russian Federation'. *Government Information Quarterly*, 39(1), 101627.

Tenner, E. (1997) *Why Things Bite Back: Technology and the revenge of unintended consequences*. New York, NY: Vintage Books.

Teo, T. S., Devadoss, P. and Pan, S. L. (2006) 'Towards a holistic perspective of customer relationship management (CRM) implementation: A case study of the Housing and Development Board, Singapore'. *Decision Support Systems*, 42(3), 1613–27.

Thompson, V. A. (1965) 'Bureaucracy and innovation'. *Administrative Science Quarterly*, 10(1), 1–20.

Tierney, K. (2014) *The Social Roots of Risk: Producing disasters, promoting resilience*. Stanford, CA: Stanford University Press.

Tolbert, C. J., Mossberger, K. and McNeal, R. (2008) 'Institutions, policy innovation, and E-government in the American States'. *Public Administration Review*, 68(3), 549–63.

Torfing, J., Peters, B. G., Pierre, J. and Sørensen, E. (2012) *Interactive Governance: Advancing the paradigm*. Oxford: Oxford University Press.

Turner, B. A. and Pidgeon, N. F. (1978) *Man-made Disasters*. Oxford: Wykeham Publications.

Tursunbayeva, A., Pagliari, C., Di Lauro, S. and Antonelli, G. (2021) 'The ethics of people analytics: Risks, opportunities and recommendations'. *Personnel Review*. https://doi.org/10.1108/PR-12-2019-0680.

UK Government Office for Science (2016) 'Distributed Ledger Technology: Beyond block chain'. London. https://assets.publishing.service.gov.uk/government/uploads/system/uploads/attachment_data/file/492972/gs-16-1-distributed-ledger-technology.pdf.

Van Dijk, J. (2007) 'Mafia markers: Assessing organized crime and its impact upon societies'. *Trends in Organized Crime*, 10(4), 39–56.

Van Eck, B. M. A. (2018) *Geautomatiseerde Ketenbesluiten & Rechtsbescherming: Een onderzoek naar de praktijk van geautomatiseerde ketenbesluiten over een financieel belang in relatie tot rechtsbescherming*

[Automated chain decisions and legal protection: A study into the practice of automated chain decisions about a financial interest in relation to legal protection). Doctoral dissertation. Tilburg: Tilburg University.

Van der Pot, J. H. J. (1994) *Steward or Sorcerer's Apprentice? The evaluation of technical progress: A systematic overview of theories and opinions*. Delft: Eburon.

Van der Wal, Z. 2017. *The 21st Century Public Manager*. London: Palgrave Macmillan.

Von Schomberg, R. (2013) 'A vision of responsible research and innovation'. In Owen, R., Bessant, J. and Heintz, M. (eds), *Responsible Innovation: Managing the responsible emergence of science and innovation in society*, 51–74. John Wiley & Sons.

Wang, S. and Feeney, M. K. (2016) 'Determinants of information and communication technology adoption in municipalities'. *The American Review of Public Administration*, 46(3), 292–313.

Weaver, R. K. (2014) 'Compliance regimes and barriers to behavioral change'. *Governance*, 27(2), 243–65.

Weitz-Shapiro, R. and Winters, M. S. (2017) 'Can citizens discern? Information credibility, political sophistication, and the punishment of corruption in Brazil'. *The Journal of Politics*, 79(1), 60–74.

Wenger, E. (1998) *Communities of Practice: Learning, meaning, and identity*. Cambridge: Cambridge University Press.

Wenger, E., White, N. and Smith, J. D. (2009) *Digital Habitats: Stewarding technology for communities*. Portland, OR: CPsquare.

Wermink, H., van Wingerden, S., van Wilsem, J. and Nieuwbeerta, P. (2015) *Etnisch gerelateerde verschillen in de straftoemeting* [Ethnic related differences in sentencing]. The Hague: Raad voor de rechtspraak.

Westergren, U. H. and Holmström, J. (2012) 'Exploring preconditions for open innovation: Value networks in industrial firms'. *Information and Organization*, 22(4), 209–26.

Willems, D. and Doeleman, R. (2014) 'Predictive Policing–wens of werkelijkheid'. *Het Tijdschrift voor de Politie*, 76(4), 5.

Williamson, A. and Fung, A. (2004) 'Public deliberation: Where are we and where can we go?'. *National Civic Review*, 93(4), 3–15.

Wilson, F. (1995) 'Managerial control strategies within the networked organization'. *Information Technology & People*, 8(3), 57–72.

Wilson, J. Q. (1989) *Bureaucracy: What government agencies do and why they do it*. New York, NY: Basic Books.

Winner, L. (1993) 'Upon opening the black box and finding it empty: Social constructivism and the philosophy of technology'. *Science, Technology & Human Values*, 18(3), 362–78.

Winograd, T. and Flores, F. (1986) *Understanding Computers and Cognition: A new foundation for design*. Norwood, NJ: Ablex.

Worthy, B. (2015) 'The impact of open data in the UK: Complex, unpredictable, and political'. *Public Administration*, 93(3), 788–805.

Wright, B. E., Moynihan, D. P. and Pandey, S. K. (2012) 'Pulling the levers: Transformational leadership, public service motivation, and mission valence'. *Public Administration Review*, 72(2), 206–15.

WRR (Scientific Council for Government Policy) (2011) *iGovernment*. The Hague/Amsterdam: Amsterdam University Press.

WRR (Scientific Council for Government Policy) (2021) *Opgave AI. De nieuwe systeemtechnologie*. The Hague: WRR.

Yackee, J. W. and Yackee, S. W. (2006) 'A bias towards business? Assessing interest group influence on the US bureaucracy'. *The Journal of Politics*, 68(1), 128–39.

Yang, K. (2008) 'Examining perceived honest performance reporting by public organizations: Bureaucratic politics and organizational practice'. *Journal of Public Administration Research and Theory*, 19(1), 81–105.

Yeung, K. (2017) '"Hypernudge": Big Data as a mode of regulation by design'. *Information, Communication & Society*, 20(1), 118–36.

Yeung, K. (2018) 'Algorithmic regulation: A critical interrogation'. *Regulation & Governance*, 12(4), 505–23.

Yi, H., Berry, F. S. and Chen, W. (2018) 'Management innovation and policy diffusion through leadership transfer networks: An agent network diffusion model'. *Journal of Public Administration Research and Theory*, 28(4), 457–74.

Young, K., Ashby, D., Boaz, A. and Grayson, L. (2002) 'Social science and the evidence-based policy movement'. *Social Policy & Society*, 1(3), 215–24.

Zouridis, S. (2000) *Digitale Disciplinering: Over ICT, organisatie, wetgeving en het automatiseren van beschikkingen* [Digital Disciplining: About ICT, organization, legislation and automating decisions]. Delft: Eburon.

Zouridis, S. and Leijtens, V. L. (2018) 'Makkelijker kunnen we het wel maken, beter voorlopig niet: Wat de Belastingdienst kan leren van institutionele crisistheorie' [What the Tax and Customs Administration can learn from institutional crisis theory]. *Bestuurskunde*, 28(3), 89–94.

Zuboff, S. (1989) *In the Age of the Smart Machine: The future of work and power*. New York, NY: Basic Books.

Zuboff, S. (2019) *The Age of Surveillance Capitalism: The fight for a human future at the new frontier of power*. New York, NY: Public Affairs.

Zuurmond, A. (1994) *De Infocratie. Een theoretische en empirische heroriëntatie op Weber's ideaaltype in het informatietijdperk* [The Infocracy: A theoretical and empirical reorientation on Weber's ideal type in the information age]. Den Haag: Phaedrus.

# Index

Lightning Source UK Ltd.
Milton Keynes UK
UKHW020300221222
414310UK00004B/58